What Folks Say About Seattle

Looking at the local surroundings, I felt that Seattle was in a pit, that to get anywhere we would be compelled to climb out if we could.

> —R. H. Thompson, city engineer who was responsible for the Denny Regrade (circa 1900)

Seattle: Not a solution to a problem, an alternative to having problems.

> —Alan Furst, author, 1983

The Market, not Mount Rainier, is Seattle's soul.
> —Mark Tobey, artist

Seattle . . . The Moist Marvel of Puget Sound.
> —Chicago Tribune

If I were a member of this community, really I should get weary of being looked on as a sort of aesthetic dustbin.
> —Sir Thomas Beecham, conductor, 1941

It will stop raining, won't it?
> —Richard Eberhart, poet, 1967

Seattle should join the list of cities which have adopted a limitation of building height—Chicago, Boston, Washington, Buffalo, Cleveland, Minneapolis, and Los Angeles—and prevent the ills which unlimited license in this respect is sure to entail. The majority of the rooms in skyscrapers require to be lighted artificially, the sunlight being shut out, and must also be ventilated artificially. As a result, they are both dark and damp, and are therefore breeders of tuberculosis.
> —Virgil G. Bogue's Plan of Seattle, 1910

EIGHTH EDITION

The

SEATTLE

GuideBook

by Archie Satterfield

A Voyager Book

The Globe Pequot Press

Old Saybrook, Connecticut

About the Author

Archie Satterfield is the author of more than twenty books on travel and history. His subjects include World War II, Alaska and the Yukon, the Pacific Northwest, and aviation. A former newspaper and magazine editor, he now devotes all his time to writing books and articles and traveling throughout the world.

Mr. Satterfield is a member of the Society of American Travel Writers and the Authors Guild.

Maps by Hartwig E. Petersen
Illustrations by Sandy Haight

Cover photograph by Nick Gunderson/Allstock

Library of Congress Cataloging-in-Publication Data

Satterfield, Archie.
    The Seattle guidebook / by Archie Satterfield.—8th ed.
        p.   cm.
    "A Voyager book."
    Includes bibliographical references and index.
    ISBN 0-87106-161-9
    1. Seattle (Wash.)—Description—Guide-books. I. Title.
F899.S43S27   1991
917.97'7720443—dc20   91-15250
                                                      CIP

Manufactured in the United States of America
Eighth Edition/Second Printing

Contents

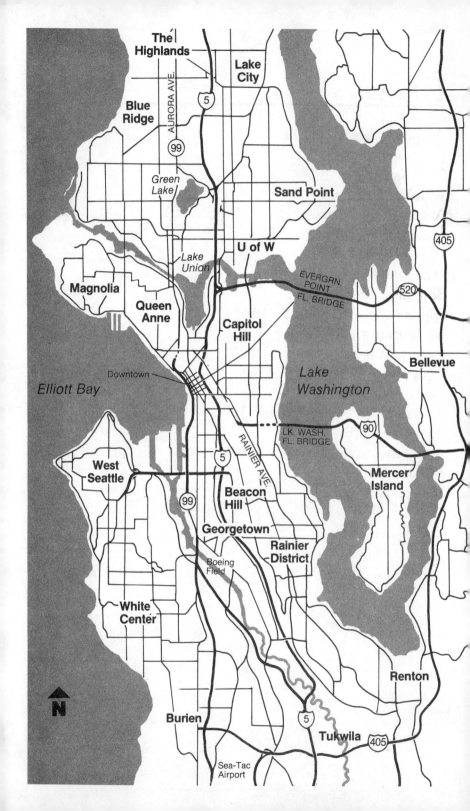

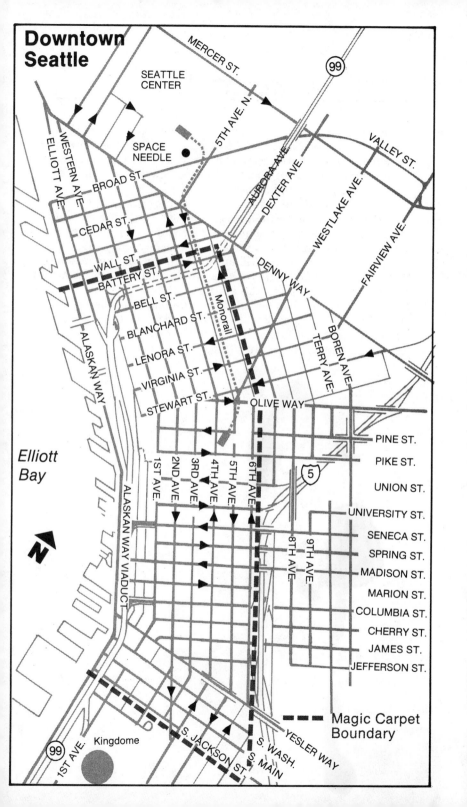

Acknowledgments

Each entry in this book represents the cooperation of the business or agency mentioned, and to each I wish to express my appreciation; however, I have accepted no gratuities from any restaurant, hotel, tour operator, or theater. In fact, few if any employees of places listed here would recognize me.

My debt to Merle Dowd is perpetual for bringing the idea of this book to me. With the first edition of *The Seattle GuideBook* Merle and Anne Dowd founded their publishing company, the Writing Works, and the book has sold steadily since 1975.

I am also grateful to William R. Hunt for sharing some of his Seattle historical material with me, to Jerome Richard for helpful suggestions, and also to the staff at the Seattle Public Library, Main Branch, for their assistance in finding information for the almanac section, especially the chronological material. Their card index on Northwest history is one of the city's greatest resources, and I wanted to publish everything in it.

Introduction

Fall is the best time for me to revise this book because the period from October until April is, it seems, the true essence of Seattle and the Puget Sound basin: short days, lots of fog and low clouds, frequent gentle rain, and mildly cool temperatures. Hardly a page goes by that I don't remind myself how fortunate I am to live here. It sounds smug and self-congratulatory, but I certainly did not feel that way about San Diego or Dallas or St. Louis when I lived in those cities.

Many of us who love the region without reservation consider the summer months an interruption in our lives, even though that is when most visitors come and when more copies of this book are sold. During the summers we tend to spend a lot of money on sunglasses, worry about skin cancer, and complain that our houses are too hot in the afternoon sun.

During the two years since the last revision of this book we have seen a housing boom hit Seattle, which drove prices up about 30 percent in a year. We saw many of our favorite small towns become suburbs, not only of Seattle, but also of San Francisco and Los Angeles. I know people who commute to Seattle the 100 miles from Ellensburg and the 85 miles from Bellingham, and most feel blessed that they can live in such nice small cities and work in such a nice large one.

Still, we old-timers worry about the influx of newcomers for a variety of reasons. In addition to increases in living expenses and housing prices, one of the major concerns is the change in attitudes that newcomers either bring with them or encourage by sheer numbers. One of the favorite complaints of old-timers is about the decline of courtesy on the streets and freeways; for example, failing to use turn signals, blocking cars from entering traffic and changing lanes, not honoring crosswalks, and not obeying the jaywalking laws (these laws especially offend most newcomers).

One friend has a no-fail way of knowing when he has met a newcomer to Seattle. Immediately after the introductions, the stranger will ask, "What do you do?"

At a dinner party I heard what became my favorite complaints about Seattle. The first was that Seattle people are so polite they are boring ("I miss the sarcasm in New York," the woman said). The other was that Seattle people, especially the police, take the jaywalking laws seriously. The complainers sympathized with Police Chief Fitzsimons when he told of his arrival in Seattle to interview for the job with Mayor Charles Royer. Fitzsimons said he was standing at the window of his Olympic Hotel room looking out into the rainy night when he saw something that completely baffled him: Standing at a traffic light, waiting for it to change, were two or three people. There wasn't a car in sight on Fourth Avenue, but they stood at the light waiting. Nothing at all like his native New York City.

My favorite newspaper columnist, Jean Godden of the *Times*, keeps a running list of the quintessence of Seattle. Reprinted here, with her permission, are a selection of her Seattle-isms:

Frango mints from Frederick & Nelson
Seattle's misty rain; it cushions our mornings.
J. P. Patches, the TV clown who charms kids and adults.
Ye Olde Curiosity Shop.
An Early Winters Gortex parka.
The *Post-Intelligencer's* globe.
The L. C. Smith Tower, still Seattle's classiest structure.
Sunny Jim peanut butter, which causes adults to salivate.
Waiting for the Interurban, the funky Fremont statue that has come to represent the city's soul.
The Pike Place Market. Where else could you buy dried chanterelles, fresh ink fish, a 1930s beaded dress, a "Slugs of Mystery" T-shirt, and thirty-eight kinds of doughnuts?
Seafair pirates. Though some people describe them as typifying quintessential silliness, they are definitely "Seattle."
The sword fern, a wild plant that is more handsome than many domesticated shrubs.
Skid Road, now Yesler Way, where they used to skid logs down the hill (and don't call it Skid Row while near Seattle).
Boeing 747.
Strawberry daiquiris, the mother's milk for young urban professionals.
Unlimited hydroplanes, the excuse for the rowdiest party of the summer.
Geoduck, the big clam that is the epitome of Puget Sound.
Ferries. It doesn't matter that the Walla Walla sometimes runs on one Walla; the boxy boats are still the essence.
The Space Needle, a kitschy spaceship on stilts.
Chief Seattle's statue.
The horsetail, a spidery plant that leaps through asphalt driveways—the quintessential Seattle weed.
Seattleites' marshmallow bodies (because we seldom see enough sun to turn our blubbery bodies any tanner than library paste).
An open drawbridge, saluting gray skies—the quintessential Seattle gesture.

Seattleites never carry umbrellas, never wash their cars, never shine their shoes, never turn on their windshield wipers until the rain is pouring, and never walk around wearing a badge or name tag.

Seattleites are apt to cultivate beards, wear hiking boots or running shoes with their business suits, and get a speeding ticket in the Arboretum.

They seldom visit the Space Needle, seldom exhibit decolletage or expanses of skin, seldom smile spontaneously while walking along streets (basically they're shy), seldom ride the monorail, and seldom wear husband-and-wife look-alike outfits.

They can describe forty-two shades of gray and they think a perfect day is 68°, partly sunny, with a light breeze from the north.

Here is a sampling from Godden's Seattle dictionary:

Kellogg Building: The Columbia Center, because it has more flakes than a box of cereal.

Native: A Californian, Minnesotan, or Iowan who has lived in Seattle more than six months and knows how to pronounce Sequim (or Puyallup).

Darth Vader Building: The Fourth and Blanchard Building, a dark, triangular structure of the post-apocalypse school of architecture.

Diaper Run: The 10:10 A.M. ferry from Bainbridge, favored by shoppers and parents en route to the pediatrician and orthodontist.

The Mountain: Mount Rainier on a clear day. On such a day people arrive at work gushing that "the mountains are really out today."

The Counterbalance: The steep part of Queen Anne Avenue, because a streetcar operated by counterbalance weights once ran up the hill.

Reader Beware

This book is not for a perfectionist, either to write or to read. It is the nature of a book with so many lines of detail—phone numbers, addresses, hours and days of opening—that changes may occur as the book goes to press, or, equally painful, shortly after publication. It is inevitable, and I have had to learn to live with it.

For your own protection against the whims and disasters and changes in the telephone system, I strongly recommend calling well in advance before visiting any of the businesses or attractions listed. Some listings have hardly changed in ten years; others change once or twice each year; and some simply disappear entirely.

Some Vital Statistics

Area Code: 206.

Latitude and longitude. At the Federal Office Building downtown, Seattle is 47°36′32″ north latitude and 122°20′12″ west longitude. The magnetic declination is 23° east.

Elevations. At an official datum point, 1st Ave. and James St., the elevation is 18.79 feet. The highest elevation is 512 feet, just south of Myrtle St. and west of 35th Ave. SW. (For other elevations, see How Many Hills? on pages 176–178.)

Land area. Within the city limits are 92 square miles, including 3.07 square miles of water.

Water areas. Elliott Bay, a part of Puget Sound, is 125 miles from the Pacific Ocean and covers 5,299 acres, with a usable shoreline of 54 miles. Puget Sound contains about 31 cubic miles of water, of which 1½ cubic miles move with each tide. The sound covers 2,500 square miles and has 2,200 miles of shoreline. Elliott Bay depths range from 150 feet to 900 feet. Its primary tributary, the Duwamish River, is an important industrial and shipping area.

Lake Washington is 27 miles long and approximately 3 miles wide, covering 22,138 acres. Lake Washington and Lake Union are connected with Elliott Bay by the Ship Canal and the Hiram M. Chittenden Government Locks at Ballard, which are operated by the U.S. Army Corps of Engineers. Lakes Washington and Union together have 139 miles of shoreline. The two lakes and the locks comprise 25,000 surface acres. The lakes are 26 feet higher than the sound.

And Some Not-So-Vital Statistics

Seattle has two hundred thousand households, of which 92 percent have television sets and 90 percent have telephones.

Harbor Island, at 396.7 acres, is the second largest man-made island in the world. (San Francisco's Treasure Island covers 402 acres).

The color television tube, the electric guitar, and the automobile headlight lens were invented in Seattle.

"Firsts" include the first gas station, in 1907 (corner of Holgate St. and E. Marginal Way), first international airplane flight (Seattle to Victoria, British Columbia), and first covered shopping mall (Northgate).

The Evergreen Point Floating Bridge is the longest floating

Why People Live Here

REASONS FOR LIVING HERE	Strong	Mild	No Effect
Grew up here	47%	6%	46%
Family and friends here	64	18	18
Cultural opportunities	37	37	26
Pro sports teams	17	30	53
Parks, outdoor recreation	66	21	12
Civic attractions	40	33	27
Schools, universities	48	25	27
Less crime	24	35	40
Job opportunities	29	36	34
Hospitals, health care	47	30	23
Natural beauty of area	89	7	3
Relaxed life-style	55	24	21
Transit system	24	31	45
Lack of pollution	37	37	23

PROBLEMS LIVING HERE	Strong	Mild	No Effect
Traffic congestion	25%	43%	32%
Crime	32	47	21
Too many people	21	38	40
Schools, universities	11	22	66
Provincialism	5	29	64
Pollution	25	40	35
Lack of cultural life	4	26	69
Lack of job opportunities	20	34	46
Poor transit system	12	22	66
Lack of good restaurants	5	13	81

Source: *Seattle Post-Intelligencer* poll

bridge in the world at 1.4 miles. In 1940, the Mercer Island bridge (actually the Lacey B. Murrow Bridge, named for a widely respected engineer who was the brother of Edward R. Murrow, the radio and television commentator) was the first concrete bridge to float on anchored pontoons.

Thirty to forty tons of San Francisco's Telegraph Hill were carried here in early days as ships' ballast and dumped into Elliott Bay for landfill.

The record for public drunkenness may be held by a Seattle resident, with 401 jailings totaling 10,680 days and $1,365 in fines. The city's very first ordinance, in fact, dealt with public drunkenness.

The Space Needle is 605 feet high.

One in six Seattle residents owns a boat, and the city's houseboat population is the largest east of the Orient.

In 1980, the city's six drawbridges opened thirty-nine thousand times for an average of three minutes each.

Suicide leaps from the Aurora (George Washington Memorial) Bridge numbered 123 from 1930 to 1979. Sixty-six jumps were made in the 1959–79 period. Nine died in 1972. Only eight have survived the fall. The bridge accounts for 2 percent of King County's suicides.

The earliest known photograph of the city was of 1st Ave. S., taken in 1864.

The first public golf course in the United States was Seattle's Jefferson Park, which opened in 1915.

Seattle has 2,570 miles of curbed streets. Each year street sweepers go over the arterials 54 times and residential streets 5 times, making Seattle one of the nation's cleanest cities. Also, each year 242 stairways are swept 3 times, 260 litter cans are emptied 250 times, and 261 cans in outlying areas, emptied 75 times. Annually, about 260 "swath miles" of hay are cut by mower and about 8 acres by hand to make fire hydrants visible.

Sightseeing

View from Gas Works Park

Seattle lies in one of the most beautiful settings in the world. The salt water of Puget Sound forms Seattle's western boundary, and Lake Washington is its eastern edge. These bodies of water give the city its famed hourglass shape and residents a choice of views. Westward the view is across the sound and the sprinkling of low islands to the Olympic Mountains, which are stunning on days with brilliant sunsets. The Cascade Range forms the eastern horizon, with its string of jagged peaks so beautiful to see as they emerge out of the night when dawn comes up behind them; and the string of volcanoes—Mount Baker, Glacier Peak, Mount Rainier, and from some favored viewpoints, the remains of Mount Saint Helens, which erupted in May 1980.

Closer in the city is Lake Union, a combination working and residential lake where seaplanes take off and land, where seagoing ships, sailboats, motorboats, kayaks, windsurfers, houseboats, ducks, parks, restaurants, and yacht brokers coexist more or less in congeniality.

Seattle is an active sightseers' paradise, and following is a selected list of sights to see and ways to see them.

Air Activities

Airports. Unless you are a frequent airplane traveler, a few hours at Seattle-Tacoma International Airport can be very interesting, what with all its shops; the dramatic art; and the international flavor, with people going and coming from the Arctic, the South Pacific, the Orient, Europe, and the other Americas. One good place for jet viewing is on the North Concourse.

For smaller stuff and a more intimate atmosphere, try the little-brother airport at Boeing Field, where smaller jets are mixed in with pleasure aircraft and helicopters. A few World War II fighters and trainers can be found there, and you can go upstairs to the restaurant and bar and watch the varied air traffic.

You'll have to go out of town for large collections of antique aircraft, particularly Snohomish, Puyallup, Monroe, and Arlington.

Airshows. Some of the regional airshows are primarily static displays of vintage, World War II, and modern military aircraft. Other shows feature aerobatics, pylon races, flybys, and demonstrations of military precision jet-formation maneuvers by the U.S. Navy's Blue Angels, the U.S. Air Force's Thunderbirds, and the Canadian Air Force's Snowbirds.

Among the scheduled airshows are Thun Field in Puyallup; Auburn Airport's Breakfast Fly-in and Airshow; Kitsap Airport Evening Fly-in, Airshow and Salmon Bake; Rotary International Air Fair at Paine Field in Everett; Renton Air Fair; and EAA-AAA Fly-in at Arlington.

Sky divers, gliders, and experimental aircraft can be seen on weekends at the Issaquah Sky Sport Airfield in Issaquah.

The Museum of Flight at the southwest end of Boeing Field has many special events throughout the year, including antique fly-ins, experimental aircraft shows, and military exhibits. (See Museum of Flight information, chapter 8.)

Ballooning. Several firms offer rides, and some include a champagne brunch after the flight. Included are the Great Northwest Aerial Navigation Company, 7616 79th SE, Mercer Island (232–2023), Climb on a Rainbow Balloon Flights (364–8876), and Balloon Depot, 16138 NE 87th, Redmond (881–9699).

Scenic Flights. Several firms offer half-hour to one-hour flights over Seattle and Puget Sound, and this is one of the best ways to get your bearings quickly as well as to appreciate the great beauty of the region. Prices begin at about $60 for a three-passenger flight for half an hour. On Lake Union, the Lake Union Air Service (950 Westlake N., 284-0300) and Chrysler Air (1325 Fairview E., 329-9638) offer flights. On Lake Washington, Kenmore Air (6321 N.E. 175th, 486-8400) also runs scheduled flights to the San Juan Islands. Several operate out of Boeing Field, such as Galvin Flying Service, 763-0350, and Flight Tech, 762-1151.

Alki Point

It was here that the first settlers landed in Seattle in 1851—or at least the Denny Party, which gets credit for being the first party of Seattle settlers—and local historians love telling everyone about it, although it wasn't very exciting. They arrived, built a town, and that was that. Today Alki Point and the miles of beach, the lighthouse, and a cluster of elderly but charming beach houses make up one of the more pleasant places to walk and sunbathe in Seattle. It is a prime boat-watching area, with ferry traffic, sailboats, sailboards, yachts, and freighters that round the point on their way somewhere. Many residents fish off the piers, while others simply walk along the 2-mile promenade with the north wind frequently chilling them while the gulls wheel and shriek overhead. The street is a particular favorite with teenage cruisers during the warm weather. For information on the Alki Point Light Station, see "Lighthouses" in this chapter.

Aquarium

Seattle's Aquarium, north of Waterfront Park on Pier 59, offers a unique and unusual look at Puget Sound marine life—both animal and vegetable. No collection of fish in big bowls or performing seals and killer whales, the Aquarium's innovative displays recreate shore and underwater habitats. A huge viewing dome takes you into an underwater world filled with sea life from the sound: sharks, several species of salmon, perch, rockfish, flounder, and cod, along with some more unusual creatures such as octopuses, sculpins, starfish, barnacles, and varieties of shellfish. An actual fish ladder leads down to Puget Sound, where the salmon fingerlings are released seasonally. After a normal life cycle, each fall the salmon make their way from the ocean, through the sound, and up the ladder to the Aquarium—the only aquarium in the world to be connected directly to life in the ocean. In the meantime, visitors may look up through a glass-bottom portion of the fish ladder to watch salmon fingerlings swimming overhead. Whether viewed from below the surface or above, playful seals and sea otters entertain constantly. The Aquarium is not limited to water creatures, but also houses ducks, wrens, sea stars, and crabs in a salt marsh. Nearby, a beach and pond are home to shorebirds. Water anemones, sand dollars, and urchins are only a few of the saltwater creatures visible. A tide rises and falls at three-hour intervals to expose barnacles, mussels, and similar shellfish at tide lines. Seattle's Aquarium embodies the newest ideas to permit the staff to engage in research and education while exhibits entertain. Open daily 10:00 A.M.–5:00 P.M. winter, 10:00 A.M.–7:00 P.M. summer. Adults $3.25; $1.50 for ages 13–18 and 62 and older; $.75 for children 6–12; children under 6 free with an adult. Annual family pass costs $25 and entitles holder to bring in two guests on each visit and to receive newsletter (call 625-4357). Summer classes for adults and children are scheduled (call 625-5030).

Arboretum

This is undoubtedly one of the most beautiful places in Seattle, and, as beautiful places should be, the Arboretum is designed for people to enjoy it. The 200-acre nature preserve is located in Washington Park on Lake Washington Blvd. near the University of Washington, which oversees its welfare. One of the visual crescendos is the Japanese Garden. Visit the garden during the spring or fall, though it is a visual delight any time of year. Virtually all types of Pacific Northwest ornamental plants are displayed throughout the Arboretum, along with many imported from other countries. Although the freeway leading to the Evergreen Point Floating Bridge rips through the northern edge of the park, and bits and pieces of an abandoned freeway project hang out over some sections of the marshes like remnants of a lost civilization, the Arboretum remains essentially a naturalist's treasure trove. The Waterfront Trail connects to the Foster Island Nature Trail (see separate listing); the other popular trails are Azalea Way and Loderi Valley, where masses of rhododendrons are planted. It is open from 8:00 A.M. to sunset year-round; no admission charge. The Japanese Garden is open 10:00 A.M.–8:00 P.M. in summer, 10:00 A.M.–6:00 P.M. in spring, autumn, and winter. Entry fees are $1.50 for adults, $.50 for children 18 and under and for seniors 65 and over, $5 for school groups, and $10 for family pass. For information on guided tours and occasional plant sales, call 543-8800 or 325-4510. The tea ceremony in the Japanese tea house is performed the third Sunday of every month, April through October; call 684-4725 for times.

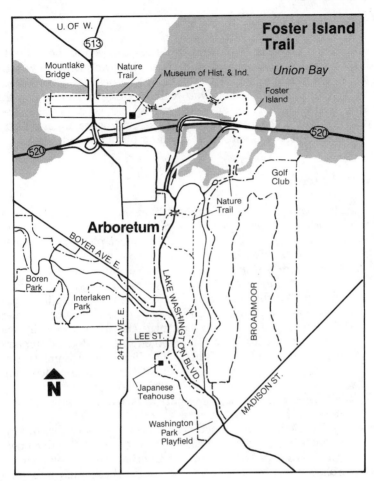

Automobile Trips

The best source, obviously, is the AAA Automobile Club of Washington at 330 6th N. (448-5310), but you must be a member to receive the benefits of stacks of maps, brochures, discounts on publications, and other material. Perhaps the best way to see Seattle is to follow the scenic route signs along routes laid out by the Seattle Engineering Department, which I have used in the Scenic Drives in this chapter. For other ideas, check separate listings, such as "Viewpoints."

Bird-Watching

You don't have to be a member of the Seattle Audubon Society (Joshua Green Building, 523-4483) to be a bird-watcher, and Seattle has several prime areas for you. Among the best are Green Lake, Schmitz Park, Foster Island Nature Trail, Discovery Park, and the entire Arboretum. With so much water and so many marshes, you'll obviously see lots of ducks, geese, and other aquatic birds, but robins, sparrows, and other dry-land birds abound.

Boat-Watching

Since Seattle claims the highest boat ownership per capita of any city in the nation, it only follows that watching boats steam, roar, sail, chug, and slip by is one of the most pleasant pastimes. Obviously you can watch them from any spot along the waterfront or lakes, but here is a selection of what I consider the prime spots:

Fisherman's Terminal. Just off 15th W. on Salmon Bay, this is where a majority of the deep-sea fishing crafts tie up. You'll see gill-netters, seiners, trollers, tenders, and other types of commercial boats moored here. Frequently the fishermen will have their nets and other gear stretched out on the dock for repairs, which delights photographers. The Terminal Administration Building has a seafood restaurant (Chinook's), a coffee shop, and shops specializing in commercial fishing gear.

Hiram M. Chittenden Locks. Commonly known as the Ballard Locks (see separate listing).

Opening Day Boat Parade. Each year, on the first Saturday in May, the yachting season in Seattle more or less officially opens with a parade of boats from Portage Bay, where they form up, through the Montlake Cut and under the bridge into Lake Washington. The parade, sponsored by the Seattle Yacht Club, usually begins about noon and lasts two hours as the sailboats, punts, cruisers, canoes, steam-powered boats, rowboats, racing shells, and whatever join the parade. The best places—those directly along the route—are at a premium, and you'll have to arrive early with your blanket or chair, picnic lunch, and binoculars. If you can't make it early enough for a waterside seat, you might try one of the dead-end streets on the northeast side of Capitol Hill, especially those leading off E. Shelby, Boyer, and Fuhrman E. Others are found on Vista Point, E. Roanoke, and Delmar Drive E. The best spots of all are along the Waterside Trail that parallels the cut between Portage Bay and Lake Washington, and the Foster Island Nature Trail (see separate listings); get there early to find a spot.

Shilshole Bay. This is the major pleasure-boat moorage on the salt-water side of Seattle, and you'll see everything from dinghies to seagoing yachts. It is also a restaurant center, with Quinn's Fishmarket & Bar, Ray's Boathouse, and the Golden Tides in the area. Adjoining the marina is Golden Gardens Park, with beach viewing on one level and a viewpoint high up on the bluff. This is a favorite hot-weather hangout for the young at heart.

Waterfront Park. See separate listing under "Parks."

Fish-Watching

This may be stretching sightseeing a bit, but there are many, many people who continue to marvel at the homing instinct of salmon. And who can stand on the rim of a pool in a fish hatchery watching the thousands of fingerlings swirling around without becoming almost hypnotized by the motion? Ed Munro Seahurst Park, 13th SW and SW 144th off Ambaum Road, is a relatively new King County park that has fish ladders, research facilities, and a holding pond for fish. Other good spots are Hiram M. Chittenden Locks, Seward Park for rainbow trout, and the Seattle Aquarium.

Foster Island Nature Walk

This is an excellent place to send or take out-of-town visitors, children, or the spry elderly and is perhaps the best place in Seattle to watch boats, feed ducks, and hike all at the same time. The 1½-mile round-trip begins at the lower end of the Museum of History and Industry parking lot (stop in at the museum and see two major attractions in the same afternoon). The trail begins at the water's edge and immediately swoops upward over one of the numerous arching bridges built high enough to allow canoeists to pass beneath. The trail is on top of the squishy marsh and sort of floats on the bog. This wide, smooth trail leads almost to the water's edge, with some side trips on dead-end spurs and benches for sitting or what have you. Bikers and joggers are strongly discouraged, to avoid pedestrian collisions. The trail follows one of the busiest boat lanes in Seattle: Lake Washington–based vessels must go past it and through the narrow channel called Montlake Cut in order to enter Lake Union and the Hiram M. Chittenden Locks en route to the sound. Plaques telling of the interrelationship between water, weeds, birds, fish, and aquatic animals line the trail, which ends on the mainland in the Arboretum property. For the serious boat-watcher, an alternate trail leads up a bank overlooking the

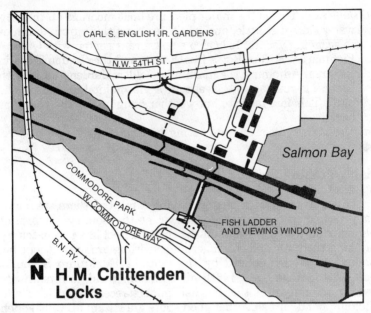

Montlake Cut, where platforms for boat viewing were thoughtfully built.

Hiram M. Chittenden Locks (Ballard Locks)

"So what," said the jaded traveler. "The boats come in, they drop down as the water goes out, the gates open, and they go away." If you want to look at it that way, that's all there is to the spectacle most locals call the Ballard Locks. Yet it is a spectacle that most people keep going back to see year after year for no better reason than that it is (1) free and (2) fun. All pleasure boats headed for salt water from Lakes Union and Washington must pass through the locks, as must the commercial boats ranging from tugs towing log booms to the ships that berth on the lakes. If nothing else, you can marvel at the patience of the loud-voiced but tolerant locks employees who must shepherd the weekend sailors into the locks and keep them from sinking each other. Nearly 2,000,000 visitors stroll through the 7-acre botanical gardens surrounding the locks each year, and from 80,000 to 100,000 vessels go through the twin locks each year. During one peak year (1962, during the world's fair here), the count included 47,748 pleasure craft, 9,645 fishing boats, 10,597 tugs, 8,460 barges, 350 ships, 1,868 government vessels, 918 passenger vessels, and 649 foreign vessels.

Construction on the canal and locks began in 1911, first by lowering Lake Washington from 29.8 feet above sea level to 21 feet above. Salmon Bay was elevated to the same level (21 feet). Lake Union remained at the same level, where the locks maintain it today. When vessels go through the locks, they are raised or lowered, depending on their direction, from 6 feet to 26 feet, which represents the tidal fluctuation.

The locks also permit salmon to migrate both through them and past them via a fish ladder, so they can continue their ancient route through Lake Union and Lake Washington to the rivers that feed the lakes. Visitors may watch the migration from outdoor overhead walkways above the ladder or through an underground fish-ladder viewing window and stand almost nose to nose with salmon, steelhead, and other fish. The heaviest runs of tourists and fish occur during the months of June and July, when sockeye salmon start their migration. Chinook run in August and September and coho in October and November.

Visitors are welcome every day between 7:00 A.M. and 9:00 P.M. while the locks operate. A visitors' center near the main entrance shows how locks operate and tells of other Army Corps of Engineers projects. Hours: daily 11:00 A.M.–8:00 P.M. June 15–September 15; 11:00 A.M.–5:00 P.M. Thursday–Monday September 15–June 15, closed Tuesdays and Wednesdays (783-7059).

The locks are reached from downtown Seattle either via Aurora N. to the Fremont exit, then west on NW Leary Way to Market St., and west on it to NW 54th; or north on 15th W. to NW Leary Way.

Houseboats

Seattle has the largest houseboat population east of the Orient. There was a time when all houseboats on Lake Union and Portage Bay were modest—little more than shacks on floats, with sewage dumped directly into the water. Some houseboats are still modest, but no longer are they free spirits; they are hooked to sewage lines. The largest collection of houseboats, and the widest variety in style and price, is found on the east shore of Lake Union. You can cruise slowly by car on Fairview N. along the lakeshore to look at them. Over on Portage Bay just off Lake Washington are the high-rent houseboats with A-frames, chalets, and two- and three-story residences, which make the bay a favorite neighborhood for young professionals. You can drive along Fuhrman E. from the University Bridge for a closer look. The way to get the best view of all, of course, is to rent or borrow a boat and cruise slowly past them. The line between window peeking and sightseeing is a fine one in such situations.

Lighthouses

"Lonely as a lighthouse keeper" may apply in some parts of the world—even some parts of Puget Sound—but not in Seattle. The two here are quite metropolitan in setting; indeed, the Alki Point Light Station is right in the middle of a neighborhood and a heavily used public beach. In spite of this, there is still that aura of loneliness to any lighthouse, the feeling of an outpost on the tip of some remote, dangerous shore.

The Alki Point Light Station (932-5800) at 3201 Alki was established in November 1881. A coastguardsman is on duty to answer questions from noon to 4:00 P.M. Saturday, Sunday, and some holidays. Group tours can be arranged Tuesday–Friday.

West Point Light Station (282-9130) is at the far western tip of Discovery Park via a 1-mile walk down a steep bluff road, past the sewage treatment facility (no noticeable odors) and out onto the point, which is cluttered with driftwood, rocks, and sand. Hours are the same as for Alki Point.

Scenic Drives

Whether you are a native or a visitor to Seattle, one of the best ways to become thoroughly acquainted with the geography of the city is by following scenic routes laid out by the city engineering department. Each of the four drives is marked by small "Scenic Drive" signs attached to street signs that are relatively easy to follow.

The drives range from 30 to 40 miles in length, and each can be covered in about three hours' driving time, allowing for stops at particularly interesting spots, such as parks and viewpoints.

Viewpoints

Some say the best views are from West Seattle, where you can look one direction to see the Olympics and the other direction to see Seattle's skyline stretched out like a painting in a doctor's waiting room. Others prefer Queen Anne Hill, with views of the city stretched out below, dimpled by Lake Union. Whatever your preference, Seattle has a viewpoint for it, and it is little wonder that view property has climbed as high as waterfront property in some areas.

The Parks Department has wisely bought up some prime viewpoints and decorated them with artworks, walls, sidewalks, and

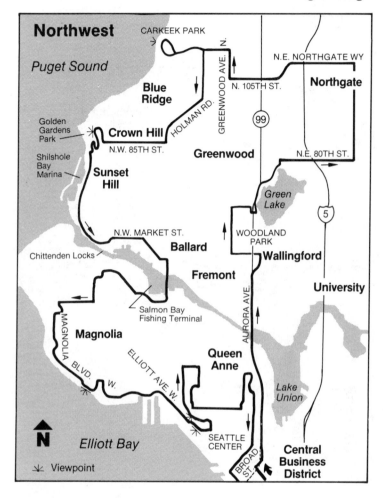

other amenities so that visitors and residents without view property can still see the sights.

In addition to those listed below, others exist on public property if you want to do a bit of exploring. Look for dead-end streets on Queen Anne Hill or overlooking Lake Washington (one of the best, with a stunning view of Mount Rainier, is on a dead-end street in Washington Park). You may have the feeling you're walking on private property, but if you're on a street, it belongs to you.

Others are part of the package in city parks, such as Lincoln Park, the Foster Island Nature Walk, Golden Gardens, and Discovery Park.

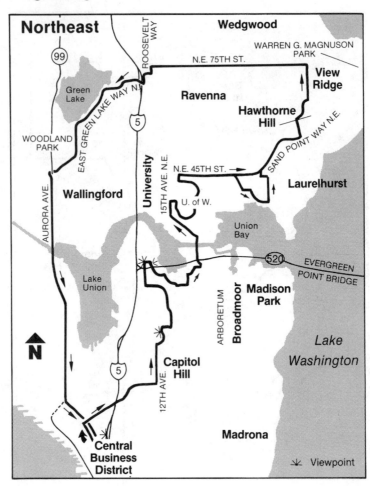

CAPITOL HILL

Bagley Viewpoint, 10th E. & E. Roanoke. Looks out over Lake
   Union to Queen Anne Hill.
Capitol Hill Viewpoint, 15th E. & E. Olin Pl. View to the east over
   Evergreen Point Bridge, Lake Washington, and on a clear day
   to the Cascades.
Four Columns, Pike & Boren at Interstate 5. View westward over
   downtown to the Olympics.
Louisa Boren Lookout, 15th E. & E. Garfield. Another eastward
   view with both Lake Washington floating bridges in sight.

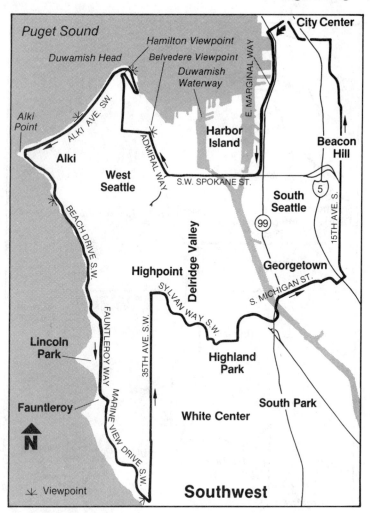

QUEEN ANNE HILL

Betty Bowen/Marshall Viewpoint, 7th W. & W. Highland Dr. This one is only a few blocks west of Kerry Viewpoint, across the street from Parsons Gardens. It looks across Magnolia and Puget Sound.

Kerry Viewpoint, W. Highland Dr. & 2nd W. A great view over Seattle Center, the Space Needle, downtown Seattle, and, on a clear day, Mount Rainier.

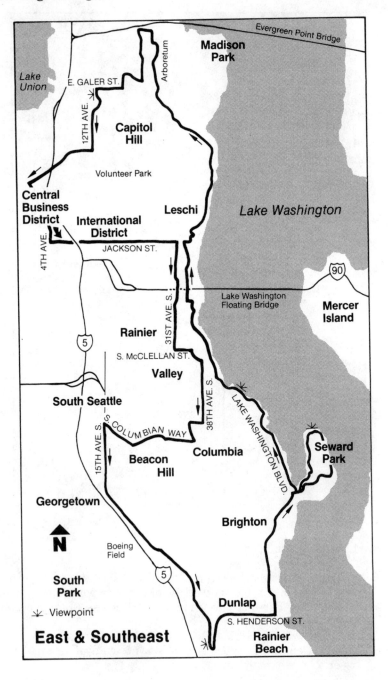

Evergreen Point Bridge

Madison Park

Lake Union

E. GALER ST.

12TH AVE.

Arboretum

Capitol Hill

Volunteer Park

Central Business District

International District

4TH AVE.

JACKSON ST.

Leschi

Lake Washington

90

Lake Washington Floating Bridge

Mercer Island

Rainier

31ST AVE. S.

S. McCLELLAN ST.

Valley

South Seattle

5

15TH AVE. S.

S. COLUMBIAN WAY

38TH AVE. S.

LAKE WASHINGTON BLVD.

Columbia

Beacon Hill

Seward Park

Georgetown

N

Brighton

Boeing Field

South Park

5

Dunlap

⋇ Viewpoint

S. HENDERSON ST.

East & Southeast

Rainier Beach

WEST SEATTLE

Belvedere Viewpoint, SW Admiral Way & SW Olga. This is perhaps
the most popular viewpoint in Seattle due to its total pano-
rama of the city skyline plus the industrial activity on Harbor
Island. During beautiful weather it is sometimes difficult to
find a parking place.
Hamilton Viewpoint, north end of California SW and SW Donald.
This, too, is popular but not quite as accessible as Belvedere.
It shows more of Puget Sound plus the skyline.
Schmitz Viewpoint, Beach Drive SW & SW Alaska. This one is on
the water level, a public oasis among the privately owned
stretches of inaccessible beach.

Guided Tours

Alaska Sightseeing Tours, Fourth and Battery Bldg. (441–8687). At
last, a cruise ship calls at Seattle on a regular basis. Due to the
federal laws prohibiting foreign-built passenger ships from
traveling between American ports without touching at a foreign port, all of the two dozen or more cruise ships to Alaska
have been departing from Vancouver, B.C.

Now, however, an American-built ship bound for Victoria,
Ketchikan, Petersburg, and Sitka will leave Seattle's Pier 70
each Saturday from May through September. The ship is the
former Pacific Northwest Explorer, built for the defunct Exploration Cruise Lines and now renamed the *Spirit of Alaska*.
The 158-foot vessel has forty outside cabins, bow thrusters,
and a ramp to permit landings on wilderness beaches.

Costs range from $1,295 to $2,695 per person.
American Sightseeing of Seattle (624–5813). This is one of the larger
tour packagers in Seattle, offering tours of the city, Boeing
plant, Museum of Flight; out-of-town trips to Mount Rainier,
Tillicum Village, and Snoqualmie Falls; and overnight trips to
Victoria and the Olympic Peninsula. Call for information and
rates.
Anchor Excursions (282–8368). Mainly for groups, this firm offers
its beautiful boat, the 49-foot *Snow Goose*, and the even larger
(240-passenger) *Islander*. It emphasizes educational trips and
has marine biologists and other specialists on staff for trips.
Call for information.
Blake Island and Tillicum Village (329–5700). If you like salmon,
boat rides, islands, and Indian culture, this could well be the

main event in Seattle sightseeing. The 473-acre island lies between Vashon and Bainbridge islands and is owned entirely by the State Parks Department for use as a marine park. Tillicum Village, a concession, is the only building on the island and is one of the best eateries on Puget Sound. The longhouse-style building will seat up to one thousand, and as you enter, you will see your salmon being cooked in the traditional Indian fashion. It is filleted and held over the wood fire on cedar sticks until it is peach and golden brown, after being basted in lemon butter. The menu consists of tossed salad, relishes, salmon, baked potato in foil, green beans almondine, hot bread, wild blackberry tart, and soft drinks. During the meal, Indian dancers perform traditional North Pacific Coast interpretive dances on a large stage decorated with totemic art. An Indian craft shop is located in the lobby, and carvers frequently work on totems and smaller items in the longhouse. The tour leaves from Pier 56 on a sightseeing boat three times daily during the summer at 11:30 A.M., 4:30 P.M., and 6:30 P.M., and at 1:30 P.M. and 4:30 P.M. (sometimes) on Sundays. During the winter, October 13–April 30, it is open on weekends only. Prices: adults, $32; senior citizens, $29; children (ages 6–12), $12; and toddlers (ages 4–5), $5. Group rates available. The tour lasts four hours.

Chinatown Discovery (447-9230). This popular tour takes you through the heart of Seattle's International District, and in spite of the tour's name, it shows why the district is called International rather than Chinatown. The Japanese and Philippine influences are apparent, as is the Pacific islands contribution. You will see the major businesses there, go on a tour of Wing Luke Museum, drink green tea and eat Japanese cookies, and see historical data on the district. Included in the price is a *dim sum* lunch in a Chinese restaurant. Cost: $18 adults, $16 seniors, $12 children 12 or under.

Gray Line of Seattle (624-5813). This is the largest tour company in Seattle and offers a wide selection of escorted bus and boat tours. Gray Line offers two-hour and six-hour narrated tours of Seattle as well as specialty tours, such as the Chocolate and Wine Sampler, which includes stops at a chocolate factory and a winery. Pickup at several downtown hotels is included. Also offered are overnight trips to Victoria, Mount Rainier, Mount Saint Helens, and the Olympic Peninsula. During the summer months Gray Line runs a motorized trolley in the downtown district that connects the major hotels with Pioneer Square and the waterfront.

Harbor Tours (623-1445). Four boats, *Goodtime I, Goodtime II, Goodtime III,* and *Spirit of Alderbrook*, make one-hour tours along Seattle's waterfront. The tours begin at Pier 56 and cruise north to Pier 90 below Magnolia Bluff, then back south to the Harbor Islands shipyards for a close-up of vessels under construction or being repaired. Half of the boats' seats are on open decks so it is wise to bring warm clothing. Season: May 1 to late September. Cost: adults, $7.50; teens, $5.00; seniors and groups, $6.50. Special Japanese language tours available if reservations are made one week in advance. Daily trips begin at 11:00 A.M.

Jazz Tours, Washington Jazz Society, P.O. Box 24284, Terminal Annex, Seattle, Washington 98124. Each summer and autumn the Washington Jazz Society charters the ancient, appealing passenger boat, *Virginia V,* for a combination jazz concert and Puget Sound tour. The jazz isn't avant-garde and purposely so, because the society wants to appeal to a wide cross section of music lovers. Because the jazz tours are so popular, it is best to obtain tickets well in advance. Write to the Washington Jazz Society for information.

Kingdome Tours (340-2128). The major-league stadium located just south of Pioneer Square also includes a sports museum, and the tour takes you through the museum as well as into the press box, the VIP lounge, the locker rooms, and out onto the Astroturf playing field. The tour is operated three times a day, unless events prohibit one or more of the tours. Times are 11:00 A.M., 1:00 P.M., and 3:00 P.M., Monday–Saturday, May–October. No 11:00 A.M. tour November–April. Cost: $2.50 for adults and teens; $1.25 for senior citizens and children under 12. Call for information.

Skagit Tours, Seattle City Light Skagit Tours, 1015 3rd Ave., Seattle, Washington 98104 (625-3030). This tour is quite a distance out of town but is a Seattle fixture because it is operated by Seattle City Light. In fact, it is one of the few tours operated by a municipal agency and one of the most popular tours in the Seattle area. The tours are of City Light's hydroelectric project in the heart of the North Cascades. The main tour is a four-hour trip through the project, including a ride on the incline lift from one level to the next, a boat trip on Diablo Lake, tours through the Ross powerhouse, and an all-you-can-eat family-style meal. The tour starts at the company town of Diablo, 137 miles northeast of Seattle on the North Cascades Highway. Cost: adults $21; seniors $19; children ages 6–11 $10. Children age 5 and under are free (request no-charge tickets when making reservations so the tour operator can keep track of visitors).

In addition, City Light offers self-guided nature walks in the same area:

Gorge Powerhouse-Ladder Creek Falls, free.

Trail of the Cedars, free.

A museum with slide show is in the town of Newhalem.

Tours operate from the third Saturday in June until Labor Day weekend with reservations available starting in April.

Underground Tour (682-4646 or 682-1511). One of Seattle's most popular tours, the late Bill Speidel's Underground Tour is also one of the most offbeat. The underground in question is an engineering fluke that resulted when Seattle went on a land-leveling binge after the turn of the century. The first of several hillsides was sluiced down toward the sound to flatten out the town and build port docks where only mudflats existed before. In the process, the ground floors of several buildings became basements. The streets were raised and sidewalks built level with the second stories. For a while merchants tried to keep their doors open, but customers had to climb up and down stairs or walk along dark, narrow walkways. Before long, the ground floors (now basements) were abandoned. There they lay for decades until the late John Reddin, a *Seattle Times* colum- nist, rediscovered the underground and wrote a column about it. Bill Speidel, publisher of *The Seattle Guide*, a weekly visi- tor's guide, leaped at the chance to start an offbeat tour that merged nicely with his self-published humorous books about Seattle and its past.

The tour begins in Doc Maynard's Tavern at 610 1st Ave. with a short, humorous version of Seattle's history. The tour then goes through several underground passageways beneath businesses and streets. It ends in Speidel's Underground Mu- seum, where you can buy artifacts and, of course, Speidel's books. Several tours daily during summer months. Tickets: adults, $4.00; $2.75 senior citizens; $2.00 children ages 6-12; $3.25 students ages 13-17. Special group rates available. Prices subject to change. Call for information.

Victoria Clipper, Pier 69 (448-5000). The Seattle-Victoria boat ser- vice was confusing at the time this was written because one shipping company, Stena Line, had just closed shop and a labor union had seized one of the ships. Stena had angered traditionalists by taking the beloved *Princess Marguerite* out of service and had run into tax problems with the IRS over gambling. So now only Victoria Clippers offers waterborne transportation between Seattle and Victoria.

The company runs three water-jet–powered catamarans (*Victoria Clipper I, II,* and *III*) between Seattle and Victoria daily. Three round trips are made during the summer, one trip during the winter months, and two trips during the spring and fall seasons. The catamarans are fast—they travel at 15 to 31 knots—so the trip takes only two and a half hours. The boats have two decks each and carry a maximum of 285 and 300 passengers respectively.

Summer prices in 1990 were $73 round-trip for adults, $63 for seniors and children. During the winter the price dropped $10 in both categories. Various package tours are available through the company.

Walking Tours

Pioneer Square

Seattle is full of enclaves with a special historical, trade, or shopping interest for visitors and residents. These spot locations can really only be appreciated on foot. Zipping by in a car does not allow you to savor the flavor of the atmosphere or the people. While there are many isolated areas with their own charm, these are among my favorites.

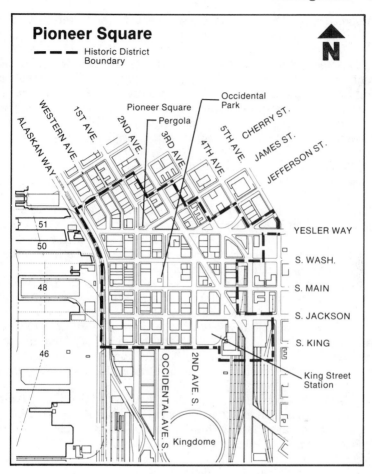

Pioneer Square

Pioneer Square is one of those pleasant anachronisms in twentieth-century America, an era in which our enlightened society appears intent upon demolishing everything that might be considered old-fashioned. The wrecking-ball renters were forced to avoid Pioneer Square, and it remains an oasis of elegant brick amid aluminum, glass, concrete, and asphalt parking lots.

It is Seattle's birthplace. It was the area chosen in 1852 when the original settlers abandoned Alki Point because of the hard, windy winters and poor moorage for visiting sailing vessels. The small harbor of Elliott Bay offered better protection, and the local

Indians, led by a compassionate chief named Sealth, were generous with both land and information.

After they settled in, the settlers offered free land to a sawmill man named Henry Yesler to set up his rig on the waterfront, and he went to work leveling the forests on surrounding hills. He built a skid for the logs down what is now Yesler St., and it became known as Skid Road, a term that was absorbed into American English as *skid row*. Seattleites are as sensitive about calling it *skid row*, instead of *skid road*, as San Franciscans are when they hear the word *Frisco*.

When the whole town burned in 1889 because a glue pot spilled in the basement of a cabinet shop, the rebuilding began before the ashes of the wooden buildings cooled. But this time people were a little smarter. They used bricks. Then, with the rebuilding expanded to include construction of a bigger and better waterfront, the city began raising the streets in the downtown area by regrading hills, both to build the port and to eliminate the lumps that made downtown traffic nightmarish.

Some of the streets were raised as much as 18 feet, which turned the first floor of the brick buildings into basements. At first the sidewalks remained at the original level with stairs up to the street for crossings, but gradually the sidewalks were paved over, sometimes with thick glass skylights, and dimly lit, dank arcades resulted. But the first floors were soon abandoned and left as basements. This phenomenon can be seen today in the *Underground Tour* (see under "Sightseeing").

As the city spread out over the hills to Lake Washington and north and south like a locust invasion, the Skid Road section became what we associate with skid roads—cheap hotels, wino havens, and something of a city within a city, a bowery, a place where nice people did not go.

The rehabilitation of Skid Road was a gradual thing, and the name was changed by its supporters to Pioneer Square. There were some close calls with the wrecking balls, but in 1970 it was declared a historic district by the city, and city, state, and federal funds began arriving.

Although it is spreading in all directions, the area is generally defined as being bordered on the north by Cherry, the south by Jackson, the east by 3rd, and the west by Alaskan Way. The core of the district is along the brick street of Occidental Way S., which has been turned into a mall and park.

It has some sixteen art galleries, about the same number of restaurants and cafes, three or four bookstores, twenty or thirty specialty shops, and several taverns.

Begin the walk at 1st and Yesler and walk beneath the pergola in *Pioneer Square Park*, once a major streetcar stop and a place to meet friends. The pergola was originally one of the "new" Seattle's most ornate pieces of ironwork but fell into a sad state of disrepair along with the rest of the district. A grant from United Parcel Service restored it to its former elegance.

Also in the park is a tall totem pole carved by Tlingit Indians of southeastern Alaska. It is a replica of one collected by a group of businessmen on a jaunt to Tongass Island, Alaska, in 1899 (actually, they stole the pole). The Tlingits agreed to carve a new one after the original was damaged by fire, then charged an exorbitant fee as revenge for the way the original was taken.

Across Yesler is the *Merchants Cafe*, and directly east of the park is the *Pioneer Building*, one of the finest brick buildings of the era.

Antique stores and taverns abound, and some have the most intriguing and worthless but necessary junk you're likely to see outside a trivia museum.

The visitor center of the *Klondike Gold Rush National Historical Park* is open at 117 S. Main. It is the first element of a park that will eventually run all the way to Dawson City, Yukon. It features old movies about the Klondike and dispenses information on hiking Chilkoot Pass.

At the corner of 1st and Main stands the *Grand Central Building*, one of the prime restoration projects in the district. It was formerly a hotel, but the owners invested private capital to expose the old, gorgeous brick and refurbish it to accent its rich architecture. Inside are a used bookstore, numerous galleries and craft shops, speciality shops, and restaurants. Some Pioneer Square visitors see this building and explore no further.

The rear door of the Grand Central opens onto *Occidental Park*, a curious mixture of cobbled park and ugly architecture. A shelter of sorts was built on one corner that looks as though the architect got confused and stopped in mid-design. The angular parasol (I think that is what it is supposed to be) is the most out-of-character piece of architecture in the district and resembles a cross between a service-station sign on a freeway ramp and the bones of a billboard.

A block east on S. Main is the bricked-in oasis called *Waterfall Garden Park*, another gift from United Parcel Service, which was founded in Seattle.

Stay on Occidental and follow the brick street down to an area of quality galleries, decorator shops, and the *Seattle–First National Bank*, with its museum atmosphere.

Other points of interest include the *Iron Horse Restaurant* at 311 3rd S., a restaurant-tavern where railroad photos and artifacts are displayed and slides of old steam engines are projected on the

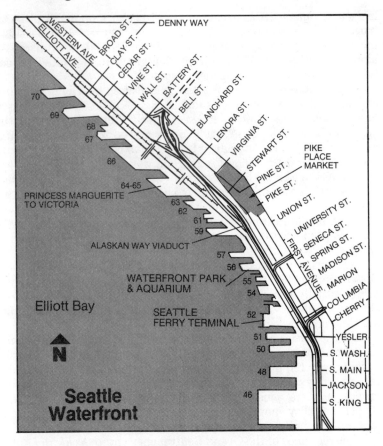

wall. Sit at the bar so that your drinks will be delivered on a train set running up and down the bar.

From Pioneer Square you can walk to the Kingdome or the International District, wander up 1st for a walk on the wild side, or swing down and take in the waterfront. Or you can cut up a block past the parking garage at Yesler and James that looks like a sinking ship, and return to the downtown area via 2nd—if you're walking only. Second is a one-way street going south away from town.

Waterfront

While other port cities around the country knew that their waterfronts had charm, with a tangy air scented by salt water, creosote, and fish, Seattle not only ignored its waterfront, it built an early American freeway, called the Alaskan Way Viaduct, like a wall of China around it. The wall still stands, its traffic noise making conversation well-nigh impossible at times, and it serves as a concrete screen to keep office workers from gazing out across the sound when they should be typing or posting bills.

Fortunately, somebody got wise and stubborn and began changing the waterfront from a blighted area to one with exotic shops, stand-up fish-and-chips bars, and even a city park.

Begin your exploration at Pier 70 at the foot of Broad St. because your chances of finding a parking spot are better there. Plan on buying something, maybe lunch for starters, while ambling around the two-story converted warehouse. The cavernous building houses a variety of shops and lots of parking on the upper level. Most of the shops are on the lower level, restaurants and gift shops in particular. The *Pier 70 Restaurant and Chowder House* is popular and has a great view of Elliott Bay. Other major tenants include import shops and the *Northwest Senior Craftsmen* outlet, where you can find a variety of gift items, including Byron Fish's famous painting, "Free at Last."

Now take a walk south past working piers, past Pier 69 where the ships bound for Victoria dock each evening between runs, to Pier 59. There you'll see a plaque on the concrete guardrail marking the spot where the steamship *Portland* landed on July 17, 1897, with nearly two tons of gold from the Klondike. Its arrival kicked off the stampede to the Klondike through Seattle and almost overnight lifted Seattle out of a depression that had begun four years earlier. Also on Pier 59 is the Omnidome Theatre, a restaurant, and a book and gift shop.

Right next door is Seattle's *Aquarium* and newest major park named, of course, the *Waterfront Park*. It isn't a traditional park. It has no grassy lawns, but it does have a large angular bronze fountain, a pavilion with a design borrowed from Stonehenge, and lots of space for sitting, walking, and looking.

Next door, for those who didn't bring their brown bag or picnic lunch, is *SourDough's Deep Dish Pizza Co.* on Pier 57, called *Miner's Landing*. They serve a wide variety of seafood and will put it in containers for picnics. The eatery shares the pier with one of the largest import houses on the waterfront, *Pirates Plunder*.

The next stop is Pier 56, *Trident Imports* (elephant bells, South Pacific furniture, clothing, and a lot of things you won't need but will want), and *Elliott's on the Pier* restaurant, with inside and outside dining and an outdoor fish bar with food to go.

Next is the *Seattle Harbor Tours* office and dock. Pier 54 is fronted by *Ye Olde Curiosity Shop*, which the staid and cautious

National Geographic once called "Seattle's most fantastic store, perhaps. . . ." The most popular and grotesque exhibit is called Sylvester, a 6-foot-tall, 137-pound mummy found in the Gila Bend Desert in 1895. Poor Sylvester. . . . The shop also has Indian, Aleut, and Eskimo artwork; elephant and walrus ivory; and to keep Sylvester company, a collection of shrunken heads from Ecuador. Beside it is *Ivar's Acres of Clams*, one of the city's most popular restaurants and the place that got the Ivar Haglund eating empire off and running.

Pier 53 is the home port for Seattle's two great fireboats, the *Alki* and the *Duwamish*, the latter with the largest pumping capacity (twenty-two thousand gallons a minute) of any fireboat in the world. On summer Saturdays and Sundays and when special events are held in the area, the fireboats pull out into the bay and spray their hoses like floating peacocks. You'll need a camera to prove to friends back home how beautiful water spraying off a boat can be.

Pier 52 is the *Washington State Ferries* dock for those bound "overseas" to the islands or the Kitsap Peninsula. Feel free to ride the escalator up to the top deck, or ride it after completing the waterfront tour and get up to 1st Ave. on the skybridge that leads from Pier 52 over the streets and beneath the Alaskan Way Viaduct.

The most interesting part of the waterfront ends here. The piers keep going south a mile or so, but guests aren't welcome, except at the Coast Guard Station and Museum on Pier 36; so you might as well turn around and forget about seeing the rest of the waterfront unless you go on a harbor tour.

From the waterfront you can either retrace your steps, continue on to a 1st Ave. tour headed north to your point of origin, or head down to Pioneer Square, only three or four blocks away.

An alternative to all this walking, at least for a one-way trip, is to ride the trolley car that went into operation in 1982. It runs on old railroad tracks beside Alaskan Way and costs $.60.

Pike Place Market

Pike Place is a two-plus-block-long street that curves north from the western end of Pike. The market is largely built on stilts out over the edge of a bluff that looks across Elliott Bay. From this vantage a number of the market's restaurants offer excellent views from windows facing west.

Starting originally in 1907 as a place where vegetable and fruit growers gathered to sell their produce to city dwellers, the market has grown into a small city all its own. As the number of farmers decreased or industries took over their lush Kent Valley farmlands for factories and parking lots, artists and craftsmen moved into empty stalls along with restaurants, antique shops, and a startling variety of small specialty businesses. Today, more than one hundred shops, individuals, produce sellers, and even a modern bank operate at the west end of Pike and in the main arcade facing Pike Place from both sides. Warrenlike lower levels with steps and ramps at odd junctions invite strollers and visitors to browse, wonder, and buy.

The market's fresh-fruit and -vegetable sellers and the variety of restaurants draw thousands of visitors daily. Seattleites regularly shop here for home-grown produce. Many experienced Pike Place shoppers walk the length of the main arcade checking quality and prices of lettuce, cabbage, cukes, and seasonal fruits. On the way back they pick up those items mentally selected on the first pass. Competition remains keen. At the end of the day a merchant-farmer, or one of the hardworking offspring, may drop in a few radishes with heads of lettuce or quote a special price for more than one item. It's a friendly place that teems with a cross section of humanity.

Change is endemic to the market. Shops open and close irregularly. At the north end of the main arcade and outside to the west when the sun shines, craftsmen and artists set up a sales counter or table for the day. The count varies from day to day, with more craftsmen showing their wares during the summer and in the weeks before Christmas. The market includes antiques, plants, meat, fish, gifts, grocers and delis, bakeries, restaurants, and spice shops.

Many Seattleites consider the market their favorite place. A stroll through makes it easy to understand why.

Following is a selective list of the establishments that have been around the longest and appear to be permanent fixtures:

Athenian Inn, Main Arcade. Many of the working people of the market hang out here, and it is known for its rather straightforward menu and great view of Elliott Bay.

Copacabana Cafe, Triangle Building. When a Bolivian family was encouraged to leave that country after the governmental winds changed, Seattle gained an excellent restaurant that has been a market fixture for many years. It is perhaps Seattle's only Bolivian restaurant and always offers high-quality food.

Corner Market, Pike Place and 1st, has been restored and rehabilitated. Merchants in this market include a beauty salon, a caterer, a crumpet place, flower shop, herb shop, an oriental market, bookstore, meat markets, and restaurants.

DeLaurenti's Italian & International Food Market. A deli with bakery that sells slices of pizza, espresso, and a variety of sandwiches.

Emmett Watson's Oyster Bar, 1916 Pike Pl. A small, courtyard spot owned by the newspaper columnist. It features raw oysters, imported beer, smoked salmon and trout, and lots of conversation.

Il Bistro, Lower Post Alley. Another unpretentious place with excellent food and bar. Light Italian food, relaxed, and rather expensive.

Starbucks Coffee and Tea, 1912 Pike Pl., rates a visit just to sniff the enchanting odors, an advertising come-on unbeaten by anything in print.

Sur La Table, 84 Pine, offers unusually fine cooking ware.

Seattle Center

Although the center wasn't built until 1962, it is difficult to remember Seattle without it or to imagine what the city would be like if we didn't have it. The recreational, cultural, and entertainment center of Seattle, it is the most exciting "people" place in the Northwest. It was the site of the Century 21 World's Fair, one of the few world's fairs in history to pay its own way.

The city went all out to make it beautiful, and the 74 acres offer a combination of imaginative architecture, lush green grass and trees, and public art. Fountains gurgle and splash wherever one turns. It was designed to be used rather than stared at. Office workers go there for picnic lunches or walks, and it is one of the highest-priority items on every visitor's agenda.

For information on galleries, children's theaters, and the monorail, see the appropriate listing elsewhere in this book. For general information, call 625-4234.

Alweg Monorail. When the monorail was built during the world's fair here in 1962, there was talk of its being extended from downtown Seattle to Seattle-Tacoma International Airport. For reasons known only to politicians, the extension never came and probably never will, even though it is popular, quiet, and fast. Today it runs back and forth along a 1.2-mile track from Seattle Center to Westlake Mall, between 4th and 5th at Pine. It makes the trip in ninety seconds and offers shoppers and visitors the alternative of parking near the center and riding the monorail to and from downtown. Hours: Sunday–Thursday, 9:00 A.M.–9:00 P.M.; Friday–Saturday, 9:00 A.M.–midnight. One-way charge is $.60; senior citizens, $.25; children under 5 free.

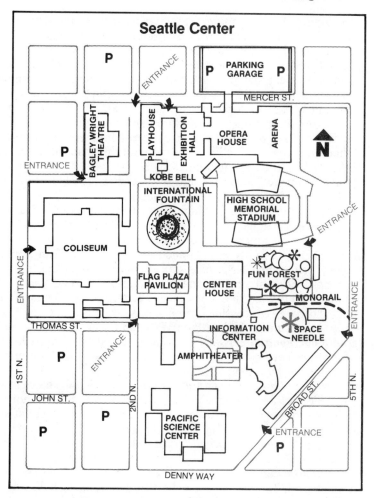

Seattle Center

Arena. This building is used more frequently for conventions than spectator sports. It is connected to the Display Hall for convenience during large exhibitions and conventions as well as high-school graduation exercises. The Arena seats up to six thousand.

Bagley Wright Theatre. This $10-million theater, paid for in part with private donations, was named for one of Seattle's most active philanthropists for the arts. It has two performing theaters, with the main stage seating 860. The PONCHO Forum seats 170 and offers workshop productions of new plays and the experimental "Dollar Theater," where rehearsals can be seen for a dollar.

Center House. Another major building, Center House was originally called the Food Circus Building. Inside this gigantic old fortress, which formerly was an armory, the Center House Court indoor park features restaurants in an atmosphere where you can eat your food at tables and engage in people-watching. The children's theater is here. Above, boutiques ring the surrounding overhead area, and the Fountain Level downstairs features a variety of shops and boutiques and a children's museum. The Seattle Center administrative offices, including the invaluable lost-and-found office at the Information Office, occupy the second floor.

Coliseum. Many rock concerts and trade shows are held here. The ice shows also appear in the Coliseum.

Flag Plaza Pavilion. The pavilion was a popular spot during the Seattle world's fair and now is used for exhibits, such as flower shows, festivals, and similar special events.

Fun Forest. Children are reason enough to go to the Fun Forest. They can clench their fists and eyes and get scared on the Zipper, the Matterhorn, the Wild Mouse, bumper cars, and numerous other rides. For the less strong of heart and stomach, there are concession games of baseball, dart and ring tossing, miniature golf, the Moon Walk, and others.

International Fountain. Electronically operated and lighted, the fountain features a constantly changing pattern of water accompanied by music.

Laserium. This cosmic laser-light concert is held in the Science Center building. Admission to the Science Center is not included, except for matinees. Buy your ticket separately at the entrance. Admission is $2.50 Tuesday, $5.00 Wednesday–Sunday. Closed Mondays. Call for hours and special group rates (443-2850).

Mural Amphitheater. This large outdoor stage area has a giant mosaic mural, *The Seattle Scene* by Paul Horiuchi, as a backdrop. The stage is surrounded by a pool and has a sloping grass amphitheater. Free concerts are held here: rock, pop, jazz, and classical. It is a centerpiece for the Bumbershoot Festival held each summer.

Opera House. Home of the Seattle Symphony and most musical events, such as the Seattle Opera and traveling symphonies and ballets, the Opera House has great acoustics, is air-conditioned, and seats 3,100.

Pacific Science Center. With its broad, shallow pools and soaring futuristic arches, the Science Center occupies the southern end of the center and has been very successful in translating science into everyday—and fun—terms. Five buildings make up the complex. Highlights: Eames/IMAX Theater, where films are shown and meetings held; the Sea Monster House, a replica of a Northwest Indian ceremonial house; the mathematics area, where you can operate computers, play games, and study the matter of probability and other heavy subjects; full-scale models of manned and unmanned spacecraft that you can climb into to see how astronauts live; and the Star Lab, an 8,000-square-foot overhead domed screen that shows the mysterious galaxies and makes you feel, indeed, small.

In addition to all this, the center hosts frequent traveling exhibits of photos, artwork, and artifacts. A scientific game area allows visitors to push buttons that make weird things happen inside machines.

The Balcony Book and Gift Shop stocks everything from nature and science books to puzzles, shells, toys, and Indian and Eskimo crafts.

Admission: adults 15–64, $5; children 5–14 and seniors, $4; children 3–5, $3. Hours: 10:00 A.M.–5:00 P.M. daily in the winter and 10:00 A.M.–6:00 P.M. in summer. For information call 443-2001 or 2880.

Playhouse. Used by the Intiman Theater and the Gilbert and Sullivan Society, it seats 890 and has a beautifully landscaped courtyard. Frequent photo and art exhibits are hung in the lobby.

The Space Needle. The revolving restaurant and viewing deck occupy the top of the tall, rather elegant tripod that has become a symbol of Seattle. The ride to the observation platform costs $3.75 for adults and $2.00 for children 5–12. The height of the Space Needle is 605 feet above ground level, and the restaurant is at the 500-foot level. The steel structure weighs 3,000 tons, and the foundation sinks 30 feet into the ground, anchored by 5,800 tons of concrete. The restaurant's outer ring of tables makes a 360-degree revolution every hour and seats 275. Elevators travel upward at the rate of 800 feet per minute, taking 43 seconds to reach the top.

Art in Public Places

Waiting for the Interurban *by Richard Beyer*

Public art in Seattle, as elsewhere, has caused a few uproars because people have never been able to agree on what constitutes art. Are those rocks along Lake City Way and in Myrtle Edwards Park art or, as some critics have insisted, just a way to get paid for dumping rocks in public places?

We will never agree on what constitutes art, but there is no doubt that people respond to certain pieces around the city, such as the many fountains—particularly the International Fountain in the Seattle Center with its 217 nozzles that spray water upward in intricate designs while music is played on the elaborate sound system.

The city's public art isn't restricted to fountains by any means, although we seem to have an abundance of them, due in part, perhaps, to the abundance of rain here.

The following list isn't complete because so many new ones are being added and new commissions granted.

SEATTLE CENTER

Amphitheater. Freestanding glass mosaic mural of fifty-four concrete slabs in sixteen shades, by Paul Horiuchi.
Central Plaza. International Fountain, which represents a giant sunflower and has 217 nozzles, by Kazuyuki, Matsushita, and Hideki Shimizu.
Coliseum, North Court. Two Chinese concrete lions, carved under supervision of the Taiwan Handicraft Promotion Center. *Evolution of Man, Flight of Gulls*, and *Seaweed*, cast bronze sculptures in 40-foot by 120-foot basin, by Everett Du Pen.
Flag Plaza Pavilion, Grand Stairway. *Flame #2*, sculptured bronze on a marble base, by Egan Weiner. Stairway fountains, by Lawrence Halprin and Bob Price.
The Lagoon. Water Sparkler, a fountain with 145 garden sprinklers set in the illuminated lagoon and run on a tape sequence, by Jacques Overhoff. *Variety Club Fountain*, copper sculpture and seascape pool with life-size beachcombing children, by Tom Hardy.
Mercer Street Parking Garage. Monolithic sculptured concrete panels on corner walls, by Charles W. Smith.
North Mall. Julius C. Lang Memorial Fountain, in a lighted pool, by Francoise Stahly.
Northwest Square, which faces the Playhouse Courtyard. *Sea Shell Fountain*, twelve tridacna shells and freeform cement, by Philippine artisans.
Pacific Science Center, Northwest Garden. *Gamma*, a sculptured concrete fountain, by Jack C. Fletcher. Northeast Pool, *Great Gull*, a bronze sculpture, by G. Alan Wright.
Playhouse, Grand Courtyard. *Fountain of the Northwest*, an illuminated bronze sculpture, by James FitzGerald. Also a river rock sculpture, *Barbet*, by James Washington.

DOWNTOWN

Federal Building, 2nd & Madison. Stone sculpture, *Landscape of Time*, by Isamu Noguchi.
Fidelity Lane, 1622 14th. *Rosetree*, bronze sculpture, by Tom Hardy.

Financial Center, Pacific National Bank of Washington, 1215 4th. Sculpture, *The Divers*, by Roy Stenger.

IBM Building, 1200 5th. Fountain, bronze, 1964, by James FitzGerald.

King County Administration Building, 500 4th. *Merchant Seamen*, murals, formerly hung in Marine Hospital, by Kenneth Callahan.

Logan Building, 5th at Union. Hammered bronze sculpture, *Morning Flight*, 1959, by Archie M. Graber.

Naramore Fountain, 1100 block of 6th. Bronze, 1967, by George Tsutakawa.

Norton Building, 801 2nd. *Totem*, welded copper sculpture, by Harold Balazs. *Restless Bird*, cast stone sculpture, by Philip McCracken.

Pioneer Square Park. Pergola, built ca. 1909, restored, by Julian F. Everett. Totem pole, replica of one brought from Tongass, Alaska, in 1899, burned in 1938, replaced in 1940, by Tlingit Indian carvers.

Plymouth Chapel, 1200 block of 6th. Stained glass created by California studio to specifications of architect John Morse.

Prefountaine Place, Yesler & 3rd. Fountain, dedicated 1926, by Carl F. Gould.

Public Safety Building, 600 block of 4th. Memorial to Gold Star Mothers (Carrara marble), 1951, by Dudley Pratt.

Rainier National Bank, 1402 15th. Aluminum and walnut sculpture, by Charles W. Smith.

Rainier National Bank, 510 Olive Way. Red cedar sculpture, *Progress*, ca. 1956, by Dudley Carter.

Rainier National Bank, 1110 2nd. Walnut and colored-glass screen, by James FitzGerald.

Seattle City Light, 1000 block of 3rd. Glass mosaic mural, *Water into Electricity*, 1959, by Jean Cory Beall.

Seattle Ferry Terminal, Alaskan Way at Marion. Joshua Green Fountain, by George Tsutakawa.

Seattle-First National Bank, 1001 4th. Bronze sculpture, *Vertebrae*. 1968, by Henry Moore. Two small fountains by George Tsutakawa. Paving mural, *Sea Marks*, by Guy Anderson. Two granite sculptures carved in relief benches, by James W. Washington, Jr. Bronze sculpture, *Penelope*, by Emile-Antoine Bourdelle. Hanging sculpture, stainless steel wires, by Harry Bertoia.

Seattle Municipal Building, 600 4th. Two bronzed walnut screens, ca. 1959, by Everett Du Pen. Pylon fountain, bronze and cast mosaic-stone, 1959, by Glen Alps.

Seattle Public Library, 1000 block of 4th. Screen (etched brass, bronze, fused glass), 1960, by James FitzGerald. Granite sculpture, *Kinship of All Life*, Creation Series #6, 1968, by James W. Washington, Jr. Casein and rice-paper collage, *Thrust Fault*, by Paul Horiuchi. Treated sheet-steel screen, *Activity of Growth*, 1960, by Glen Alps. Bronze sculpture, *Pursuit*, 1960, by Ray F. Jensen. Cedar sculpture, *Alice*, 1967, by James Wegner. Copper alloy, *Fountain of Wisdom*, 1960, by George Tsutakawa.

Washington Building, 1325 4th. Abstract sculpture, by James FitzGerald.

Westlake Square Park, 6th at Stewart. Fountain, ca. 1965, by Jean Johanson.

CENTRAL SEATTLE

Jefferson Terrace, 800 Jefferson. Abstract aluminum sculpture, *Tall Shape*, by Glen Alps. Thomas Jefferson Memorial Fountain, bronze, 1969, by James FitzGerald.

Kerry Park, West Highland Dr. Kinetic, volumetric space-frame, steel, by Doris N. Chase.

Madrona School, 1121 33rd. Three carved cedar abstract sculptures for children, 1961, by Henry Rollins.

Magnolia Branch Library, 2801 34th W. Abstract sculpture, by Glen Alps.

Museum of History and Industry, 2161 E. Hamlin. Cast-iron sculpture, *Man in Space*, by Armando O. Orozco.

Myrtle Edwards Park, north of Pier 71. Stone sculpture, *Adjacent, Against, Upon*, by Michael Heizer.

Regrade Park, 3rd & Bell. Concrete sculpture, *Gyro Jack*, by Lloyd Hamrol.

Seattle University, library, 12th & E. Columbia. Two paintings, by Paul Horiuchi.

Volunteer Park, Seattle Art Museum terrace. Black granite sculpture, *Black Sun*, 1969, by Isamu Noguchi. Chinese tomb figures: rams, camels from approach to tomb of fifteenth-century Ming prince; tigers, warrior, and civil officer from tomb of Manchu noblemen, seventeenth or eighteenth century. Stainless steel sculpture, *Fifteen Planes*, by David Smith. East of Seattle Art Museum: cedar sculpture, *Rivalry of the Winds*, by Dudley Carter. Wading pool environs: Children's play sculpture, 1962, by Charles W. Smith.

Washington Park (Arboretum) Tea Garden. Stone lanterns, Japanese.

NORTH SEATTLE

Ballard Branch Library, 5711 24th NW. Copper alloy fountain, *Of*

Sea and Life, 1963, by Howard Duell. Wall sculpture of lami-
nated wood, 1963, by Archie M. Graber.
Lake City Branch Library, 12501 28th NE. Bronze semicircular
gates, 1965, by George Tsutakawa.
Northgate Shopping Center, 5th NE and NE Northgate Way. Giant-
plant fountains, Totem Pole Pool, bronze, 1963, by George Tsu-
takawa.
N. 34th & Greenwood. Cast aluminum sculpture, *Waiting for the
Interurban*, by Richard Beyer. (To the disgust of modern-art
enthusiasts, this is the most popular piece of art in Seattle.)
Northwest Hospital, 1551 N. 120th. Totem pole, by Don Keys.
Pacific National Bank, 4501 15th NE. Steel sculpture, by Charles
W. Smith.
Safeco Plaza, Brooklyn Ave. NE & NE 45th. Bronze fountain, 1973,
by George Tsutakawa.
University of Washington, 15th NE overpass. Bronze sculpture, *Girl
with a Flat Hat*, by Philip Levine. E. 41st entrance: statue of
George Washington, bronze, ca. 1909, by Lorado Taft. Suzallo
Quadrangle: *Broken Obelisk*, Cor-Ten steel sculpture, by
Barnett Newman. Rainier Vista: Drumheller Fountain, 1961,
by Lawrence Halprin.
U.S. Post Office, NE 43rd & University Way NE. Two murals, by
Jacob Elshin.
Woodland Park. Totem pole, Chief William Shelton, Tulalip Indian
Reservation. Birdbath, brick with carved bird insets, by Rich-
ard Beyer.

SOUTH SEATTLE

Belvedere Place, Admiral Way at Olga. Totem, replica of Haida pole,
by Fleischman and Morgan.
Burien Library, 14700 6th SW. A. N. Thompson Memorial Foun-
tain, 1972, by George Tsutakawa.
Hilton Inn, near Seattle-Tacoma Airport. Painting, *Space Owl*, by
Jane G. Johnston. Coffers, by Irene McGowan. Painting, by
Paul Horiuchi. Sculpture, by James Wegner. Raccoon mural,
by Patricia K. Nicholson. Frieze, by Archie M. Graber. Metal
wall sculpture, by Gordon Anderson. Mural, by Guy Anderson.
Lake Washington Floating Bridge, east tunnel entrance. *Pacific Rim
Motifs*, concrete tablets, by James FitzGerald.
Mount Baker Park, Lake Washington Blvd. S. Granite reproduction
of ancient Japanese lantern, 1923.
Seattle-Tacoma International Airport. Acrylic painting, *Spectrum
Delta II*, by Francis Celantano. Four acrylic paintings, *Kalpa*,
by Christopher English. Sculpture in glass and neon, *Infinity*

Column, by John Geise. Acrylic painting, untitled, by Thomas Holder. Ebony, vermilion wood, and ivory sculpture, *Tent Frame*, by Paul R. Jenkins. Central Plaza sculpture, enameled aluminum, by Robert Maki. Oil painting, *Garden Zipper*, by Alden Mason. Wood sculpture, *Night Flight I*, by Louise Nevelson. Serigraph on mirror-coated Plexiglas, *Star Quarters*, by Robert Rauschenberg. Room with computer-controlled sound and light, untitled light display, by James Seawright and Peter Phillips. Acrylic painting, *York Factory A*, by Frank Stella. Acrylic sculpture, untitled, by John Wharton.
Seward Park, Lake Washington Blvd. S. Torri, Gateway of Welcome, presented by local Japanese-Americans in 1939.
Southwest Branch Library, 9010 35th SW. Wall sculpture, *Mother Reading with Child*, by Charles W. Smith.
Water Operations Center, 2700 Airport Way S. Stainless steel fountain, 1975, by Ted Jonsson.

Individuals and Events Commemorated by Public Monuments

* John McGraw (1850–1910) is represented by a full-length figure in bronze, at the triangle of Stewart St., 5th, and Westlake, which was dedicated in 1913. McGraw rose from policeman to King County sheriff, then became a banker, state governor, and president of the Seattle Chamber of Commerce. The statue is the work of a New York sculptor, Richard Brooks, and was financed in large part by Alden Blethen, *Seattle Times* publisher. At that time the newspaper was produced in the triangular building near the statue, hence the name, Times Square. The inscription reads: "This commemorates the services of an energetic and wise leader in many enterprises undertaken for the general welfare, especially the project for connecting Lake Washington with tide water by ship canal."
* James R. Ellis of Metro and Forward Thrust fame is honored by a plaque in Freeway Park.
* A bronze bust of the Empire Builder, James J. Hill (1838–1916), the energetic builder of the Great Northern Railroad, stands on the University of Washington campus. Finn H. Forlich was the sculptor of this monument, which was dedicated at the Alaska-Yukon-Pacific Exposition in 1909.
* Edward Grieg (1843–1907) is represented by a bronze bust on the University of Washington campus. The Norwegian composer is the only artist honored by a Seattle monument.
* A Chinese memorial on the Weller St. Playfield is dedicated to

ten Chinese-Americans who gave their lives in defense of this country.

- A Spanish-American War memorial, *The Hiker*, represents the soldiers of the 1898–99 war and guards the entrance to the Woodland Park Zoo.
- Judge Thomas Burke (1849–1925) was memorialized in a dedication in 1930 at Volunteer Park. The inscription reads: "Patriot, jurist, orator, friend, patron of education. First in every movement for the advancement of the city and the state. Seattle's foremost and best-beloved citizen."
- A bronze statue of George Washington, by Lorado Taft, stands on a twenty-five-foot pedestal provided in 1971 for its present position on the University of Washington campus. Originally cast for the 1909 Alaska-Yukon-Pacific Exposition, it received its original pedestal in 1939, constructed as a WPA project. Students love to paint the statue green in keeping with the state's fire-prevention theme, Keep Washington Green.
- William Henry Seward (1801–72) is represented by a full-length bronze figure erected in 1909 in Volunteer Park in front of the conservatory. As secretary of state, Seward was instrumental in the purchase of Alaska and thereby earned the gratitude of Seattle. The 2,000-pound bronze, the work of a New York sculptor, Richard Brooks, was originally unveiled at the Alaska-Yukon-Pacific Exposition in 1909 and moved to the park in 1910. Its cost of $15,000 was paid by private donations.
- A bronze statue of Christopher Columbus was donated by the city's Italian-American community and placed in Waterfront Park at Pier 57. Douglas Bennett designed the $75,000, 6½-foot figure showing a robed, helmeted Columbus leaning on a staff, peering into the distance from his ship. A lack of realism and a certain starkness of Columbus's features that mitigate against a heroic appearance induced the Arts Commission to recommend rejection of the gift when it was first offered. Bennett, a local sculptor, explained that a man seventy-one days out of port searching for a New World might well look gaunt and anguished. For Columbus's rival as discoverer, see Leif Erikson at Shilshole Bay.
- *Waiting for the Interurban*, a group of patient commuters at the north end of Fremont Bridge, was sculpted by Richard Beyer.
- A bronze bust in Denny Park commemorates the controversial Mark A. Matthews, pastor of the First Presbyterian Church, who enlivened Seattle from 1902 to 1940. Alonzo Victor Lewis was the sculptor of the monument, raised in 1942.

- *The Doughboy*, a huge bronze figure by Alonzo Victor Lewis, stands in the Seattle Center. The statue, dedicated in 1932, lacks an inscription identifying it as an official World War I memorial because some city officials resented the victorious soldier's triumphant smile and his war trophies.
- President Warren Harding's memorial in Woodland Park was dedicated in 1925.
- Father Prefontaine, a Catholic priest of the pioneer era, is commemorated by a monument at Prefontaine Place.
- Chief Seattle (1786–1866) is honored by a bronze bust atop a drinking fountain in Pioneer Square and also by a full-length statue at Tilikum Pl. on 5th Ave. near Denny Way. The statue, designed by James A. Wehn, was dedicated in 1912, then again in 1975 when it was moved out of storage after improvements were completed in the little triangular park.
- Leif Erikson stands in bronze at Shilshole Bay. The sculpture by August Werner was dedicated in 1962. Norwegian organizations, which contributed the monument, resisted charges made in 1962 that Erikson was a murderer and an indifferent Christian.
- Since 1952 the Yukon Club and the Propeller Club have placed twenty-two bronze plaques along the waterfront to commemorate historic events, including the 1897 arrival of the *Portland* with Yukon gold; the first West Seattle ferry landing in 1888; and the site where the ship *Decatur* fired on Indian attackers in 1856. Other plaques commemorate the original Colman Dock (1909); Joshua Green; Dr. Alexander DeSoto and his hospital ship *Idaho*; the Great White Fleet visits of 1908; the *Willapa*, the first sailing vessel built by the Alaska Steamship Company; the Coast Guard cutter *Bear*; and the Moran brothers, builders of the battleship *Nebraska* in 1904 and other ships.
- A plaque honoring ten American crewmen of a B-17 shot down over Warsaw on September 18, 1944, was placed in the Public Safety Building Memorial Plaza in 1966. The plaque hangs opposite the wall dedicated in 1951 on which the names of Seattle's war dead are engraved. This memorial was designed to replace the plywood pylon that marked Victory Square on University St. during World War II. Lake City veterans of World War II are honored by a plaque at 125th NE and Bothell Way NE. Among the other monuments to servicemen is one at the Veteran's Memorial Cemetery, N. 111th at Aurora.
- Will Rogers (1879–1935) is honored by a plaque at NE 137th St. near 15th NE.
- The pioneers who landed at Alki are honored by a stone pylon

carved from Plymouth Rock and brought to its Alki location
by a motorized caravan in September 1926.

- An 11,900-pound stone with plaque at 34th NW near W. 75th,
  sponsored by the Halibut Fishermen's Wives Association, hon-
  ors fishermen lost on the boat *Jane* in September 1959. Dedication was in March 1961. The inscription reads: "Dedicated to
  the men of the Seattle fishing fleet who reaped their living
  from the sea and found their final rest beneath its waves."

Other plaques around the city honor Herman B. Bagley, physician, and other promoters of the Lake Washington Ship Canal;
Henry L. Yesler, pioneer mill operator; Catherine P. Blaine, the
city's first schoolteacher; the site of the blockhouse used dur-
ing the 1853 Indian war; peace between Japan and the United
States (stone lantern given by Yokohama in 1930 in gratitude
for earthquake assistance); Arthur A. Denny's log cabin; Car-
son D. Boren's log cabin; Louisa Boren Denny; the 1909
Alaska-Yukon-Pacific Exposition; the Fuller donation of the
Seattle Art Museum; William E. Boeing; W. W. Conner; the
Statue of Liberty (replica at Alki); Russian veterans of World
War I (Washelli Cemetery).

Sports and Recreation

Myrtle Edwards Park

Many people in Seattle are so recreation minded that they know little and care less of what goes on inside the city limits; the city is a condition they tolerate five days each week, a place to live and work between outings. With the possible exception of outdoor ice skating in the winter (it's too mild here), there probably is no sport played anywhere else in the nation that isn't available in Seattle.

But that is only the beginning. Outside the city, within sight on a clear day, are the Olympic and Cascade mountains, where you can rock climb, hike, car camp, canoe, kayak, swim, ride horses, or simply pause and look. And within sight of the city, even right in the city, you can walk on beaches, dig clams, or fish for salmon, lingcod, and sole. Other diversions include sailing, water-skiing, swimming, cruising, scuba diving . . . the list is very long.

Because Seattle is surrounded (almost) by water—fresh to the east, salt to the west—and the mountains are less than an hour's drive away and more than twelve million acres of them are in public ownership, it is easy to understand why many residents treat the city simply as a launchpad for fun.

Interestingly, with all this self-propelled sports activity, Seattle has also become a success story in spectator sports, and each professional team—the Seahawks, SuperSonics, Mariners, and others—receives enthusiastic support in terms of seats sold.

Archery

This isn't one of the major sports in Seattle, in part because it isn't particularly strenuous. But there are public ranges: one at Magnuson Park, at Sand Point Way NE and NE 65th, and one at Carkeek Park at the west foot of NW 110th St. The park has six practice ranges, but you'll have to bring your own targets.

Badminton

This is by no means a major sport in the area, but community centers organize leagues if sufficient demand exists. Call the local community center for details.

Baseball

For years Seattle had the Rainiers baseball team as part of the Pacific Coast League, the Triple A variety of baseball, and games were played in Sicks Stadium on Rainier Ave. S. Then, with the wisdom that brings smog to cities, Seattle decided to become a "major league" city. They got into the American League with the Seattle Pilots—for one year. Then the franchise was sold and Seattle sports fans screamed "Foul!" In one of those legal maneuvers that only attorneys can understand, Seattle interests took the American League to court. But instead of suing them to get the league out of town and behind bars, or at least several million dollars poorer, Seattle took them to court to bring them *back* to town. And Seattle won. The city got an expansion franchise out of the case and a promise from the apologetic baseball league that the city would have a team. And we do . . . sort of. The Mariners.

The team began playing in April 1977, after selecting thirty players from existing American League teams. The ownership has changed, but the club's dismal record and penchant for bad trades have not. Fan loyalty is not excessive.

Late in the 1990 season the Mariners acquired all-star Ken Griffey, Sr., to join his son Ken, also an all-star, a first in major league baseball. It wasn't long before they hit back-to-back home runs, also a major league first.

We also have the college teams at the University of Washington and Seattle Pacific College, plus uncounted dozens of community-center league teams, Little League teams, Babe Ruth teams, and what have you. During the season, select a community center at random if you are a baseball buff, and you'll find someone playing baseball. Sandlot baseball, unfortunately, has disappeared with real grass.

Dozens of slow-pitch leagues are formed around the city by the Parks Department, and a few fast-pitch softball teams exist.

Basketball

For several seasons Seattle had an excellent NBA team called the SuperSonics (abbreviated to Sonics). The team's once-mediocre record suddenly changed in 1978 after Lenny Wilkens came back as coach. The next year they won the NBA championship.

But they haven't been the same since. Wilkens left and was replaced by Bernie Bickerstaff, who has been trading for new faces and trying new approaches to coaching.

They play in the Coliseum. For ticket information, call 281-5850.

Among the college teams, only the University of Washington Huskies are much of a national factor now. The Seattle University Chieftans produced a number of good players; Elgin Baylor, Frank Oleynick, and Clint Richardson come to mind.

For University of Washington information, call 543-2200; for Seattle University information, call 626-5305.

Seattle Pacific University has another popular team on the small-college circuit, the Falcons. For information, call the athletics office at 281-2085.

For the participant rather than the spectator, the Parks Department each fall organizes fast-break, slow-break, and half-court leagues, as well as an occasional open night for drop-ins to organize their own games.

Call your local recreational center or call park headquarters at 625-4671.

Bicycling

Getting acquainted with Seattle's outstanding views, water-front and boating activities, and people by bicycle offers more action than walking and more intimate experiences than driving. As you pedal along a beach or pump up and down hills to take in old neighborhoods with interspersed viewpoints, you can absorb each experience before a new one interrupts.

All of Seattle and its suburbs are laced with planned bicycle routes. Many are marked with the familiar two-wheel symbol of the bike trail. Every type of trip can be experienced, from easy, level rides around Green Lake to the up-and-down challenging rides on Queen Anne Hill and Mercer Island. Rental bikes are available, mainly at Green Lake and in some of the shops listed below.

BICYCLE TRIPS

Following are only a few of the most popular bicycle trips or tours around Seattle and neighboring islands and suburbs. Two or three excellent bicycle-tour books on the area are available.

Bicycle Sundays. During summer months a 6-mile stretch along Lake Washington is closed to auto traffic from 10:00 A.M. to 5:00 P.M. every third Sunday. Check with the Seattle Parks Department or police before you go freewheeling.

Burke-Gilman Trail. This 12½-mile premium bicycle and hiking trail represents a concept that has been watched closely by other cities. The city and county took over an abandoned stretch of railroad bed that ran from Gas Works Park on Lake Union to Kenmore, taking a swing through the edge of the University of Washington campus and along the west shore of Lake Washington. After the city and county acquired it, the roadbed was cleared of rails and ties, graded smooth, surfaced, and given to bikers, walkers, and runners. From the city, start at Gas Works Park on Lake Union and follow the marked bikeway around Lake Union, through the University of Washington campus to University Village shopping center. At this point the trail intersects the bikeway to Green Lake, or you may make a loop trip back to Gas Works Park. Continuing on the Burke-Gilman Trail at University Village, you will pass Warren G. Magnuson Park, Matthews Beach Park, and a rest area at NE 130th, then go around the northern tip of Lake Washington to Kenmore Logboom Park. Auto parking, rest rooms, and picnic tables are available at all parks on the trail.

Green Lake Ride. Probably the most popular bicycling path in Seattle, a trip around Green Lake is 2.8 miles and is mainly flat.

You're likely to encounter many walkers and joggers but no motor traffic. Traffic moves counterclockwise around the lake. Green Lake Park East and West includes fishing, swimming both in the lake and in a pool, playfields, and picnic areas. The Green Lake Ride offers a destination from the University of Washington along the Ravenna Park bicycle path. The ride is generally easy and takes about one-half hour. Bike rentals are available near the lake. Restaurants and shops are nearby.

Lake Washington Ride. A succession of waterfront park areas along Seattle's eastern edge gives low, level riding on paths and streets from the University of Washington's Arboretum to a circle tour of Seward Park.

Magnolia View Ride. High above Puget Sound, Magnolia Bluff offers views of the Olympics, the shipping in Elliott Bay, West Seattle, and Mount Rainier, as well as Seattle's downtown.

Queen Anne Hill Ride. Cycling around Queen Anne Hill affords a look at one of Seattle's oldest residential areas with viewpoints interspersed for a look in all directions.

Shilshole Bay-Salmon Bay Rides. These two rides are located along both sides of the Salmon Bay waterway from Fisherman's Terminal to Shilshole Bay and Golden Gardens Park on the north side of the waterway and along Commodore Way to Discovery Park on the south side of the waterway.

Waterfront Park Bike Path. (See Myrtle Edwards and Elliott Bay parks under "Parks.")

West Seattle Beach Ride. Begin at the west end of the Spokane St. Bridge over the Duwamish Waterway on Harbor Ave. SW near SW California Place. You'll be looking at an ever-changing view of Elliott Bay, the Olympics in the background, and across the water to Seattle's downtown skyline, so pick a clear day. Your ride will be level on the water side of Harbor and Alki avenues around Duwamish Head, along Alki Beach and Park, past Alki Point Lighthouse, on to Schmitz Viewpoint Park, and beyond to Lincoln Park and the landing for ferries to and from Vashon Island. Generally an easy trip, it is about 12 miles and two hours round-trip. Turn around at any point for a shorter trip. Picnic areas, rest rooms, food shops, and take-out foods are available along the route.

Other rides within the city limits include Capitol Hill, Laurelhurst, Lake Union, and Seattle City Center. Nearby are interesting trips around Mercer Island, Bainbridge Island, Whidbey Island, Newport-Lake Sammamish, and Vashon Island. Experienced cyclists can circle Lake Washington in about 50 miles of varied riding.

BICYCLE CLUBS AND INFORMATION

Various clubs offer touring, racing, and information sharing about bicycles. Cascade Bicycle Club sponsors a twenty-four-hour hot line (522-BIKE). Leave your name and telephone number on the recording, and someone will return your call and answer any questions on biking. The *Bicycle Paper* (P.O. Box 842, Seattle, Washington 98111) is published monthly from April to September and costs $4.50 a year. It is available at most bike shops. Other organizations to contact for information are:

City of Seattle Engineering Department publishes a Bicycle Guidemap, free; send 65¢ in postage to: Seattle Engineering Dept., 900 Municipal Bldg., Seattle, Washington 98104-1879. Attn: Bike Map.

Washington State Bicycle Association: call 329-BIKE. Lists of racing organizations may be obtained from this association.

Washington State Highway Department locates sixty-one different routes for bicyclists and publishes maps. Write Bicycle, Engineering Services Division, Highway Administration Building, Olympia, Washington 98504.

BICYCLE RACES

Races are held at King County Marymoor Park in Redmond on Friday nights at 7:30, April through November. For training-ride schedule, call 329-BIKE. An entry fee is charged, and the sponsor is the Marymoor Park Velodrome. The track is banked at 25 degrees and is open to the public every day.

BICYCLE RENTALS

Alki Bicycle Co., 2722 Alki SW (938-3322). Near the Alki Ave. bike path.

The Bicycle Center, 4529 Sand Point Way NE (523-8300). Near Burke-Gilman Trail.

Gregg's Greenlake Cycle Inc., 7007 Woodlawn NE (523-1822). Close to Green Lake path and near Burke-Gilman Trail.

Sports Exchange, 2232 15th W. (285-4777).

Rental rates at most shops range upward from $3.00 an hour depending on the type of bike.

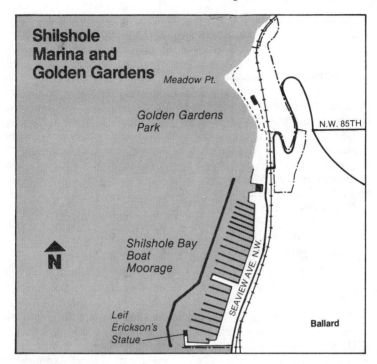

Shilshole Marina and Golden Gardens

Meadow Pt.

Golden Gardens Park

N.W. 85TH

N

Shilshole Bay Boat Moorage

SEAVIEW AVE. N.W.

Leif Erickson's Statue

Ballard

Boating

BOAT RACING

Each summer Seafair sponsors an unlimited hydroplane race on Lake Washington, usually in early August. It is one of the most popular events in the city in spite of the loud groaning by residents of whatever lakeside neighborhood the city and Seafair decide to take over for the weekend. Seafair also sponsors smaller-class hydroplane races, usually on Green Lake, earlier in the summer.

One of the most beautiful types of boat racing is the shell races held in the Lake Washington Ship Canal occasionally throughout the year with the University of Washington crew competing against other college crews.

Sailboat Racing. Sailing detractors say watching sailboat races is as exciting as watching grass grow or watching paint dry. A lot of people disagree. The Seattle Yacht Club, 1807 E. Hamlin (325-1000), and the Corinthian Yacht Club, with clubhouses on Shilshole Bay and Leschi Park on Lake Washington (322-

7877), are the major clubs. Both sponsor numerous races throughout the year. Check the newspapers or call the clubs.

BOAT RAMPS AND MOORAGES—PUBLIC

Duwamish Waterway. 1st S. & S. River.
Lake Washington. Atlantic City, S. Henderson & Seward Park S.; Lakewood Moorage, Lake Washington Blvd. S. & S. Genesee; N. & S. Leschi Moorages, Lakeside S. off E.-Alder; Sayres Memorial Park, Lake Washington Blvd. S. & 46th S.; S. Ferdinand & Lake Washington Blvd. S.; S. Day & Lakeside S.
Puget Sound. Don Armeni Boat Ramp, Harbor Ave. SW off SW Maryland; Eddie Vine Boat Ramp, north end of Seaview Ave. NW; Seacrest Boat House, Harbor SW & S. Washington (day).
Salmon Bay and Lake Washington Ship Canal. 14th NW & Shilshole NW; N. 36th, Corliss N. & Northlake Way.

BOAT-RENTAL PRICES

Whether you want to sail, fish, scuba dive, water-ski, sightsee, or simply go for a boat ride, there's a place somewhere in the Seattle area to rent a boat of your choice. You can rent yachts for extended Puget Sound cruises, with or without skippers and crews; you can rent a kicker boat with motor and fishing gear to go after salmon (and dogfish, of course) off Whidbey Island and Point No Point; you can join a sailing club and take instructions; you can rent a paddleboat at Green Lake; and you can canoe through the Arboretum.

Before giving you a sampling of places to rent boats, here is a rough estimate of rental prices:
Canoes. These range from about $3.50 an hour at the University of Washington Canoe House to $5 at private firms.
Kicker boats. For the uninitiated, these are simply outboard boats with a twenty-horsepower motor, used in Puget Sound for salmon and bottom fishing. They cost roughly $15 a day without motor. Boats and motors go for about $8 per hour. Most rental places also have fishing gear available at about $5 a day, some slightly higher. Rental places open around 4:00 A.M. for the early risers who want to get their salmon before going to work.
Paddleboats. At Green Lake these rent for $6 an hour and up.
Rowboats. At Green Lake these rent for $5 an hour.
Sailboats. The smaller models, for day use only (up to 16 feet) average about $10 an hour. The 25- to 30-foot models run from

$80 a day and up, with better prices for a weekly rental. When you get into this class and larger, some charter firms require you to use your own skipper at an additional cost.

Water-ski boats. For obvious reasons, it is hard to find a boathouse that will rent these high-powered craft, because they are accident-prone and expensive to repair. Those few places that do rent them charge upward from $25 an hour or $75 to $100 a day, depending on the size of boat and motor.

BOAT-RENTAL LOCATIONS

The Boathouse, 9812 17th SW (763-0688). Rents canoes.

Goodtime Charters, Pier 56 (623-1445). Charters for large groups, three-hour minimum. Price ranges from $875 to $3,375, depending on group size. Can take from one hundred to three hundred aboard the cruise boats.

Green Lake. Rentals on east end of lake (527-0171). Rowboats and paddleboats.

Kelly's Landing, 1401 NE Boat St. (547-9909). Rents up to 22-foot sailboats, canoes, and small sailboats. Open seven days a week April to September.

Ledger Marine Charters, 1500 Westlake N. (283-6160). Charter boats, power and sail, 26-footers and up, with one-week minimum. Can provide skippered charters for one-day group trips.

Northwest Marine Charters, 2400 Westlake N. (283-3040). Charters both sail and power boats from 26-footers. Special arrangements can be made for skippered one-day outings.

Sailboat Charters & Rentals Unlimited, 2046 Westlake N. (281-9176). Charters and rentals.

Seacrest Boat House, 1660 Harbor SW (932-1050). Kicker boats, rented half days or all day, motors, and bait.

University of Washington Waterfront Activities Center (543-9433). Somewhat difficult to find. Turn right into parking lot north of Montlake Bridge near Husky Stadium, and follow the Montlake Cut (east) to the end of the lot at a new building. Canoes are for rent by the hour or day.

Wind Works Sailing School Rentals & Charters, 7001 Seaview NW (784-9386). Cruising sailboats from 26 to 40 feet for trips through Puget Sound, the San Juans, and Canadian Gulf Islands. Skippered charters available.

SAILING LESSONS

Pick a beautiful summer day in Seattle and you'll see hundreds, if not a thousand or more sailboats flitting across Lake

Washington and Puget Sound. Sailing is nearly as popular as power boating and certainly a lot quieter. A number of sailing courses are available through private clubs and organizations such as the University of Washington Alumni Association. Public courses are easier to enroll in, and only these are listed. For information on others, contact the Coast Guard Auxiliary, the Power Squadron, a community college, or a private yacht club.

American Red Cross. In cooperation with the city parks, the Red Cross offers classes open to anyone 13 years or older who can pass the Red Cross swimming test. The course includes twenty-four hours of instruction, twelve in the classroom and the rest on water. To register, call the Parks Department, 100 Dexter N., Seattle, Washington 98101 (625-4671); or the Red Cross, Box 24286, Seattle, Washington 98124 (323-2345).

Center for Wooden Boats offers basic classes on Lake Union (382-2628).

Corinthian Yacht Club offers a variety of classes (322-7877).

Elliott Bay Yacht Center offers basic, coastal cruising, and bareboat charter lessons (285-9499).

Green Lake Small Craft Center offers basic lessons for adults and teens (684-4074).

Bowling

There are some three dozen bowling centers (they aren't called "alleys" anymore) in Seattle, more in outlying areas, many of which have restaurants and nurseries. Most also have billiard tables (few pool halls remain in Seattle). Check the Yellow Pages for a complete list of nearby lanes.

The following organization will assist you with league and tournament information: Seattle Bowling Association, 1512 NE 117th (365-2973).

Boxing

Although Seattle has produced a few contenders in the middle- and heavyweight classes (Eddie Cotton, Boone Kirkman, and Pete Rademacher) and some regional boxers, such as Brett Summers and Greg "Mutt" Haugen, are getting national exposure, Seattle has never been much of a factor in boxing. Gyms are scarce, and most lean toward the health spa or Oriental martial arts, the latter popularized by the late Seattle native, actor Bruce Lee.

Bridge

At least three bridge clubs exist in Seattle, and an occasional tournament is held in the Seattle Center. For information and instruction, call the Seattle Bridge Center, 557 Roy (282-6414).

Chess

The Main Library of the Seattle Library system, 5th & Madison, offers free chess games Wednesdays from 1:00–6:00 P.M., Room 219. For information on other clubs, call the library (625-2665), since others meet on an infrequent basis in branch libraries.

Curling

The Granite Curling Club, 1440 N. 128th (362-2446), offers free instruction. Season runs from October through April. Initiation fee: $25, dues $12 per month, $2 per game. Call for schedules and competition.

Fishing

It has often been said that to understand the Northwest mystique, you first must go winter steelheading when the temperature is below freezing and you have to keep dipping the rod into the water to clear the ice off it, and you stand there shivering and never catch a fish. Or you must catch some sea-run cutthroat or a salmon headed for the spawning beds, or dig a clam, or go out in Puget Sound in a kicker boat before dawn and sit in a fogbank, lost and wondering if a freighter is going to run you down. If the Northwest has a mystique, fishing and all that goes with it are part of it.

Fisheries biologists say there are some 150 species of fish in Puget Sound and about 36 in Lake Washington (including the saltwater fish that migrate in). Thus, most anglers go after the more spectacular fish—the salmon, steelhead, and sea-run cutthroat trout—and there isn't so much competition for the bottom fish that are equally good on the dinner table.

These lesser-known marine fish include cod, hake, flounder, sole, perch, and surf smelt. The freshwater fish include rainbow trout, largemouth bass, sunfish, mountain whitefish, and crayfish.

Also of major importance to sport fishermen are the marine shellfish. Who among us doesn't love Dungeness crab? Unfortunately, there are few places right in town to take shellfish, such as clams, geoducks, crab, shrimp, octopus, and squid. They are found at various places along Puget Sound and Hood Canal. Perhaps the most comprehensive source of information on public access to the state's shorelines and the fishing available is the book *Washington Public Shore Guide*, by James W. Scott and Melly A. Reuling, published by the University of Washington Press. It lists shoreline that is available for public use throughout the state and how to catch most kinds of shellfish found on the shorelines.

The city and county have spent a great deal of money building fishing piers around Puget Sound, and it is always interesting to walk out onto them and watch the action and talk to the fishermen. You will find people of all ages and social backgrounds on the piers, and during January and February the piers are filled with people of Oriental descent fishing for squid, which are in great abundance then.

The seasons are too complicated to list here, so your best bet is to check in at a sporting goods store for information on seasons, license fees, and tips on where to fish for which species. In most cases you'll have to drive out of town, especially for clam digging and stream fishing. However, there are numerous piers maintained by the Seattle Parks and Recreation Department where no license is needed.

PUBLIC FISHING

Green Lake. Fish anywhere on the lake or at three piers: NE corner near the ball field (juveniles only); NW corner near "Duck Island"; and SW corner by the former Aqua Theater.

Lake Washington. Madison Park at the foot of E. Madison; just south of Madrona Beach near the foot of E. Jefferson; Mount Baker Park, N. Leschi Moorage, Lakeside S. and Alder E.; S. McClellan and 35th S.; and Seward Park, Lake Washington Blvd. and S. Juneau.

Puget Sound. Waterfront Park at the end of Pier 57. A public fishing pier and popular place for father-and-son teams of bottom fishermen. Also on the waterfront, the public seawall just north of Pier 70 is popular. Others include the Alki Ave. breakwater and the pier at the south end of Golden Gardens Park.

Ship Canal. South side of Hiram M. Chittenden (Ballard) Locks.

CHARTERS

Ocean Charters. Charter boats in the Pacific off the coastal towns of Westport, Ilwaco, Sekiu, and Neah Bay in particular have become a major industry. There are many in Seattle who do not consider their year complete without at least one trip out into the ocean for salmon, just as there are many tourists who come here with that one thing in mind. In most cases, it is possible to arrange for a charter-boat trip from Seattle via toll-free numbers to the coastal towns. More and more charter firms are stressing other fish now instead of only salmon, so check with the firm to see what they suggest you go after.

In addition to the day trips, there are tuna and albacore charter boats from the coastal towns. Check chambers of commerce, sporting goods stores, and the *Fishing and Hunting News* for details. The charter season for salmon runs from around May 1 through September.

Puget Sound. Bait, tackle, and (usually) coffee are provided on these local salmon charter boats. They will also take you bottom fishing if requested. Local charter companies are: *Viking Star Charters*, 2442 NW Market St., #239 (622-2393); *Major Fishing Charters* at Ray's Boathouse on Shilshole Bay (783-8873); *Bendixen Charters*, Shilshole Marina (285-5999); *Ballard Salmon Charters* (789-6202) operates out of Shilshole and provides everything needed, including coffee, tea, and hot chocolate; and *Major Marine Tours*, 1415 Western Ave. (292-0595) operates out of Pier 54 and provides all equipment, with a barbecued-chicken picnic thrown in. Rates begin at $45.

Football

PROFESSIONAL

Seattle Seahawks. The National Football League team has been Seattle's most popular team for several years, in part because the original owners, the Nordstrom family, remained out of sight and let professionals run the team. In late 1988 the team was sold to two Californians, one of whom, Ken Behring, is very visible on the sidelines. It is clear, however, that changes will be made. Home games are played in the Kingdome, almost always before more than 60,000 fans. Office: 11220 NE 53rd, Kirkland (827-9777); ticket sales: 827-9766.

UNIVERSITY OF WASHINGTON

The Huskies have been coached by Don James for more than a decade, have gone to a variety of bowls, including the Rose Bowl, and have almost as loyal a following as the Seahawks. Ticket information: 543-2200.

Golf

The Greater Seattle area has more than a dozen private golf courses and some two dozen public courses. It is best to call the public courses in advance for reservations.

As with everything, greens fees are on the rise, but a sampling recently gave these costs:

Nine to eighteen holes starts at $10. Annual golf cards are $195 for fifty rounds per year, $85 for senior citizens.

GOLF COURSES

Ballinger Park, 23000 Lakeview Dr., Mountlake Terrace
    (775-6467) 9H.
Bellevue Municipal, 5450 140th NE Bellevue (451-7250).
Foster, 13500 Interurban S. (242-4221).
Greenlake, 5701 W. Green Lake Way N. (632-2280), par 3.
Interbay, 2501 15th W. (281-7556), 9H par 3, driving range.
Jackson Park Municipal, 1000 NE 135th (363-4747).
Jefferson Park Municipal, 4101 Beacon S. (762-4513).
Tyee Valley, 2401 S. 192nd (878-3540).
Wayne, 16721 96th NE, Bothell (485-6237).
West Seattle, 4470 35th SW (935-5187).

PRACTICE GOLF RANGES

Harris-Conley, 1440 156th NE, Bellevue (747-2585).
Interbay, 2501 15th W. (281-7556).
Jefferson Park, 4101 Beacon S. (762-4513).
Puetz Evergreen, 11762 Aurora N. (362-2272).

Gymnastics

This isn't one of the major sports in Seattle, but instruction and competition are sometimes offered by the Parks Department (625-4671), Seattle Pacific University (281-2000), and the University of Washington's Continuing Arts Education (543-2300); also, the YMCA (382-5010) and the YWCA (447-4868). For privately owned schools, check the Yellow Pages.

Handball, Squash, Paddleball

Some private clubs (Washington Athletic Club and the host of newer franchise clubs) offer these sports. Otherwise, your best bet is the YMCA, listed elsewhere in this section.

Hang Gliding

This sport, which is about as dangerous as executing a swan dive from a jet, is popular among the daring, but there are few places it is practiced near Seattle. The best spot, according to enthusiasts, is near Morton, where each weekend in good weather hang gliders from all over the Northwest gather to "hang out." The Pacific Northwest Hang Glide Association has been formed. For information, call Recreational Equipment Inc. (323-8333).

Hiking

This is one of the most popular sports in Seattle and the whole Northwest, with at least 250,000 (at last count) participating in it. The government owns some 12 million acres of the state, much of which is available to hikers and climbers. If you have no experience in hiking, or "backpacking," as it often is called, your best bet is to join a club or take a course in the highly specialized and potentially dangerous sport. With hypothermia a major problem even in summer, you should know what you're doing before you strike out across the forest floors, glaciers, and peaks.

ORGANIZATIONS

The Mountaineers, 300 3rd W. (284-6310). Seattle's oldest hiking organization, this club offers courses and trips in the whole range of outdoor experiences: short hikes, expedition hikes, rock climbing, mountaineering, bicycle trips, canoeing and kayaking, and skiing and snowshoeing in the winter. (Hunting is a real no-no, although fishing is OK.)

The Sierra Club, 1516 Melrose (621-1696). The Seattle chapter goes on frequent outings, usually in connection with an area it is attempting to save.

The Washington Alpine Club, Box 352, Seattle, Washington 98111.
   This club sponsors ski instruction and occasional caravans for
   camping trips to other parts of the state, as well as the climbs
   for which it was named.

OUTFITTERS

Several firms in Seattle specialize in wilderness trips and
mountain climbing for the inexperienced.

Rainier Mountaineering, Inc., Paradise, Washington 98397 (long distance 1–569–2227). Rainier Mountaineering has the National
   Park Service concession for leading climbs on the king of
   mountains.

REI Mountain Schools, P.O. Box C88126, Seattle, Washington
   98188. Month-long courses are offered from April through September, with instruction in all the basics of backpacking; how
   to choose a pack and boots as well as survive on freeze-dried
   food. Climbing and alpine travel courses also. For information,
   call Recreational Equipment Inc. (323–8333).

Courses are offered by the Parks Department, most community colleges, and at Recreational Equipment Inc. on Thursday
evenings. If you want to find out in advance how you'll enjoy rock
climbing before investing in a course, try yourself out on the 25-
foot-tall Schurman Rock in Camp Long, 5200 35th SW. Make reservations first: 684–7434.

EQUIPMENT

Packs, boots, climbing gear, and sleeping bags are available at
the major outdoor-recreation stores in Seattle. Recreational Equipment Inc., 1525 11th (323–8333), has the best selection and prices.

GUIDEBOOKS

All hikers, whether novice or expedition class, feel naked in the
Northwest unless they have the excellent series of guidebooks published by The Mountaineers on various sections of the mountains
around the state and the classic hiking-climbing text, *Freedom of
the Hills*. The guidebooks include *Trips and Trails*, *101 Hikes*, *102
Hikes*, and the *Footsore* series for the lowland hiker.

Guidebooks frequently accomplish two things: they point out
the most spectacular sights, and they bring hordes to those attractions. To avoid crowds (and to satiate your hunger for gorgeous

maps), contact the various forest rangers in the state and the national parks. They will supply maps with marvelously detailed trails, streams, and major features shown.

The National Park Service and National Forest Service have combined forces to furnish information on questions such as up-to-date trail information, cutting of Christmas trees and firewood, and environmental concerns. They also supply maps ($1 each) and answer questions at Forest Service-Park Service Joint Recreation Information, 1018 1st (442-0170).

Hockey

For some reason, professional hockey hasn't done well in Seattle. The Totems were here for a number of years but had to give up and fold. Then came the Breakers, a semiprofessional team in the Western Canada Hockey League, primarily for players on their way up, but it, too, folded. Seattle now has a team, The Thunderbirds, of the Western Hockey League. For information, call 728-9124.

Horse Racing

Longacres, a fixture for decades, was sold to The Boeing Company in the autumn of 1990. The track will operate through the 1991 season; then it will close so Boeing can build an office complex on the site. Investors are talking of building another track in the Seattle–Tacoma area. Call Longacres for information (226-3131).

Horseback Riding

There are no riding stables or trails in the city limits, but there are several on the outskirts of town.

RIDING STABLES

The best public riding area for those who own horses is Bridle Trails State Park in Kirkland. Stables in the Seattle area include:
Aqua Barn Ranch, 15277 SE Renton–Maple Valley Highway, Renton (255-4618).
Gold Creek Stables, 16528 148th NE, Woodinville (483-2878).
High Lonesome Ranch, 233 144th NE, Redmond (868-5072).
Kelly's Riding and Boarding Ranch, 7212 Renton-Issaquah Rd. SE (392-6979).

Lake Serene Pony Farm & Tack Shop, 3915 Serene Way, Lynnwood (743-2112).

Horseshoe Pitching

Pits are available at Lincoln Park; Woodland Park; Rainier Playfield, Rainier Ave. and Oregon St.; and Broadway Playfield, 11th Ave. and E. Pine. Bring your own shoes, though.

Kayaking and Canoeing

Saltwater kayaking has become one of the most popular sports in the Seattle area, as well as the rest of the Inside Passage between Puget Sound and southeast Alaska. In fact, it has probably eclipsed the more dramatic freshwater version of the sport.

The major source of information is the Washington Kayak Club, P.O. Box 24264, Seattle, Washington 98124 (433-1983). Several shops along Lake Union specialize in kayaks and help sponsor outings and instruction.

Kingdome

The King County Multipurpose Stadium (called the Kingdome) was approved by voters in 1968, but the site-selection rhubarb that followed delayed construction several years. When a site was selected on the edge of Pioneer Square at King St. and Occidental, a new element was introduced to Seattle's skyline.

Now the sterling statistics: It covers 9.1 acres and is 250 feet high and 660 feet in diameter. It will seat 64,772 for football games, which includes 15,057 chair seats with armrests, 39,233 on the sidelines, and 25,489 in the end zone. For baseball games, it will seat 59,623, including 13,082 chair seats with armrests, 16,649 between first and third bases, and 41,799 between the foul lines. (For a tour, see the listing in "Guided Tours," chapter 1.) For personality shows, it will seat approximately 80,000.

It has 17 restrooms for men, 15 for women; 87 water fountains; 2 freight elevators; and 51 concessions. It has a sports museum and space for 2,700 cars on the site. Shuttle buses run north and south from the stadium.

The professional football and baseball teams play in the Kingdome.

Lawn Bowling

Jefferson Park Golf Course, S. Dakota & Beacon.
Queen City Lawn Bowling Club, 6018 Whitman N. (782–1515).
Seattle Parks Department Woodland Park, N. 63rd & Whitman N.

Model Airplane Flying

Carkeek Park.
Genesee Playfield, 43rd S. & Genesee.
Interbay Playfield, 17th W. & W. Barrett.
Marymoor Park in Redmond has a model airport opening at dawn in
    the spring and summer months; shows and races are held
    there.

Model Boat Racing

The west shore of Green Lake. These tiny hydro races are held at
    infrequent intervals. Check with the Parks Department for
    information and clubs (684–4075).

Polo

   The Seattle Polo Club isn't actually in Seattle. It is at NE 116th
& 150th NE, Redmond. Free matches are held throughout the summer on the outdoor field and during the winter in the *Central Park
Stables* at Bridle Trails State Park. For information, call 827–2900.

Rugby

   This sport is played on an intramural basis by some schools,
particularly private schools, and some clubs. Call the Seattle Parks
Department for current information (684–4075).

Running

   Like most cities, Seattle has become addicted to running, and
there's hardly a level stretch of pavement or grass in the city that
doesn't have running-shoe marks on it.

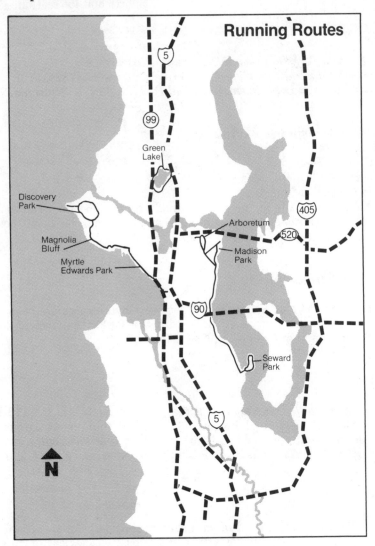

Some of the best running routes in Seattle:

Arboretum, begin from the main entrance on Lake Washington Blvd. and Madison. You can run 1.75 miles one way through one of the most beautiful areas in the city.

Discovery Park. With several choices of routes, you can run up to sixteen miles through the park—nearly all of it on grass instead of pavement.

Green Lake, Aurora Ave. N. and NE 65th. Here is a popular and well-known run, where you'll see hordes of other runners, walkers, strollers, and bikers on the 3.2-mile circuit.

Madison Park to Seward Park, start at intersection of Madison and McGilvra Blvd. This 14.4-mile run goes along Lake Washington.

Seattle Waterfront, beneath the Alaska Way Viaduct. Running beneath the viaduct is a good way to stay out of the weather. By starting downtown at the hotel at 6th and Pike, for example, you can run to Myrtle Edwards Park, a strip park that follows the waterfront from near Pier 70 to Pier 92, then back to the downtown area. Total distance covered is 5.4 miles.

Seward Park, Lake Washington Blvd. S. and S. Orcas St. A 2.5-mile loop route follows the shoreline nearly all the way around this peninsula park that juts out into Lake Washington.

Waterfront to Magnolia Bluff. This 11-mile run takes you along the bluff with its spectacular views of the sound, Mount Rainier, and the city's skyline. Start at the hotel at 6th and Pike and extend the waterfront run by going up the long hill across the bridge and up to Magnolia Bluff.

You'll see runners on virtually every street in the city, even those that are almost too steep for walking, so you'll be welcome anywhere.

For information on running and races, call the Runners' Hot Line at 524–RUNS.

Seafair

This community festival used to be a parade, the hydroplane races, and pirates running around making a lot of noise. It has grown up a bit to include these things plus an almost year-round schedule of events. Among them are tug-of-war contests, the milk-carton boat race on Green Lake, the beautiful Bon Odori festival in the International District, bicycle competitions, soap-box derbies, golf tournaments, kite-flying contests, art exhibits, and on and on—even a chess tournament. If you don't like parades and don't like your meals disturbed in restaurants by clowns dressed as pirates, this clearly is not your type of event. But there are thousands, if not millions, who consider the main Seafair parade the highlight of the year, and it has become as much a part of Seattle life as rain and skiing and bicycle Sundays. For information, call your local papers or Seafair, 414 Pontius Ave. N. (623–7100).

Skating

Roller skating has been discovered here as well as in the rest of the world, but we're not quite as well-wheeled as Venice, California. Yet.

The victories of Rosalynn Sumners, formerly of Edmonds, in international figure skating have brought some new attention to that kind of skating as well, but far from a boom.

Highland Ice Arena, 18005 Aurora N. (546-2431).

Lynnwoods Sno-King Ice Arena, 19803 68th W., Lynnwood (775-7511).

Roll-A-Way Skate Center (roller), 6210 200th SW, Lynnwood (778-4446).

Southgate Roller Rink, 9646 17th SW (762-4030).

Skiing

Snow conditions vary widely in the mountains around Seattle, ranging from the wet and heavy "Snoqualmie Premix" to fluffy, dry powder at the top of the "Internationale" at Alpental. The closest consistent dry snow is some distance from Seattle: Mission Ridge, thirteen miles outside of Wenatchee, and Mount Baker, 60 miles east of Bellingham.

In spite of the frequently heavy snow and light rain that turns the slopes into cold mashed potatoes, skiing attracts thousands every winter weekend. Downhill skiing has survived competition from cross-country skiing and shows no signs of weakening.

Busloads of students in private and PTA-sponsored ski-school classes keep expanding the numbers crowding the slopes on Saturdays and Sundays. The crush of skiers on those two days prompted operators to install lighting on the slopes and keep the lifts running until 9:00 or 10:00 P.M.

Some of the best skiing on uncrowded slopes with no lift lines is available on weekdays. Most areas operate seven days a week during the main season, and some operate until midnight on weekends.

All areas offer lessons by professional instructors operating from established ski schools; they operate ski shops for repairs and rentals, and each has a day lodge for lunches, beverages, and snacks. Each has a ski patrol.

Lift-ticket prices can range upward from $25.

DOWNHILL SKIING

Three ski areas under the same management operate in the

Snoqualmie Pass summit area where Interstate 90 crosses the Cascade Range. The pass is forty-six miles east of Seattle, with at least four lanes all the way. Unless chains are required or one or more lanes are blocked by traffic or avalanches, you can easily drive to the summit in an hour. All three areas are served by a free shuttle bus.

Crystal Mountain Resort, 76 miles southeast of Seattle on Highway 410. This is one of the state's most ambitious ski areas and is considered a destination resort, in part because it has year-round programs. A bar and restaurant are at the warming hut on top of the highest chair, and a cafeteria is in the day lodge. Overnight facilities offer restaurants, bars, swimming pools, dormitories, and apartment suites and condominiums. For information, call 1-634-3771.

Pacific West Mountain Resort (formerly Hyak), a short distance east of Ski Acres. This recently renamed ski area offers extensive cross-country skiing as well as downhill. For information, call 462-SNOW.

Snoqualmie Summit and *Ski Acres*, 46 miles east of Seattle on Interstate 90 in the Snoqualmie Pass Summit area. These two areas are side by side, and skiing conditions are quite similar. *Alpental* is the newest of the three and the most challenging, with steeper slopes, in addition to modest slopes suitable for beginners and intermediates.

   For information, call 232-8182. Lodging is available within walking distance of the slopes; condominiums are located near Alpental and Ski Acres.

Stevens Pass, 70 miles east of Seattle on Highway 2. This popular area is reached by the last two-lane blacktop transcontinental highway in the United States. It is open every day and many evenings. No overnight accommodations at the summit; the closest are in Leavenworth and Skykomish. For information, call 634-1645.

White Pass, 105 miles from Seattle on Highway 12. This one is almost beyond the range for a day trip, but it has overnight facilities and a broad selection of classes as well as restaurants and lounges. It is open daily and has night skiing three nights a week and during school vacations. For information, call 1-509-453-8731.

SKI TOURING

   Ski touring, Nordic skiing, cross-country, or whatever it is being called at the moment, has settled in to become a staple in the Northwest mountains, and more and more downhill areas are either adding Nordic trails or increasing those already available.

Most of the national forests have areas set aside for this sport, but you don't really need them; find an interesting place and strike out across the landscape.

SNOW REPORTS

Weather and snow conditions at favorite areas assume major status, and four services provide daily or twice-daily reports via telephone. Most of the local radio stations also broadcast snow-condition reports on a daily schedule that varies with each station. For telephone reports in season:

Avalanche Report (526-6677).
Cascade Ski Report (634-0200).
Crystal Mountain Ski Report (634-3771).
Northwest Ski Report (634-0071).
Sno-Line Pass Report, October 1 through March 31 (1-976-7623).

Numbers are often busy, so keep trying.

Scuba Diving

Scuba diving around the Seattle area began where the city began, at Alki Beach. Some of the best diving in the Seattle area can still be found there and at nearby Seattle park access areas. Entry can be made all along the 3-mile waterside strip starting at the 1600 block of Harbor Ave. SW around to 64th SW and Alki SW. Smaller access sites are along Beach Dr. SW, off Golden Gardens Park north of Shilshole, and on the beach areas of Discovery Park. Scheduled underwater tours with sea-life identification by park personnel are offered at Discovery Park. Call Parks Department (684-4075) for more information.

Skin divers are represented by a statewide council and a number of clubs with interests in underwater photography, bottle recovery, scientific study, sightseeing, and exploration.

Soccer

Few games have been accepted in Seattle as quickly as soccer. For a period in the mid-1970s it was as much a part of Seattle's recreational profile as tennis. The Seattle Sounders pro soccer team was popular, and things seemed great. But for some reason the team floundered, then folded. The closest professional soccer now is in Tacoma. The game continues its popularity in schools and league play around the region, but its charm has faded a bit.

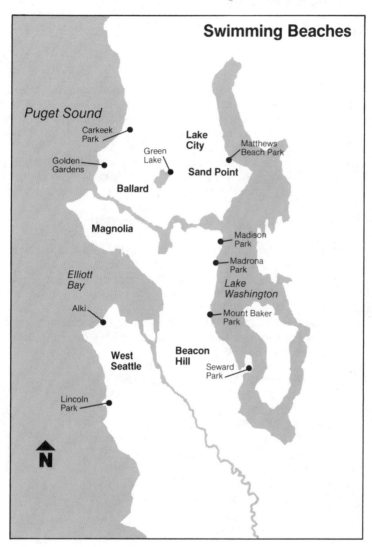

Swimming Beaches

Puget Sound

Carkeek Park

Lake City

Matthews Beach Park

Green Lake

Golden Gardens

Sand Point

Ballard

Magnolia

Madison Park

Madrona Park

Elliott Bay

Lake Washington

Alki

Mount Baker Park

West Seattle

Beacon Hill

Seward Park

Lincoln Park

N

Stargazing

The University of Washington observatory near the north campus entrance is open to the public on summer evenings. On clear nights look through a six-inch telescope or a spectroscope that shows the spectrum of bright stars. There is also a free slide show on cloudy evenings.

Swimming

BEACHES

Green Lake. There are two separate beaches here, also managed by
the Parks Department.
Lake Washington. The Parks Department has six public swimming
beaches along this lake: Madrona, Madison, Mount Baker,
Matthews, Pritchard, and Seward parks.
Puget Sound. For the extremely hardy, there are public beaches here
if you feel you must swim in the sound: Alki, Golden Gardens,
Carkeek, and Lincoln parks.

SEATTLE CITY PARKS AND RECREATION DEPARTMENT

Pools under the directorship of the Parks Department are all
indoor except one and are open year-round for lessons and public
swims. Fees for public swims are $1.25 for adults, $.75 for 18 years
old and under. Call the individual pool for scheduled swim times.
Ballard, 1471 NW 67th (684-4094).
Colman (50-meter Olympic size), an outdoor pool connected with
Lincoln Park, open June through Labor Day only, Fauntleroy
& Cloverdale (684-7494).
Evans, 7201 E. Green Lake Dr. N. (684-4961).
Helene Madison, 13401 Meridian N. (684-4979).
Meadowbrook, NE 107th & 30th NE (684-4989).
Medgar Evers, 500 23rd (684-4763).
Queen Anne, 1st W. & W. Howe (386-4282).
Rainier Beach, Rainier S. & S. Henderson (386-1944).
Southwest, 2801 SW Thistle (684-7440).
YMCA pools: Downtown, 909 4th; West Seattle, 4550 Fauntleroy
SW; and East Madison, 1700 23rd (461-4888).
YWCA pool, downtown at 5th & Seneca (447-4868).

Tennis

Almost overnight tennis became *the* game in Seattle, and the
city was hard put to keep up with the demand for more public
courts. After spending a small fortune on backpacking gear, canoes, kayaks, and other relatively expensive sports, the surge of
tennis, with its very low investment, resulted as much from eco-
nomics as from Billie Jean King and Seattle's Tom Gorman.

INDOOR FACILITIES

There are many private facilities or clubs in Seattle and the vicinity requiring monthly or yearly membership dues.

Seattle Tennis Center, Martin Luther King Jr. Way S. and S. Walker St. (684-4764). A Seattle Parks and Recreation facility, this is the first publicly owned indoor center in the area. There are ten indoor courts and four adjacent outdoor courts. The center is open every day from 7:00 A.M. to 10:30 P.M. Reservations may be made up to a week in advance.

RESERVATION SYSTEM

The Seattle Parks and Recreation Department has established a reservation system for nine outdoor tennis courts scattered around the city. These may be made in person up to a week in advance at the Seattle Department of Parks and Recreation's Public Information/Scheduling Office at 5201 Green Lake Way N. or by calling 684-4082. Courts that may be reserved are:

Ballard Pool, NW 67th & 14th NW.
Bitter Lake, N. 130th & Greenwood.
Broadway, E. Pine & 11th.
Lincoln Park, Fauntleroy SW & SW Webster.
Lower Woodland (two courts). Stoneway N. & Green Lake Way N.
Meadowbrook, NE 107th & 30th NE.
Mount Baker, S. McClellan & 35th S.

A note of caution: Your fee will not be refunded if it rains.

At last count, nearly 550 courts at 175 different locations in and around Seattle reflect the game's popularity, so the reservation system definitely should be considered before challenging a friend, getting dressed, and finding you've no place to go.

Following is a list of the Seattle Parks and Recreation courts.

LIGHTED COURTS

Alki, 58th SW & SW Stevens—(2)
Ballard Pool, NW 67th & 14th NW—(4)
Bitter Lake, N. 130th & Linden N.—(4)
Bobby Morris, 11th E. & E. Pine (formerly named Broadway)—(3)
Garfield, 23rd E. & E. Cherry—(3)
Genesee, 46th S. & S. Genesee—(2)
Hiawatha, California SW & SW Lander—(3)

Jefferson, 16th S. & S. Dakota—(2)
Laurelhurst, NE 41st & 48th NE—(4)
Lincoln Annex, Fauntleroy SW & SW Webster—(6)
Lower Woodland, West Green Lake Way N.—(10)
Madison, 34th E. & E. Lynn—(2)
Madrona, 34th E. & E. Spring—(2)
Magnolia, 34th W. & W. Smith—(4)
Meadowbrook, 30th NE & NE 107th—(6)
Miller, 20th E. & E. Republican—(2)
Mount Baker, S. McClellan & Lake Park Dr. S.—(2)
Rainier, 10th S. & S. Alaska—(4)
Rainier Beach, Rainier S. & S. Cloverdale—(4)
Volunteer, 15 E. & E. Prospect—(4)

UNLIGHTED COURTS

Atlantic City (see Beer Sheva)
Ballard Plgd., NW 60th & 28th NW—(2)
Beacon Hill, 14th S. & S. Holgate—(2)
Beer Sheva, Seward Park S. & S. Henderson—(1)
Brighton, 42nd S. & S. Juneau—(2)
Bryant, NE 65th & 40th NE—(2)
Cowen, University Way NE & NE Ravenna Blvd.—(3)
Dearborn, 30th S. & S. Brandon—(2)
Delridge, SW Oregon & Delridge Way SW—(2)
Discovery Park, 36th W. & W. Government Way—(2)
Froula, NE 72nd & 12th NE—(2)
Georgetown, Corson S. & S. Homer—(1)
Gilman, 11th NW & NW 54th—(2)
Green Lake East, E. Green Lake Drive N. & Latona NW—(3)
Green Lake West, N. 73rd & W. Green Lake Drive N.—(2)
Highland Park, 11th SW & SW Thistle—(1)
High Point, SW Graham & Sylvan Way—(2)
Hutchinson, 59th S. & S. Pilgrim—(2)
Kinnear, 7th W. & Olympic Place—(1)
Lakeridge, Rainier S. between 68th & Cornell—(1)
Leschi, 100 Lakeside Ave. S.—(1)
Lincoln, Fauntleroy SW & SW Webster—(2)
Lowman Beach, 48th SW & Beach Dr. SW—(1)
Magnolia, 31st W. & W. Garfield—(2)
Magnuson, Sand Point Way NE & 65th NE—(6)
Montlake, 16th E. & E. Calhoun—(2)
Observatory Courts, 1st N. & W. Lee—(2)
Ravenna, 20th NE & NE 58th—(2)
Riverview, 12th SW & SW Othello—(2)

Rodgers, 3rd W. & W. Fulton—(3)
Rogers, Eastlake E. & E. Roanoke—(2)
Seward, Lake Washington Boulevard S. & S. Juneau—(2)
Soundview, 15 NW & NW 90th—(2)
South Park, 8th S. & S. Sullivan—(2)
University, 9th NE & NE 50th—(2)
Upper Woodland, NE 50th between Stone Way N. & Midvale—(4)
Van Asselt, 32nd S. & S. Myrtle—(2)
Victory Heights, NE 107th & 19th NE—(1)
Wallingford, N. 43rd & Wallingford N.—(2)

Windsurfing

For some genuinely insignificant trivia, after reading this paragraph you will know that (1) the word *windsurfing* was coined by Bert Salisbury of Seattle about 1972, and (2) that I wrote the first story mentioning windsurfing on assignment for the *Seattle Times* with Roy Scully, the dean of photographers on that paper.

Windsurfing is performed on sailboards and has gradually become a major sport here in spite of the cold waters of Puget Sound and the lakes. Thanks to those cozy wet suits that permit people to go diving in the winter, windsurfing is also done year-round to some extent.

Boards rent for around $8 an hour and $20 to $30 a day. Wet suits rent for $3 to $5 an hour. Lessons run from $10 to $30 an hour, depending on whether they are private or with a group. Here are some sources for sailboard rentals or lessons:
The Bavarian Surf, 2130 Westlake N. (281-7834).
Fiorini Sports, 4720 University Village Pl. NE (523-9610).

Associations

YMCA

The YMCA of Greater Seattle offers a wide variety of programs for men, women, and children in five categories: Youth (camping, youth basketball, etc.), Family (parent-child, day care, youth shelter, etc.), Fitness (cardiovascular testing, aerobics, sports, etc.), International (refugee aid, tours, etc.), and Individual and Community Development (forums, urban issues, etc.).

YMCA association headquarters, 909 4th. Branches are:
Downtown, 909 4th (382-5010).
East Madison, 1700 23rd (322-6969).

Fauntleroy, 9260 California SW (937–1000).
Highline, 17874 Des Moines Way S. (244–5880).
Metrocenter, 909 4th (382–5013).
Shoreline, 1220 NE 175th (364–1700).
West Seattle, 4515 36th SW (935–6000).

In addition, the YMCA operates two resident camps: Camp Orkila on Orcas Island and Camp Colman at Lakebay in southern Puget Sound.

YWCA

One of the widest varieties of physical fitness and adult education programs outside the educational system is offered by the YWCA. Classes in creative writing, art, metric conversion, speech and drama, crafts, foreign languages, bridge, health, and self-improvement are among the subjects available.

Another program for downtown workers on their lunch hour is called the Brown Bag Speakers' Series, with experts from various fields speaking for a nominal fee.

Physical fitness programs include exercise classes, swimming, yoga, ballroom dancing, volleyball, judo, and karate. Several programs for children are offered.

The YWCA operates several branches. For information, call the main branch at 1118 5th (461–4888).

YWCA association headquarters, 1118 5th. Branches are:
Downtown, 1118 5th (461–4888).
East Cherry, 2820 E. Cherry (461–8480).
North Area, 13305 1st NE (364–6810).
West Seattle, 4800 40th SW (461–8489).

In addition, the YWCA operates the Rainbow Day Care & Before/After School program (461–8489).

Parks

Green Lake Park

From David Denny's first 5-acre park donation, now a grassy lawn near the center of the city, Seattle's parks today encompass nearly 4,774 acres spread from one end of the city to the other.

Multiple facilities are operated by the Seattle Parks and Recreation Department. See chapter 4 for swimming pools and tennis courts. For more information, call 684–4075. A folder showing the location of each park facility may be obtained free by writing to Seattle Parks, 5201 Green Lake Way N., Seattle, Washington 98103.

Picnic Reservations (684–4081). Shelter sites may be reserved year-round at these parks: Carkeek, Discovery, Seward, Woodland, Lincoln, and Gas Works. Fee is $5 per group of fifty.

Camp Long, 35th SW & SW Dawson (684–7434). Sixty-eight acres open to organized groups for camping and wilderness-skills programs; call the camp or Parks Department for children's camping programs.

Community Centers

Along with picnicking, flopping in the sun on green grass, swimming at a fresh- or saltwater beach, and playing softball, tennis, or half-court basketball, the Seattle and King County park systems operate community recreation centers, often in connection with a school building. The range of free and for-fee activities offered is surprising. These centers were formerly called "recreation centers," but the park departments prefer the new term to emphasize the broader concept of community activities, since sports are only a part of the program.

Each of the Seattle centers publishes four seasonal program brochures that describe and schedule programmed activities. They are available at the centers and often in community newspapers. Look, too, at the special centers for arts and crafts at Seward Park and the Pratt Fine Arts Center; for dance instruction at Madrona Park; and rock climbing at Camp Long. Poncho Theater at Woodland Park and the Bathhouse Theater at Green Lake offer programs for aspiring thespians. Most of the community centers offer similar programs, but more ambitious arts-and-crafts programs may be offered in one than another, or different sports and other activities will be in one center and not another. Call Parks Department Information (684–4081) for information.

King County Parks

Outside Seattle the King County Parks Division maintains sixty-one facilities (at last count, anyway) that offer variety—from indoor swimming pools to green grass for contemplation. Since the first King County park opened for public recreation in 1937, the park system has grown until it now encompasses 5,000 acres under the direction of 130 full-time specialists. Park sizes vary from the tiny Enetai Beach at ¼-acre just off the south corner of the East Channel bridge on I-90 to 486-acre Marymoor Park in Redmond. A major jump in King County parks resulted from the Forward Thrust bond issue of 1968, which provided $49 million to purchase and develop up to 120 new parks, swimming pools, and related facilities. (See Sports and Recreation chapter for pool listings.)

Activities at King County parks feature do-it-yourself recreation—swimming, launching your boat, sunbathing, and playing ball with friends. Organized activities continue year-round with holiday parties, storytelling, classes in everything from exercising to crafts, and outings for senior citizens and handicapped children. Sports lessons are offered on a challenging schedule at many facilities.

For complete information on programs, call 344–3982 on weekdays between 8:30 A.M. and 4:30 P.M. Or write to Department of Community Development, Parks Division, 2040 84th SE, Mercer Island, Seattle, Washington 98040 to receive recreation bulletins regularly.

Special Parks

Among Seattle's parks are special spots, unique to Seattle for one reason or another and treasured by citizens and guests alike. Each offers its own charm.

Discovery Park, main gate at W. Government Way & 36th W., south gate at W. Emerson near Magnolia Blvd. W., and north gate near W. Commodore Way & 40th W. This represents a bounty from the military and has been developed over a period of years. Seattle acquired the nearly 400 acres at the northwest corner of Magnolia Bluff from what was Fort Lawton. The land includes 2 miles of beaches, isolated forested ravines, small streams, and open meadows. Plans are to preserve much of it as a nature park. Cars and motorized vehicles are banned from the park except for designated parking areas. To explore it, you must hoof it along the trails. A ¹⁄₂-mile "parcours" or health path with fifteen exercise stations winds through woods of alder and maple. Discovery Park's comparative isolation from the city's noise, its dramatic views, varied topography, and expansive natural areas offer the visitor a chance to enjoy a wilderness experience only minutes from the city center.

Included in the multiple-use park is Daybreak Star, an Indian cultural center where you can watch Indian craftsmen at work, plus musicians and dancers. It is just inside the main gate.

Along the beach area the Coast Guard operates the West Point Light Station, open 1:00–4:00 P.M. weekends and holidays. Discovery Park is open daily from dawn to dusk. For more information on the park and times for guided nature

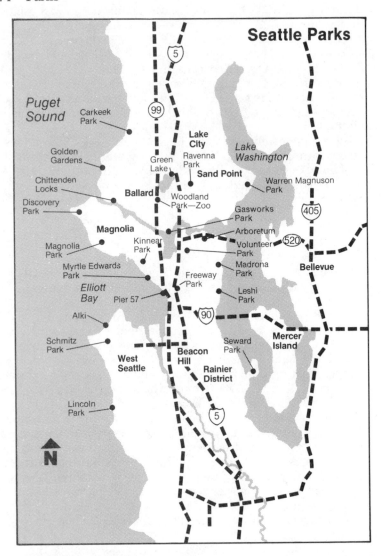

Seattle Parks

Puget Sound

Carkeek Park

Golden Gardens

Chittenden Locks

Discovery Park

Magnolia

Magnolia Park

Myrtle Edwards Park

Elliott Bay

Pier 57

Alki

Schmitz Park

West Seattle

Lincoln Park

N

Ballard

Green Lake

Lake City

Ravenna Park

Sand Point

Lake Washington

Woodland Park—Zoo

Warren Magnuson Park

Gasworks Park

Arboretum

Kinnear Park

Volunteer Park

Madrona Park

Bellevue

Freeway Park

Leshi Park

Beacon Hill

Seward Park

Rainier District

Mercer Island

walks and programs, call 386-4236. Park headquarters are at 3801 W. Government Way, Seattle, Washington 98199.

Freeway Park, bordered by 6th Ave. on the west, Spring St. on the south, University St. on the north, and, except for a boot-shaped section of pools and lawns, 8th Ave. on the east. Imagine the eight-lane Interstate 5 freeway roaring through the heart of Seattle as a natural phenomenon—a deep river canyon, for example. Forget that it once encompassed houses,

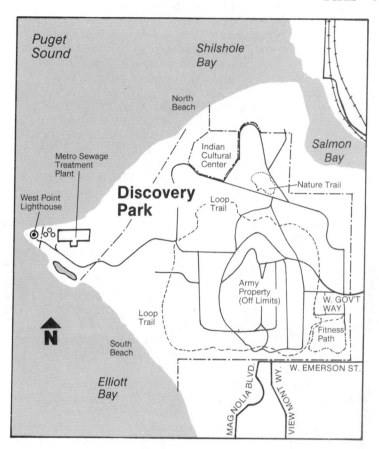

streets, trees, and lamp posts. With this concrete river canyon
effectively splitting the town in half, something was needed to
tie the town back together and to provide a place for people
to relax, to eat a brown-bag lunch, to sit beneath trees, and to
play.

This, in essence, is what went through the minds of the
planners who were responsible for Freeway Park. First, they
put a big lid over the freeway to create a 5.4-acre platform on
which to build the park. They poured tons of concrete; installed
miles of pipe; then planted acres of lawn, groundcovers, path-
ways, plazas, fountains, and waterfalls. Surprisingly, the
sound of the waterfalls and fountains plus the screens of trees
and shrubs muffle the roar of the freeway that is only a few feet
below.

Between Spring and Seneca streets is a vast "box garden" where big concrete boxes installed at different levels hold plants of various species. From Seneca to University is a concrete canyon with waterfalls of different heights.

Gas Works Park, on Pacific Ave. at the north end of Lake Union. The park gets its name from the remains of a plant for manufacturing heating and lighting gas on the north shore of Lake Union. The rusting black towers added drabness to part of Lake Union's skyline for years. The park plans, very controversial at the time they were presented, called for retaining the bulbous and odd-looking contraptions needed to manufacture the gas, and the design team won; now nearly everyone is charmed by the funky old structures. The viewing mount built beside the park gives an unobstructed view of the city skyline and is a favorite place for kite flyers to stand. Also, there is a huge concrete-aggregate-and-bronze sundial on the ground, and your shadow marks the hour.

A series of cement arches from a former railway trestle serve as an entrance. An old boiler house with an overhead maze of pipes remaining is a play barn. A picnic shelter and rest rooms are also open. The shelter can be reserved for large groups with two weeks' notice. Many of the discarded pumps, large machinery, and equipment pieces are refurbished with bright paint. It is a park full of recycled industrial equipment that is spooky, grotesque, and entertaining.

Green Lake, near Woodland Park Zoo and Aurora Ave. One of Seattle's most popular parks, it is used by virtually everyone in the city at one time or another. It is popular with runners, walkers, bicyclists, rowers, swimmers, and watchers. It is a continuation of the Woodland Park Zoo property across Aurora Ave., but the four-lane street makes an effective barrier in spite of the underpass for both foot and vehicular traffic.

Myrtle Edwards and Elliott Bay parks, from Pier 71 to Pier 86. These two new adjoining parks have a 1.25-mile pathway for walking or biking along the waterfront. Benches are situated beside the pathway, and there are grassy areas for kite flying. The pathway follows the bulkheaded waterfront to the northern end where it swings past the massive grain elevators blocking the view of Elliott Bay to end at Pier 86, the import car terminal ("lemon grove," as some wags call it). Myrtle Edwards Park is at the southern end and has the controversial lumps of stone some consider sculpture.

Waterfront Park, Pier 55. It is peopled mostly by Seattleites, although visitors to the Elliott Bay docks just north of the ferry terminal also roam around the viewpoints and water access.

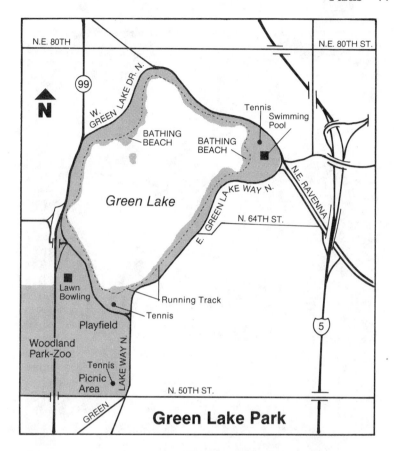

N.E. 80TH

N.E. 80TH ST.

99

W. GREEN LAKE DR. N.

N

Tennis

Swimming Pool

BATHING BEACH

BATHING BEACH

N.E. RAVENNA

Green Lake

E. GREEN LAKE WAY N.

N. 64TH ST.

Lawn Bowling

Running Track

5

Tennis

Playfield

Tennis

Woodland Park-Zoo

GREEN LAKE WAY N.

Picnic Area

N. 50TH ST.

GREEN

Green Lake Park

Seattleites love the quiet and serenity near their jobs; it is only a few steps down University or Union, then under the Alaskan Way Viaduct to the park, where they can watch the water traffic and the Olympics while eating a leisurely lunch. A glass-enclosed public viewing gallery with an outside deck is at the end of Pier 57, and the promenade extends to the Aquarium (see Aquarium listing in Walking Tours chapter).

Woodland Park Zoo. If you haven't been to the zoo lately, you haven't really been to the zoo at all because the present version shares only the street address with the old one. New exhibits are everywhere.

A Nocturnal House reverses night and day; the Swamp and Marsh feature scattered ponds and an outdoor aviary filled with ducks, herons, coots, and other water birds; gorillas

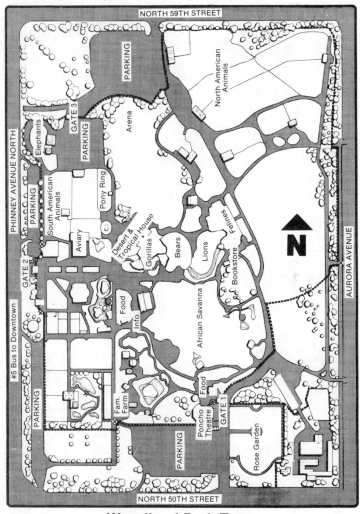

Woodland Park Zoo

roam through a tropical forest with streams, boulders, natural soils, and ample trees for climbing; and Asian monkeys leap through tropical forest islands, scampering across waterfalls to chase fellow simians.

The latest addition is the African Savanna, which has lions, hippos, pata monkeys, giraffes, zebras, springboks, a walk-through aviary, and land and water birds.

The zoo opens at 8:30 A.M. every day of the year. Closing time varies from 4:00 to 6:00 P.M., according to the season. Admission: $3 adults 18-64; $1.50 children 6-17, senior citizens, and handicapped; free under 6. Annual passes are $15 individual, $25 family (including children and their grandparents). Schools and other groups call 684-4800 for admission fees and tour information.

Transportation

Waterfront Streetcar

Seattle is known as the jumping-off place to Alaska, the Arctic, and the Orient; we are closer to Tokyo than any major U.S. city. Consequently, the Seattle-Tacoma International Airport and the Port of Seattle have a distinctly international flavor to them, with families dressed in parkas and mukluks rubbing shoulders with people wearing Hawaiian leis or speaking Chinese or Japanese.

Airlines

These major airlines use Sea-Tac Airport, connect with all other international airlines, and have either headquarters or offices in Seattle.

Air BC (433-5734).
Alaska Airlines (433-3100).
American (1-800-433-7300).
American West (763-0737).
British Airways (1-800-247-9297).
Canadian (1-800-426-7000).
Continental (624-1740).
Delta (433-4711).
Hawaiian (1-800-367-5320).
Horizon (1-800-547-9308).
Japan (1-800-525-3663).
Northwest (433-3500).
Pan Am (1-800-221-1111).
Scandinavian Airlines (SAS) (1-800-221-2350).
Thai (467-0600).
Trans World (447-9400).
United (441-3700).
US Air (587-6229).

REGIONAL AIR SERVICE

In addition to the major airlines, some of the smaller, one-engine companies have begun offering scheduled service to the smaller Puget Sound communities as well as Victoria and Vancouver, B.C., and they put you down in the heart of the cities if they are seaplanes.

The major ones are Lake Union Air, 284-0300, and Kenmore Air, 486-8400.

AIRPORT TRANSPORTATION

Getting to and from Sea-Tac, and parking there, isn't nearly the irritating experience it was before the new multimillion-dollar terminal was completed. Now it is a simple matter to drive out, park in the gigantic parking lot across from the terminal, and get to the gate as fast as you can.

Another alternative is to park your car at one of the numerous outdoor parking lots on Pacific Highway S. near the terminal, all of which provide minibus transportation to the terminal. This is especially recommended if you are going to leave your car overnight or longer, since it will cost you about one-fourth as much. The major disadvantage of the private lots is that your car will be left outside during your absence.

It is best to call the parking lots and the airport lot for prices. After computing what it will cost, you can compare that against catching a cab downtown to one of the major hotels where the Gray Line of Seattle makes pickups (Four Seasons Olympic, Westin, the two Sheratons, etc.) and taking the bus to the airport. One-way costs $6. A taxicab runs roughly $15 for the same trip. The Suburban Airporter runs from north and east of Lake Washington; the cost ranges up to $17 depending on location.

The newest kid on the airport-transportation block is the ShuttleExpress, a fleet of vans owned by San Juan Airlines that offers door-to-door service at a reasonable rate—$15 one-way to Edmonds, for example. Call 1-800-942-0711 twenty-four hours before your flight.

If you are staying in an airport-area hotel, most provide free shuttlebus service to and from the terminal with free phones in the baggage-claim area.

Some phone numbers: Gray Line of Seattle (626-6088); Sea-Tac Parking Garage (433-5307); Airport Thrifty Rent-a-Car (246-7565); Airport Dollar Park and Fly (433-6767); Suburban Airporter (232-9545).

Amtrak

Seattle is served by Amtrak, and the city's geographical location makes it a major junction. Seattle catches them going north, south, and east. The southern route from Seattle heads down the length of Oregon and California. Two choices are available from Seattle east: one across the very top of the nation and the other a bit south out of California. The depot is at 3rd & S. Jackson. For information on schedules, prices, and reservations, call 464-1930.

Buses

METRO TRANSIT

The Seattle-King County Metro bus system is one of the nation's best and is continually getting better. It is a countywide service that covers all of Seattle and runs to all suburban areas, plus additional routes to Enumclaw, Black Diamond, Issaquah, North Bend, Fall City, Carnation, Redmond, and as far east as Snoqualmie Pass on Interstate 90.

The basic fare is $.75 during off-peak hours and $1.00 during the peak rush hours. The two-zone fare (outside the Seattle city limits) is $1.00 off-peak and $1.50 peak hours. Student/youth fares (ages 5–17) are the same as the one-zone fares, and reduced fares for the elderly or disabled with a permit are $.25.

Metro offers a number of plans and fare reductions: monthly and annual passes, and an all-day weekend and holiday pass for $1.00. All except the one-day $2.50 pass can be bought by mail or through a number of financial institutions.

Drivers do not provide change, but if you place a larger amount in the fare box, the driver will, on request, give you a refund coupon that will be honored at the Customer Assistance Office at 821 2nd Ave.

Bike and Ride. Metro encourages bicyclists to make use of the system to reach their biking route, and it is part of Metro's energy- and traffic-saving program. Bike racks have been placed on many buses that run particular routes, especially to outlying areas, such as up I-90 toward Snoqualmie Pass and north to Redmond, Avondale, etc. There is no extra charge for bikes. Call Metro's information and route number, 447–4800.

Free!! Metro's best deal of all is its Magic Carpet Service, which gives free rides in the downtown area. This Magic Carpet Zone, the nation's first, is bordered by 6th Ave. and the I-5 freeway, Battery St. on the north, and Jackson St. on the south. The waterfront, obviously, is the western extreme. (No, that doesn't include free rides on the Waterfront Trolley. Sorry.)

The city reimburses Metro for this service, and all you have to do is get on and get off and forget about fares. You can board any bus from either the front or rear door in this zone, but when the bus leaves the zone, you will have to pay the normal fare. And that is one reason you always leave by the front door on Metro buses.

Park & Ride. Metro has established a large network of free, well-maintained parking lots along major arterials where you can leave your car and ride the bus to town, eliminating the horrendous parking charges in the core area. Call 447–4800 for information.

Pass Savers. Metro has a program with many regional merchants that gives Metro pass holders substantial savings when they present their Metro pass. The Pass Savers brochure lists these businesses and the discounts offered (a random sampling shows $1 off breakfast at one place, 20 percent off several dinners, $5 off membership at the Seattle Art Museum, etc.). Call 447–4800 for information.

Pets. Well-behaved dogs are welcome, but those appearing to weigh more than 20 pounds will be charged a regular people fare, but no additional zone fares. Seeing-eye dogs ride free, of course.

Cats and other pets must be in a carrier. The driver has the right to refuse a pet boarding and can force you to remove the pet from the bus or not let you and your pet enter the bus at all when it is crowded.

Script Program. This is for elderly and disabled persons and provides script for those who cannot use Metro buses for some reason—no wheelchair lifts on their route, for example. The script gives you $10 worth of rides for $5 and is good on taxicabs and van services registered with Metro. Call 447-4800 for information.

Vanpools. This program permits a group of ten to fifteen commuters to share a ride in a van owned by the Metro Commuter Pool, for which they pay a fare based on round-trip daily mileage. A 35-mile round-trip, for example, costs $40. However, prices vary depending how many people are in the van. For information, call 625-4500.

Waterfront Streetcar. A few years ago Seattle bought a vintage (meaning discarded) trolley from Australia, shipped it to Seattle, restored it, and put it to work on a stretch of unused railroad along the waterfront. It has been one of the most popular waterfront attractions. It costs $.65 in peak hours; $.55 other times. You can buy the ticket at one of the automatic ticket machines at each station. Or have a Metro transfer handy and you can ride free. If you have a Metro Reduced Fare Permit, it costs you only $.15. The streetcar runs from S. Main St. on the edge of Pioneer Square north to Pier 70. The streetcar can seat fifty-two passengers and carry another forty standees. It runs during the daylight hours only and shuts down at dusk.

For other information—routes, schedules, prices, etc.—call the twenty-four-hour information number at 447-4800.

Other useful Metro numbers: lost and found (684-1585); complaints (compliments welcome, too) (447-4824); carpool and vanpool information (625-4500); pass purchase by mail (447-PASS or 7277).

INTERCITY BUS LINES

Seattle is served by the two major transcontinental bus lines, Greyhound and Trailways. Greyhound serves other cities and towns in the state; Trailways can operate only between states, which means its buses make no stops until they reach Oregon or Idaho. Community Transit serves Seattle and communities in Snohomish County. For information call Greyhound, 8th and Stewart (624-3456), or Trailways, 1936 Westlake (728-5955).

Bridges

Evergreen Point Floating Bridge. This bridge was renamed the Gov. Albert D. Rossellini Evergreen Point Floating Bridge in August 1985 in honor of the man who served two terms as governor, from 1957 to 1965. It lays claim to being the longest such bridge in the world—1.4 miles. It offers spectacular views of the entire area, often with Mount Rainier as a backdrop. It runs past the University of Washington and over a section of the Arboretum.

Mercer Island Floating Bridge. Its real name is the Lacey B. Murrow Floating Bridge, and it was named for one of the most respected civil engineers the Northwest has ever produced. He also was the brother of the famed broadcaster, Edward R. Murrow, and both were graduates of Washington State University (then College). The mile-long bridge was completed in 1940 and was built of honeycombed concrete to connect Seattle with Mercer Island. A normal raised bridge connected the island with the Bellevue area on the east side. The four-lane bridge is in the process of growing into eight lanes with the addition of a twin floating bridge and tunnel beside the existing one, both of which cost enough to build a sister city on the moon.

Ferries

Washington has the largest fleet of vehicle/passenger ferries in the nation, and if anything is a symbol of Puget Sound, it must be those awkward-looking, open-ended ferries, which have a strange kind of grace in spite of their appearance. Next to having your own boat, they are the best way to see Puget Sound and the people who live around it. And they are certainly the best way to see the islands of the sound, surely the most charming archipelago in North America.

Ferries will take you to the San Juan Islands, the urbanized Bainbridge Island, and the stubbornly rural Vashon Island. They form moving bridges that you will share with semitrailers, delivery vans, passenger buses, bicycles, and the walk-on passengers. Waiting in ferry lines on long weekends, too, is a part of the Northwest mystique.

If you are lucky, you will see mountain climbers crawling "up" a wall by rappelling themselves along in the ferry parking lanes, pretending they are climbing when they actually are crawling across the pavement. That is only one of the cultural activities you can expect to see while waiting for the ferry.

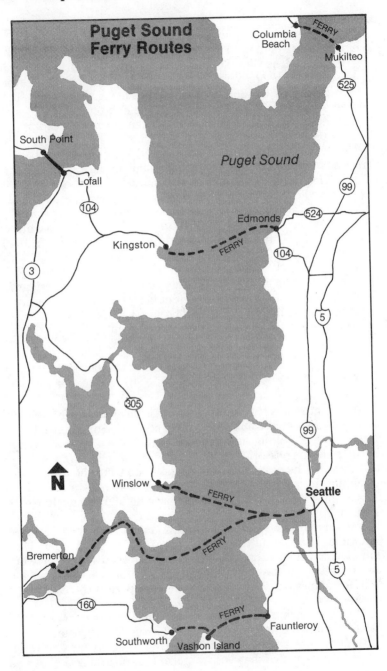

Each ferry has an observation deck and food service that ranges from the elaborate (for self-service) on the busy runs, such as the Bainbridge Island route, to the very modest, such as the crossing between Mukilteo and Whidbey Island.

They provide the most direct route to the great hiking, fishing, and sightseeing on the Olympic Peninsula; to the great historic towns of Port Townsend and Port Gamble; and to all the resorts along Hood Canal, the sound, and the Strait of Juan de Fuca.

Fares are complex and continually escalating upward, so no attempt will be made to show them here. One price break is that given to senior citizens—half price.

For information on all routes, call the ferries at 464-6400.

WASHINGTON FERRIES

Anacortes-San Juan Islands-Sidney, British Columbia. This is considered by everyone who takes the trip as one of the prime boat rides in the country. It is a premium, all-day trip from one nation to another through the gorgeous, remote San Juan Islands. The ferry leaves early in the morning (usually about 7:45 A.M.) from the Anacortes ferry terminal, winds its way through the San Juans, stops at Lopez, Shaw, Orcas, and San Juan islands, passes several others, and lands at Sidney, British Columbia.

Edmonds-Kingston, Edmonds ferry terminal, approximately 20 miles north of downtown Seattle via either Aurora N. or Interstate 5. Runs between Edmonds and Kingston, Kitsap Peninsula, the most direct route to the northern part of the Olympic Peninsula. Crossing time one-half hour, leaving approximately every seventy minutes from 6:00 A.M. to 1:30 P.M.

Fauntleroy-Vashon Island, Fauntleroy ferry dock in West Seattle at the foot of Fauntleroy Ave. near Lincoln Park. To Vashon Island only, leaving every thirty-five minutes between 5:30 A.M. and 3:00 A.M. Crossing time fifteen minutes.

Mukilteo-Columbia Beach, Mukilteo to Whidbey Island route. Leaving every twenty-five minutes between 6:00 A.M. and 3:00 A.M. Crossing time fifteen minutes. Whidbey Island is the largest island in Puget Sound and one of the largest within the United States. A trip from Seattle across the sound by ferry to the island, then up its length to the high, dramatic bridge at Deception Pass State Park, then back south again via Interstate 5 makes an excellent day trip. This is also the most direct route to Port Townsend via the Keystone ferry on Whidbey Island.

Seattle-Bremerton, Pier 52 at the foot of Marion St. To Bremerton leaving every hour on the hour from 6:00 A.M. until 9:00 P.M., less frequently thereafter until approximately 1:30 A.M. Crossing time is one hour.

Seattle-Winslow, Pier 52. To Winslow on Bainbridge Island, leaving approximately every forty-five minutes except during early morning hours. Crossing time one-half hour. Agate Passage Bridge connects Bainbridge Island and the Kitsap Peninsula mainland and is toll-free.

Vashon-Southworth, Vashon Island to Southworth, running on roughly the same schedule as those listed above. Crossing time ten minutes. (Note: Some ferries make the three-point run between Fauntleroy, Vashon Island, and Southworth, depending on the season and time of day. Check with ferry information.)

Shopping

Pike Place Market

One of the nicer things about Seattle is that you can have so much fun spending money. The city has a long tradition of superior craftsmanship in everything from houses to sailboats, and more recently it has become famous for its clothing. This clothing is mostly recreational, of course, but a few other surprises appear, such as Britannia jeans, which came out of Seattle.

Most clothing items, though, are a result of our climate—damp but mild—with one exception, and that is the quilted down coats and sleeping bags patented by Eddie Bauer nearly half a century ago. This process created a revolution in insulated clothing.

Other Seattle creations include the superb waterproofed canvas pants worn by loggers and fishermen and developed by Filson of Seattle, and a variety of woolen pants, shirts, and jackets (particularly the Cruiser jackets).

Merchandising has been a Seattle specialty that dates back to Eddie Bauer's first total guarantee—if you don't like it, send it back and you'll get all your money back, no questions asked.

That kind of merchandising has been largely responsible for the success of Nordstrom, the department-store chain that has virtually exploded into the Bay Area, Southern California, and the East Coast.

This merchandising philosophy was shared by the first major department store in Seattle, Frederick & Nelson, which was a downtown fixture for decades. Frederick's, as it was usually called, had a no-questions-asked refund policy like Eddie Bauer, and, unfortunately, many shoppers abused the system. They would buy an item for a specific weekend party then return the goods first thing Monday morning. In spite of this, the benefits of the program outweighed the disadvantages.

Unfortunately, the company went out of business in 1992 leaving The Bon Marche and Nordstrom as the primary downtown department stores.

Here is a sampling of shopping that will give you an idea of the diversity available.

Department Stores

The Bon Marche, 4th and Pine. This is one of Seattle's oldest and most-respected department stores and has one distinct plus on rainy days; you can park across the street in the parking garage, then cross over the skybridge without having to unfurl an umbrella. The Bon is more popular with the younger set for the latest in both clothing and records. Other stores are in Alderwood Mall, Bellevue, Southcenter, Northgate, and Federal Way.

Nordstrom, 1501 5th Ave. This suddenly successful chain was founded in a shoe store on the corner of Pike and 5th Ave. many years ago, and the parent store is still the anchor of the empire, except that now it covers most of the block. It is perhaps Seattle's most stylish place to shop, and quality of service remains as important as quality of merchandise. Nordstrom is at several other locations: Bellevue Square, University District, Southcenter, Aurora Village, Alderwood Mall, and Northgate.

Seattle also has the national chain stores, such as Sears, J.C. Penney, and others in the downtown area and at several shopping malls.

Clothing

WOMEN'S CLOTHING

These stores are among Seattle's most popular, and expensive.

I. Magnin, 6th and Pine (682-6111).
John Doyle Bishop Fashions, 411 University St. (682-4177).
Littler's, 1331 5th Ave., Rainier Square (223-1331).
The Mediterranean-Italian Fashions, 515 Pine St. (622-2949).
Pino's, 521 Union St. (623-8107).
Totally Michael's, 1333 5th Ave., Rainier Square (622-4920).

MEN'S CLOTHING

Brooks Brothers, 1401 4th Ave. (624-4400).
Butch Blum, 1408 5th Ave. (622-5760).
Klopfenstein's, 600 Pine St. (622-2360), also some shopping centers.
Littler's, 1331 5th Ave. (223-1331).
Michael's Bespoke Tailors, 407 Union (623-4785).
Yankee Peddler, 4218 E. Madison (324-4218), 4737 University Plaza NE (526-9656).

Those Magnificent Malls

Seattle was one of the nation's pioneers in shopping malls, particularly covered malls that provide an artificially rainless environment. Malls have become a way of life for many people who use them as entertainment centers as well as the equivalent of the village square.

Here are some statistics on the major malls in the area. I will leave it to trained sociologists to explain what effect they have or could have on our lives and culture, and I will also leave to them the chore of telling who hangs out at which.

Alderwood Mall, Interstates 5 and 405. Seventy-six acres and 136 stores. Figures on sales and number of shoppers are not released by management.

Bellevue Square, NE 8th and Main. Thirty-four acres and 198 stores with some 182,000 shoppers each week. Gross annual sales of $275 million.

Northgate, Interstate 5 and NE Northgate Way. The nation's first covered mall, it spreads over fifty-two acres with 116 stores and more than 350,000 shoppers each week, making it the most heavily used mall in Seattle proper. Sales average $200 million a year.

Sea-Tac Mall, Pacific Highway S. and 320th Ave. Fifty-one acres and 106 stores. About $50 million annual gross sales and 40,000 to 50,000 shoppers each week.

Southcenter, Interstates 5 and 405. Ninety-two acres with 127 stores and 275,000 to 300,000 shoppers each week. Gross sales are about $250 million yearly.

Downtown Covered Shopping

Rainier Square Pedestrian Concourse (Rainier Tunnel); western terminus is the Rainier Tower Building lobby on 4th Ave. The carpeted concourse continues to 6th Ave., with entrances to a variety of stores and restaurants. Included among the shops are Eddie Bauer, Littler's, Beks Bookstore, Totally Michael's, a gourmet kitchenware store, home furnishings, Crepe de Paris restaurant, and Odette's Cafeteria. Exits lead directly to the Hilton Hotel, Skinner Building, 5th Avenue Movie Theater, Washington Athletic Club, and, of course, Rainier Bank and the parking garage.

Unique Shopping Centers

In and around Seattle a sprinkling of creative and unusual enclaves of shops and specialty stores attract browsers and shoppers interested in the quaint and unusual. Some of the most interesting of these little centers are described below.

Avenue Arcade, 4518 University Way NE. An old J.C. Penney store remodeled into three levels of shops—jewelry, men's and women's apparel, gift shops, interior design, import shops, ice-cream and spice shops, and the Walking Crepe Company (a restaurant).

Capitol Hill, between Broadway and 15th, Olive and E. Roy, and down the hill toward town on Pine and other streets. Several of the shops are listed in our "Specialty Shops" section, particularly the more exclusive furniture stores such as Keeg's and Del Teet. Several cafes and restaurants are listed in chapter 9.

Pier 70, at the foot of Broad on the sound. Originally a working dock and warehouse built in 1902, this two-story wooden warehouse's exterior has been sandblasted and the interior renovated to enclose over forty shops and several restaurants. A few of the shop types are candy, import candle, jeans warehouse, jewelry, toy, book, and art gallery. One of the restaurants, the Top of the Pier, has a good view of the sound.

University District, centered at 45th and University Way NE. Not an enclosed shopping center, but a mixture of shops: inexpensive restaurants, boutiques, arts-and-crafts stores, bakeries, and the University Bookstore, one of the largest bookstores in the nation. The "in" place for the young to buy their pants, tops, clogs, and jewelry.

Westlake Center, at Pine and 5th, is the newest shopping center in town. It includes a new urban park and an office/retail complex that houses some sixty shops and fifteen eateries. The opening of the center in late 1987 finally put an end to one of Seattle's longest civic feuds, centering on what to do with the awkward little triangle that was bordered by Nordstrom's, Frederick & Nelson, and the Bon Marche. At this writing the center is still in its shakedown stage, and it's too early to tell which retail outlets and cafes will survive.

Specialty Shops

This category could go on forever because I am lumping several types of stores into one listing. The resident will likely already know many of these shops, and the out-of-town visitor will want to visit them. It is unlikely, however, that the out-of-towner will buy a love seat in Seattle to ship back home to New Orleans. So here's a grab bag of more-than-passing interest. Specialty shops tend to be clustered in places like Pioneer Square, along the waterfront, in and around the Seattle Center, and in enclaves around the city and in the suburbs.

Baby & Co., 1936 1st (448-4077) and 4234 University Way NE (547-6465). A boutique of clothing, costume jewelry, accessories, and footwear for the adult baby.

Del Teet Furniture Company, 127 Broadway E. (323-5400). Excellent contemporary furniture.

Johnson-West Music Service, 500 Denny Way (441-7741). The best selection of sheet music in town.

Keeg's, 310 Broadway E. (325-1771). Kitchenware, toys, posters, Danish furniture, mostly imports.

La Tienda Folk Art Gallery, 4138 University Way NE (632-1796). African, Peruvian, Polish, and Mexican rugs, clothing, jewelry, etc.

Made in Washington, Pike Place Market (467-0788) and Westlake Center (623-9753).

McBreen, 905 E. John (323-2336). Furniture and design services.

Opus 204, 204 Broadway E. (325-1781). Imported leather, rugs, textiles, and baskets from Africa.

Sur La Table, 84 Pine (448-2244). Cookware for the gourmet.

Teresa of Hong Kong, 1512 6th (622-0455). Oriental fashions for milady, including kimonos, pajamas, Happi coats, and ivory and jade carvings.

Tobo Oriental Imports, 504 12th S. (324-2100). Japanese variety store, crammed with handsome pots, dishes, gifts.

Toys Galore, 1525 6th (624-3350) and Southcenter (246-7060). Ordinary and extraordinary gifts for the youngsters.

Uwajimaya, 6th S. & S. King (624-6248). Japanese imports from
foods to records to printed matter. Southcenter and Bellevue
also.

Specialty Food Stores

When your family or companions gather round the table and
say "Oh yuk, THAT again!" it's time to go down to the Pike Place
Market and gather your dinner from the concentration of specialty
food shops there. But if the market doesn't appeal to you, try some
of the other shops located in and around Seattle.

A & J Meats, 2401 Queen Anne N. (284-3885). Some customers
come from Mercer Island to buy their weekly supply of meats.
Aside from their choice selection of regular meats, Al or Jerry
will make up rouladen, chicken kiev, or hors d'oeuvre trays that
make you wish you had forgotten to invite the guests.

Boehm's Candy Kitchen, 559 NE Ravenna Blvd. (523-9380), and
the original chalet store, 255 NE Gilman Blvd., Issaquah
(392-6652). Superb candies from broken chocolates to mint
truffles, English toffee, and other mouth-watering tidbits.

Brenner Bros. Bakery & Delicatessen, 12000 Bellevue-Redmond Rd.,
Bellevue (454-0600). Out of town and a little difficult to find
but worth the trip for their superb breads and bagels.

DeLaurenti Italian & International Food Market, Pike Place Market
(622-0141); 317 Bellevue Way NE, Bellevue (454-7155). An
old-style market with open bins for beans, dried fruit, and
similar foods. Not limited to, but heavily specializing in, Ital-
ian-style foods: breads, cheese, wines, and a host of items you
won't find anywhere else, plus a complete delicatessen.

Husky Deli & Catering, 4721 California SW (937-2810). Tasty bulk
ice cream and cones, imported foods including such exotic
items as reindeer meatballs.

Pike Place Deli, Pike Place Market (622-9172). Outstanding source
for foods hard to find elsewhere, such as freshly ground creamy
peanut butter, spoon cheese, sweet mustard, chow-chow pick-
les, old-fashioned deli olives, dates, imported Greek feta
cheese, and the biggest assortment of fruitcake ingredients in
Seattle.

Sivertsen's Bakery, 100 Mercer (283-3797). Their Scandinavian pastries are tops.

Starbuck's Coffee and Tea, 1912 Pike Pl. (448-8762), University
Village, University District, Broadway District, and 10214 NE
8th, Bellevue (454-0191). This is the company that pioneered
coffee in Seattle. Their coffees are roasted in Seattle; they also
sell brewing and grinding devices.

Truffles, 3701 NE 45th (522–3016). Wine, meats, tea, French cheeses; a step above your basic grocery store. Also gift boxes and baskets.

Uwajimaya. See listing under "Specialty Shops."

The Wedge, 4760 University Village Pl. NE (523–2560). Good selection of imported and domestic cheeses.

Fish Markets

There is nothing wrong with properly frozen fish, but if you want fresh seafood, here are the approximate seasons. King salmon begin arriving about May 1; silvers about June 15; sockeyes about July 1; pinks in August, especially in odd-numbered years (underwater calendars?); and chums (also called "dogs" or "falls") arrive near the end of September. Bottom fish (cod, sole, and snapper) come in year-round; fresh crabs come on the market in December.

Pike Place Market. Three seafood markets are near each other in the main floor of the market and will pack a salmon for sending across the country: City Fish Market (682–9329), Pure Food Fish Market (622–5765), and Pike Place Fish Market (682–7181).

Port Chatham Packing Company, 632 NW 46th (783–8200). Smoked salmon at its best. Also you can bring in your own catch for smoking, canning, or airmailing to the folks back home.

Totem Smokehouse Gourmet Seafood, 1906 Pike Pl. (443–1710); 7307 NE 120th, Kirkland (823–6611). Canned alder-smoked salmon, sturgeon, oysters, and clams.

Wild Salmon Fish Market, 1800 W. Emerson Pl. (283–3366). Located in Fishermen's Terminal where all the boats tie up, so the salmon don't have far to go; also crab and shrimp. Market owned by a group of salmon fishermen.

Wine

Washington has never been known for its enlightened liquor laws, although it is getting better all the time. For years the laws were so protective to the state's small wine industry that those in love with the immortal grape were forced into smuggling to accumulate a decent wine cellar. But that is changed now, and with it came a splurge of wine how-to books and columns. (Yes, we know: ask anybody lurking around the north end of the Pike Place Market. But we're talking about a different kind of wine experience.)

We won't get into the specialized material here, in part because all experts on wine share a single trait; they disagree with each other constantly. Here are a few of the major wine shops in the Seattle area:

Cellar Wine Shop, 14411 Greenwood N.

Esquin Wine Merchants, 1516 1st S.

Gourmet Shop in Lake City, 12511 Lake City Way NE.

Lacantina Wine Shop, University Village and 104 Bellevue Way SE, Bellevue.

Mondo's World, 4223 Rainier S.

Pike and Western Wine Company, Pike Place Market.

Nearly all of these shops will arrange a wine-tasting party for you in your home, in a hotel suite, a room of a restaurant, or elsewhere. They also offer classes in the basics of the art of wine. Most wine-tasting parties, by the way, are given by the shops at no charge unless extensive planning is involved. Several give 10 percent discounts on cases.

Several restaurants team up with wineries to offer special "wine-maker dinners," featuring fine food and a selection of wine. Among the restaurants offering these special occasions are Cafe Alexis; Cafe Sport; Campagne; Enoteca; Fuller's; The Georgian Room, Olympic; The Hunt Club; Le Fleur; The Mirabeau; The Other Place; Prego; and Ray's Boathouse.

There's still another way to get into wine: join the Enological Society of the Pacific Northwest. It is open to anyone over 21. Write to the society: 200 2nd N., Seattle, Washington 98109. The society has monthly programs, dinners featuring food and wine from different parts of Europe, and an annual festival held in August at Seattle Center.

If you're really hooked on wine and think you can do better than the French or the Californians by making your own, here's a list of shops that carry wine-making equipment—plus the forms you have to fill out for the federal government. There's no fee for the permits, but the government wants to know who is making wine and where, and it is a no-no to make more than two hundred gallons a year. That is usually sufficient for the average family anyway.

Arbor Wine & Beer Supply, 8824 Roosevelt Way NE.

Cellar Wine Shop, 14411 Greenwood N.

Liberty Malt Supply Company, 1432 Western.

The Party House, 10408 16th SW.

Antiques

While the Pacific Northwest isn't old enough to have its own antiques—most have been imported—there are numerous shops with excellent collections and reasonable prices. The antique business is in a growth stage, and new shops are opening frequently throughout town. For the moment, they tend to cluster in the downtown area, Pioneer Square, Capitol Hill, and north on Queen Anne Hill, Fremont, University, Ballard, and the Greenwood districts plus the Pike Place Market. Here we have listed just some of the more centrally located and unique shops.

Antique Liquidators, 503 Westlake N. (623-2740). Old English furniture received every ten days, priced low for quick turnover.

Antiques & Art Associates, 2113 3rd (728-2113). Furniture, china, glass, prints, and books.

Antiques 'N Things, 1010 4th S. (622-9117). Glass, costumes, dolls, and toys.

Furniture Spa, 7557 15th NW (784-0011). Stripping; old furniture for sale.

Washington Art Galleries, 3311 Rainier S. (725-2002). European furniture, art glass, and paintings.

Yesteryear Collection, 2500 32nd Ave. W. (284-2808). Costume jewelry, porcelain, glassware, and silver.

Outdoor Recreation

Seattle is within sight of some of the best hiking, climbing, skiing, fishing, and kayaking spots in North America. To quote a defunct TV show, "No brag, just fact." In fact, a short time ago there were at least two hundred thousand backpackers in the area, according to one store. Most have annual sales, but be prepared to camp on the sidewalk if you want first grab at these events: SNIA-GRAB, a three-day sale held in early September at Seattle Center, sponsored by Osborn & Ulland; and Recreational Equipment Inc. camping sale in April, ski sale in October.

Athletic Supply, 901 Harrison (623-8972). Complete equipment for all sports, individuals, and teams.

Fiorini Sport, University Village (523-9610). Skiing, hiking, sports clothing and equipment.

Harris-Conley Golf Shop, 1st & Seneca (624-8361). A highly rated golfer's shop.

MSR, 1212 1st S. (624-8573). Mountain Safety Research specializes in climbing gear and stoves.

North Face, 1023 1st (622-4111). Specialists in backpacking clothing and equipment.

Olympic Sports, 10700 5th NE (363-3007). Specializes in winter sports equipment but also has stock of hiking gear, tennis equipment, and water skis.

Osborn & Ulland, 1926 3rd (728-8999). One of the best shops for outfitting skiers and tennis players. Branches at Northgate, Southcenter, and Bellevue.

Recreational Equipment Inc., 1525 11th (323-8333). The "Co-op," so named because it is a cooperative that pays you back an average of 10 percent on your year's total purchases. Emphasis here is on backpacking, mountaineering, kayaking, and bicycling. Heavy emphasis on conservation. Expedition outfitter.

Warshal's, 1st & Madison (624-7301). Specializes in fishing and hunting equipment with a complete photographic department that wheels and deals in new and used cameras and accessories; for the amateur and pro.

Thrifty Places to Shop

Seattle, like many cities, offers numerous opportunities for canny money managers and thrifty shoppers to buy food, clothing, and sports equipment at significant savings. Some of the places operate all year. Others, such as Sniagrab (*bargains* spelled backward), by Osborn & Ulland, open and close on one weekend. The Children's Orthopedic Hospital guilds also host a gigantic rummage sale at the Seattle Center Exhibition Hall once a year. Watch the newspapers for news of these and similar events. Not so well known are the out-of-the-way sample shops, consignment resale emporiums, and used clothing outlets operated by charity organizations as a fund-raising activity. Irregulars and seconds are also offered at factory outlet stores, principally for outdoor wear—ski jackets and the like.

Auctions

Here's a sampling of auctions in the Seattle area, ranging from county- to city- to government-sponsored.

Bushell's Auction House, 2006 2nd (622-5833). Home furnishings, antiques, estates. Sales on Tuesdays.

Police Department (625-2051). Every two or three months, depending on the amount of goods received, the Seattle Police Department holds an auction of stolen items or unclaimed lost-and-found goods. Many bikes end up in this auction. For information, watch the local newspapers or call the police department's public information office at the number above.

U.S. Customs Service (442-4678). An auction is held each year in November of goods unclaimed or confiscated, ranging from Christmas decorations to clothing to jewelry. Call for information and a catalog, which will be sent two weeks ahead of the auction.

Vintage Clothing

Remember when you wouldn't be caught dead shopping for used (previously owned, to put it politely) clothing? Or even selling used clothing because it would be an admission that you weren't as wealthy as J. Paul Getty? Things have changed somewhat, and it is no longer in the same category as hocking the silver.

Here are a few places you can sell and buy used clothing:

Chop Suey, 1828½ Broadway.
Deluxe Junk, 3518 Fremont Pl. N.
Dreamland, 619 Broadway E. and 4302 University Way NE.
Fritzi Ritz, 1519 1st Ave.
Guess Where, 615 N. 35th St.
Isadora's, 1921 1st Ave.
Jasmine Room, 109 1st Ave. S.
Madame & Co. Collectable Fashions, 117 Yesler Way.
Out of the Past, 112 Broadway Ave. E.
RetroViva, 1511 1st Ave.
Tootsie's, 215 Union.
Vintage Clothing, 6501 Roosevelt Way NE.

NONPROFIT INSTITUTIONS

Council of Jewish Women's Thrift Shop, 1501 Pike Pl.
Deseret Industries (Mormon Church), 17935 Aurora Ave. N.
Goodwill Industries, Rainier Ave. S. & S. Dearborn St.
Shop 'N Save Thrift Shops (American Diabetes Association), 10014 15th SW.
St. Vincent de Paul and *Salvation Army*, several locations.
Thrift Korner Stores (People Helping the Rights of the Disabled), 85th & 1st Ave. NW.
Trinkets & Treasures (Epiphany Episcopal Church), 517 15th Ave. E.
Value Village (Northwest Center for the Retarded), several locations.
The Wise Penny (Junior League), 4744 University Way NE.

Galleries and Museums

Seattle Art Museum

Seattle has always had an affinity for visual art, perhaps more than any other art form, and if a Northwest school of anything exists, it is Northwest art. More visual artists are able to support themselves than composers, poets, or novelists, and galleries and museums have always been especially partial to regional artists.

As a result of this, Seattle has a lot of public art (not all of which is especially attractive to everybody, of course) and a reputation for supporting regional artists.

One of the major events in the art community, which surprised most people with its success, is the First Thursday openings in Pioneer Square. On the first Thursday of each month, a group of galleries in this historic district have their openings in the evening. They have been a resounding success, and most of the galleries are packed.

The gallery business is a tough one, and some galleries that seemed to be successful have closed, with the owners citing a general burnout because it is such a tough way to earn a living. But others thrive, or at least manage to stay open.

Here, then, is a list of the major galleries that were in operation when the book went to press.

Arthead Gallery, 5411 Meridian Ave. N. (633-5544). Limited-edition prints, sculpture, and paintings by local artists.

Cliff Michel Gallery, 520 Second Ave. (624-4484). Prints, photographs, and sculpture are featured in this gallery.

Davidson Galleries, 313 Occidental Ave. S. (624-7684). Contemporary Northwest paintings, prints, sculpture, and drawings are featured, with an emphasis on works on paper. Publishes posters and catalogs for national distribution. No reproductions. The gallery at 1915 1st Ave. in Pike Place Market specializes in antique prints, maps, manuscripts, etc.

Fire Works, 210 1st Ave. S. (682-8707). Ceramics, glass, jewelry, and crafts from the Northwest and elsewhere are displayed.

Flury & Company Gallery, 322 First Ave. S. (587-0260). Mainly photographic works, with an excellent collection of Edward S. Curtis gold-tone prints.

Foster/White Gallery, 311½ Occidental Ave. S. (622-2833). Specializes in contemporary Northwest ceramics, glass, paintings, and sculpture. Represents some of the major Northwest artists. Also has a gallery in Frederick & Nelson store in downtown Seattle.

Francine Seders Gallery, 6701 Greenwood Ave. N. (782-0355). Exhibitions of contemporary works with an emphasis on Northwest artists.

Greg Kucera Gallery, 608 2nd Ave. (624-0770). Fine-arts gallery showing local and national artists. Represents several national artists and emerging regional ones.

Hundredwaters Gallery, 115 Bell St. (441-8643). One of the newer galleries that features contemporary, often experimental, artists and has two annual exhibits of masks and new furniture.

Kindred Gallery, 424 Broadway E. (325-7950). Northwest paintings, pottery, graphics, and posters are featured.

Kirsten Gallery, 5320 Roosevelt Way NE (522-2100). A wide range of artistic styles are displayed, which range from traditional and representational to abstract works. The annual Northwest Marine Art Exhibition in July and August is a highlight for the gallery.

Linda Farris Gallery, 320 2nd Ave. S. (623-1110). Museum-caliber contemporary works by regional and national artists are featured.

Linda Hodges Gallery, 322 2nd Ave. S. (623-1110). Contemporary works by regional and nationally known artists are shown. It is one of the Pioneer Square First Thursday opening galleries.

Matzke-Runnings Gallery, 413 1st S. (622-2540). Represents and sells paintings by Northwest artists, with new shows each month. Hosts the annual Puget Sound Country juried competition in September.

MIA Gallery, 314 Occidental Ave. S. (467-8283). Sculpture, jewelry, and paintings are featured in this Pioneer Square institution.

Northwest Craft Center, Seattle Center (728-1555). A gathering place for crafts lovers with an emphasis on ceramics and wood. The center sponsors several juried shows and has one of the best craft gift shops in Seattle.

Silver Image Gallery, 318 Occidental Ave. S. (623-8116). Sells photographic prints, books, and posters. Represents regional photographers as well as established masters. Has works by Ansel Adams, Imogen Cunningham, Asahel, and Edward Curtis.

Snow Goose Eskimo Art, 4220 NE 125th St. (362-3401). Northwest Coast Indian and Eskimo art is featured. Five or six shows a year are held to show items selected on trips north by the owner, Jane Schuldberg.

Stone Press Gallery, 89 Yesler Way (624-6752). Represents regional and national contemporary printmakers. Also features work by young artists.

Stonington Gallery, 2030 1st Ave. (443-1108). Specializes in the work of contemporary Alaskan and Northwest artists, and all cultures of Alaska are represented. Limited-edition prints a specialty.

Traver Sutton Gallery, 2219 4th Ave. (622-4232 or 448-4234). Represents contemporary regional and national artists, with two or three artists showing each month. Holds the annual Pilchuck Glass Exhibition.

Museums

Bellevue Art Museum, 301 Bellevue Square (454-3322). One of the few museums located in the heart of a major shopping mall, this one stresses regional artwork and is closely allied with the Pacific Northwest Arts and Crafts Association. The museum does not keep a permanent collection on the premises, but continually rotates its collection, depending on what exhibit is planned. It presents traveling and special exhibitions as well as loaned exhibits and sells arts and crafts in its large gift shop. Hours: Tuesday–Friday noon–8:00 P.M.; Saturday 10:00 A.M.–5:30 P.M.; Sunday 11:00 A.M.–5:00 P.M. General admission is $1 for seniors and students; $2 for a family. Everyone is admitted free on Tuesdays. It is on the third floor of the covered shopping center.

Thomas Burke Memorial Washington State Museum, University of Washington campus just inside the 17th NE & NE 45th entrance (543-5590). An outstanding collection of North American Indian culture with artifacts from the Northwest Coast tribes: Bella Coola, Tlingit, Haida, Kwakiutl, and Nootka. Many masks used by dancers and shamans; spirit boards used in ceremonial dances; carved storage boxes and chests; ceremonial blankets; and wool and cedar-bark clothing. The Hall of Anthropology has a collection of fossil plants, a dinosaur footprint, several skulls for the morbid, and an outstanding collection of moths and butterflies. The Hall of Ornithology features a collection of coastal seabirds, owls, rare and extinct birds, and a push-button system that lets you hear the songs of several varieties of birds. Several exhibits are from the Pacific islands, including a large collection of tapa cloth from the Tonga Islands. Eskimo and Greek artifacts also are displayed. Free admission. Hours: Monday–Friday, 10:00 A.M.–5:30 P.M.; Saturday–Sunday, 9:00 A.M.–4:30 P.M.; closed legal holidays.

Coast Guard Museum, Pier 36 (286-9608). Opened in 1977, this is the first museum in the West to explain the work and history of the Coast Guard. Housed in the small, one-story building is a collection of navigational aids, including an octant, chronometer, and magnetic compass. Also on display are ship models, Arctic ivory, and a 4-foot-high Fresnel lens made in France for a Puget Sound lighthouse. Nearby is the Puget Sound Vessel Traffic Center, where you can watch guardsmen monitor ship traffic or on weekends join a guided tour of an ice breaker, cutter, or other ship in port. Hours: Monday, Wednesday, Friday 9:00 A.M.–3:00 P.M.; Saturday and Sunday 1:00–5:00 P.M. Vessel Traffic Center open 8:00 A.M.–4:00 P.M. daily. Free.

Charles and Emma Frye Art Museum, 704 Terry (corner of Terry & Cherry), P.O. Box 3005 (622-9250). Works by Edouard Manet, Childe Hassam, Hans Thoma, and other nineteenth-century painters, plus a few twentieth-century painters such as Andrew Wyeth and Mary Cassatt. The museum also holds frequent contemporary art exhibits, special displays, and photographic exhibits. Each year a juried Puget Sound Area Exhibition is sponsored, with cash prizes. Guided tours arranged by advance notice. Parking is free in museum lots. Wheelchair entrance at rear; ring buzzer. Free. Hours: Monday–Saturday 10:00 A.M.–5:00 P.M.; Sunday noon–5:00 P.M. Closed Thanksgiving and Christmas.

Goodwill Industries Memory Lane Museum, 1400 S. Lane (329-1000). The management thwarted antique hunters, who for years haunted the hangarlike store for bargains, by deciding to hang on to the antiques and display them in a museum within the building. Many of the objects are hanging from the ceiling beams, including coffee mills, sausage grinders, Confederate money, spinning wheels, baby buggies, sabers, grain mallets, high-button shoes, and even a stuffed armadillo. An extensive wardrobe collection is put to use in vintage fashion shows at noon in the store every Wednesday except July, August, and December and at gatherings around Seattle. Free. Hours: Monday–Saturday 10:00 A.M.–6:00 P.M.; Sunday noon–6:00 P.M. Closed major holidays.

Henry Gallery, University of Washington campus, 15th NE & NE Campus Parkway (543-2280). Originally a public art gallery, the establishment reached museum status with its permanent collection of more than fifteen hundred early nineteenth- and twentieth-century American and European paintings, prints, and ceramics. Numerous Japanese folk ceramics as well. Some thirty-five exhibitions are held each year. Cosponsors film series, lectures, concerts, poetry readings, workshops, and other special events. Admission: $2 adults, students, and seniors. Hours: Tuesday and Thursday 11:00 A.M.–7:00 P.M.; Wednesday and Friday 11:00 A.M.–8:00 P.M. Saturday and Sunday 11:00 A.M.–5:00 P.M.. Closed major holidays.

Klondike Gold Rush National Historical Park. See "Pioneer Square" in Walking Tours chapter.

Museum of History and Industry, 2161 E. Hamlin (324-1125). The best collection of Seattle's history. The spacious museum depicts events from the city's founding on a smelly tideflat to the present. Dioramas depict the founding and several subsequent events, plus photographs of the founders and their documents. Photographs and artifacts from early years are also displayed: Yesler Mill, shipyards, Klondike gold-rush era, and Boeing beginnings. The museum houses a major collection of marine equipment, such as wheels from famous ships, engines, bells, and submarine periscopes. The famous hydroplane, *Slo-Mo-Shun IV*, is also displayed. Boeing's famous B-1 seaplane that delivered the first airmail from Seattle to Victoria hangs from the ceiling. A major doll collection with a fantastic house is on display. Several antique cars, fire engines, and a cable car are in the basement level. A special room is devoted to stuffed animals (including the zoo's late gorilla, Bobo) and mounted heads from all over the world. The museum also boasts an excellent reference library with extensive photo collection; special children's events and handicraft classes; and Christmas Around the World, a special holiday program where various nationalities present their Christmas customs. Hours: every day 10:00 A.M.–5:00 P.M.. Admission: $3 adults, $1.50 children and seniors.

Museum of Flight, 9404 E. Marginal Way S. (764-5720). This ambitious museum began its life in a modest little building on the grounds of the Seattle Center. Through the efforts of a totally dedicated staff that believes in the museum's value to the community, several million dollars were raised nationally to acquire the site and put up the buildings. The centerpiece of the museum is the Red Barn, the nickname for the old boat-building plant that became the Boeing Company's first plant. It was moved about and was almost destroyed before the museum acquired it. The museum is open now, but construction continues on the Great Gallery, a steel-and-glass exhibit hall where a B-17 and other aircraft will hang from the girders. The museum also stresses the contributions from Pacific Rim nations and, of course, the Boeing Company across the street. But it is not a Boeing museum; rather, it is a world-class museum telling the story of aviation from a Pacific viewpoint. Hours: every day 10:00 A.M.–5:00 P.M.; Thursdays until 9:00 P.M. Closed Christmas day. Admission: adults and seniors, $4; teens, $3; children 6–12, $2.

Nordic Heritage Museum, 3014 67th NW (789-5707). Features the social and family life of Nordic countries and the life of immigrants to the United States. Annual Nordic Yule Fest and other events held in museum. Hours: Tuesday–Saturday 10:00 A.M.–4:00 P.M.; Thursday 10:00 A.M.–9:00 P.M.; Sunday noon–4:00 P.M. Admission: $2.50 adults; $1.50 seniors; children 6–16 $1.00; children under 6 free.

Postal Museum, Pioneer Square Station, 302 Occidental S. (623–
1908). Patron rental boxes, three-wheeled carts, documents
dating back to the last century, wooden pens with metal points,
two-cent prepaid envelopes, antique postal scales, postal regu-
lation books, canvas mail pouches, and numerous other items
are included in the growing collection. It is undoubtedly one of
the few branch post offices in the country with an attached
museum (yes, you can mail a letter there). Free. Hours:
Monday–Friday 9:00 A.M.–5:00 P.M. Closed Saturday, Sunday,
and legal holidays.

Seattle Art Museum, 100 University St. (654–3100). The new downtown 62-million-dollar museum opened on December 5, 1991,
amid raves for the architecture (by Robert Venturi), lawsuits
(by the contractor who claimed $12 million in overruns) and
embarrassment (the 48-foot, 22,000-pound Jonathan Borofsky
sculpture "Hammering Man" toppled over during its installation).

The museum is a smash hit with everyone in the national
art community. It has four floors and 155,000 square feet of
exhibit space to show off many of the museum's 18,500-piece
collection that could not be viewed regularly in the original
(and much smaller) Volunteer Park Museum.

The first floor has the Museum Store, a 299-seat auditorium, and The Restaurant, catered by the Sheraton Tower Hotel,
that serves hot and cold entrées in an outdoor-cafe setting. The
mezzanine and second floor houses traveling exhibitions. The
third floor houses the permanent collections of African,
Northwest Coast Native American, Chinese, Japanese, Korean,
and Pre-Islam Persian collections. The fourth floor presents the
Northwest "Old Masters" such as Mark Tobey and Morris
Graves, photographs, and the European collections dating from
the medieval times up through the present.

Notable collections include the Samuel H. Kress that features a ceiling fresco by Giovanni Tiepolo and the Venus and
Adonis by Paolo Caliari. The Norman Davis collection of Greek
coins is one of the most renowned collections in the world.
Perhaps the most impressive collection is the enormous store of
Oriental art left to the museum by the late Dr. Richard Fuller,
the man who built the Volunteer Park Museum and gave it to
the city.

The new museum has a rental and sales gallery where
members can rent or buy artwork. It also sponsors education
programs for adults, children, and school classes and conducts
free tours of the permanent collection, special exhibitions, and
the architecture of the building.

The former museum in Volunteer Park is closed for renovation and is scheduled to reopen in 1993. Its exhibit space will

be devoted to the museum's enormous Asian collection and is described by Asian art curator William J. Rathbun as an "Asian art retreat, someplace people can come and lose themselves in the quiet study of esthetic objects."

Annual membership costs $30 for individuals, $50 for families, $22 for students and seniors, and $125 for patrons.

Hours: Tuesday–Saturday 10:00 A.M.–5:00 P.M.; Thursday 10:00 A.M.–9:00 P.M.; Sunday noon–5:00 P.M. It is closed Mondays, Thanksgiving, Christmas, and New Year's Day.

Admission is free to members, $5 for adults, and $3 for seniors and students. Children 12 and under accompanied by an adult entrance free. The first Tuesday of each month is a free day for everyone. No admission is charged for using the Museum Store or the Café.

Wing Luke Museum, 407 7th Ave. S. (623–5124). This museum, which preserves and interprets Chinese culture, is named for a city councilman who died in 1965 when his plane crashed in the Cascades. Permanent exhibits include such diverse items as firecrackers, fans, parasols, herb remedies, unusual foods, and photographs. Special exhibits and classes are offered in brush painting. Lectures and demonstrations of techniques in origami are given. Art auctions are held each November to raise funds. Admission: $1.50 adults, $.50 children, students, and seniors. Hours: Tuesday–Friday 11:00 A.M.–4:30 P.M., Saturday and Sunday noon–4:00 P.M., and some evenings.

Restaurants

Sidewalk cafe

It wasn't too many years ago that a new restaurant opening was given approximately the same fanfare one would expect from the arrival of Queen Elizabeth. That is because until only recently the restaurant business was pretty simple—a handful of excellent restaurants and several dozen mediocre ones—and our idea of an ethnic restaurant was one that served chop suey or Italian food with parmesan cheese.

By early 1990 Seattle had more than 2,200 restaurants, and the number that survives long enough to pay interior decorating bills is increasing. Jonathan Susskind, food writer for the *P-I*, pointed out that not only are the odds against new restaurants, but many buildings used for a succession of restaurants seem to be cursed, because all restaurants in them fail.

You will quickly note that I do not use a restaurant rating system. I suppose such a system is like the democratic form of government—imperfect, but still the best available. I have yet to see a rating system, other than by expense, that is an adequate means of telling readers where to eat. Service changes from day to day, and the waiter who glowered and snarled yesterday may be back driving a taxi today; by the time my complaint about him is published, he may have a Ph.D. and be teaching at Pomona College.

Criticism of this nature is usually unfair. It is fair to criticize a record or a movie or a book, because those products are permanent. Restaurants, the meals they serve, and their staffs are not. Add to this my reluctance to even attempt to make up people's minds for them. So those of you who want to read restaurant criticism are reading in the wrong place.

I gladly refer you to the major newspapers that run restaurant reviews. Both the *P-I* and the *Times* publish their restaurant reviews on Friday in their respective entertainment sections, and the *Weekly* publishes its reviews every Thursday. In addition to this, the *Weekly*'s book-publishing arm, *Sasquatch Publishing Company*, publishes the standard works on restaurants—*The Best Places* series.

So what I have for you here is a suggestion list only. If the joint has a bad reputation, it won't be listed here. But if it has been in business awhile and seems headed for a stable future, then it is the kind of place I want to patronize and list here.

Obviously, I cannot visit all hundred-odd restaurants, cafes, delis, take-out places, and the places that specialize in Sunday brunches that would change even Ichabod Crane's profile. I don't have the time, the money, or the desire. I have compiled this list from friends' recommendations, other sources, and my own experiences.

Ethnic Restaurants

Following is a partial list of ethnic restaurants. Watch the newspapers for the opening of new ones:

Bolivian: Copacabana Cafe, Pike Place Market.

Cajun/Creole: Burk's Cafe, 5411 Ballard Ave. NW; The New Orleans Restaurant, 114 1st Ave.; Cajun Corner Cafe, 90 W. Madison; Thompson's Point of View, 2308 E. Union St.; Catfish Corner, 2776 E. Cherry St.; La Mediterranean Delicatessen, 528 Broadway; Franglor's Cajun & Creole Cafe, 5478 1st Ave. S.

Chinese: Atlas Chinese Restaurant, 424 Maynard S.; Tien Tsin Restaurant, 1401 N. 45th (also Korean); Tai Tung Restaurant, 659 S. King; Wild Ginger, 1400 Western Ave.; Honey Court, 516 Maynard S.

Czechoslovakian: Labuznik Restaurant, 1924 1st Ave.

Ethiopian: Axum Ethiopian Restaurants, 4142 Brooklyn Ave. NE; Kokeb Restaurant, 926 12th Ave.

French: Crepe de Paris, Rainier Square; Le Tastevin French Restaurant, 19 W. Harrison; Mirabeau Restaurant, top floor of Seattle–First National Bank Building; Dominique's Place, 1927 43rd E.; Maximilian-in-the-Market, 81-A Pike Place Market.

Greek: The Byzantion, 806 E. Roy; The Aegean, 1400 1st Ave.

Indian: India House Restaurant & Lounge, 4737 Roosevelt Way NE.

Indonesian: Java Restaurant, 8929 Roosevelt Way NE.

Irish: Jake O'Shaughnessey's First Established 1897, 100 Mercer St.; Kells, Pike Place Market.

Italian: Italian Spaghetti House & Pizzeria, 9824 Lake City Way NE; Italo's Casa Romana Restaurant & Lounge, 14622 15th NE; Trattoria Pagliacci, 426 Broadway E.; Al Boccalino, 1 Yesler Way.

Japanese: Askua Restaurant, 6th and Seneca; Benihana of Tokyo Restaurant, IBM Building, 5th and University; Bush Garden Sukiyaki, 614 Maynard S.; Mikado Restaurant, 514 S. Jackson; Nikko Restaurant, S. King and Rainier Ave. S.; Toshi's Teriyaki, 14705 Aurora and 372 Roy.

Mexican: Casa Lupita, 1823 Eastlake E. and 17555 Southcenter Parkway; Guadalajara Restaurants, 1429 4th, 1718 N. 45th, and 5923 California SW; Chile Pepper, 5000 University Way NE.

Middle Eastern: Adriatica Restaurant, 1107 Dexter Ave. N.; The Phoenecia Restaurant, 100 Mercer St.; Hello Belly, 10002 Aurora N.

Polynesian: Trader Vic's, Westin Hotel, 1900 5th Ave.

Russian: Kaleenka Russian Cafe, 1933 1st Ave.

Spanish: Cafe Felipe, 303 Occidental S.; La Gaviota, 174 Roy.

Thai: Thai Palace, 2224 8th; Bahn Thai, 409 Roy St.; Thai Restaurant, 101 John St.

View Restaurants

Although restaurants that advertise their "atmosphere" some-times try to sell that instead of good food and service, still there is a demand for places to eat that have a view, especially for entertaining out-of-town guests. Here are a few listed according to what you will see:

City Skyline: Salty's on Alki, 1936 Harbor Ave. SW.

Lake Union: Arnie's Northshore Restaurant, 1900 N. Northlake Way; The Canlis' Restaurant, 2576 Aurora N.; Franco's Hidden Harbor, 1500 Westlake N.; Ivar's Indian Salmon House, 401 NE Northlake Way; The Lakeside Restaurant, 2501 N. Northlake Way; Latitude 47°, 1232 Westlake N.

Puget Sound & Olympics: Athenian Inn, Pike Place Market; Chinooks at Salmon Bay, Fishermen's Terminal; Edgewater Inn, Pier 67; Elliott's on the Pier, Pier 56; Hiram's at-the-Locks Restaurant, 5300 34th NW (view of the locks); Ivar's Captains Table, 333 Elliott W.; Mirabeau Restaurant, Seattle–First National Bank Building, 46th floor.

Everywhere: Space Needle Restaurant, Seattle Center.

Brunch

Here's a list of places that offer brunch or at least serve up a better-than-average late breakfast. Watch billboards and newspapers because this market changes rapidly.

Cafe Sport, 2020 Western.
Crepe de Paris, Rainier Square.
Franco's Hidden Harbor, 1500 Westlake Ave. N.
Georgian Room, Olympic Four Seasons.
Green Lake Grill, 7200 E. Green Lake Dr. N.
Henry's Off Broadway, 1705 E. Olive.
Hunt Club, Sorrento.
The Lakeside Restaurant, 2501 N. Northlake Way.
Lake Union Cafe, 3119 Eastlake Ave. E.
Latitude 47°, 1232 Westlake N.
Rusty Pelican, 1111 Fairview Ave. N.
Salty's, 1936 Harbor Ave. SW.

Delis, Picnics, and Brown Bags

The custom picnic has been in Seattle so long now that we take it more or less for granted, and we no longer consider a trip to the local fast-food establishment as the choice for instant picnics.

Here are a few of the many delis that will serve sandwiches or will prepare a picnic basket for you.

Duke's, 236 1st W. (283-4400).

Gretchen's Of Course, 1111 3rd Ave. (467-4002) and Rainier Square (622-1188).

La Mediterranean Delicatessen, 528 Broadway Ave. (329-8818).

Leschi Food Mart, 103 Lakeside Ave. (322-0700).

Matzoh Momma Deli & Restaurant, 509 15th Ave. E. (324-6262).

Nick and Sully Carry Out Cuisine, 2043 Eastlake Ave. E. (325-8813).

Top Spots

Each year restaurant critics for the daily and weekly newspapers, and often magazines and television critics, list the top ten or twelve restaurants. Several places invariably appear on all lists.

In mid-1990, two or three of these lists were published during the Goodwill Games, and these restaurants appeared on all:

Al Boccalino, 1 Yesler Way (622-7688).

The Dahlia Lounge, 1904 Fourth Ave. (682-4142).

Kaspar's by the Bay, 2701 First Ave. (441-4805).

Il Terrazzo Carmine, 411 First Ave. S. (467-7797).

Chez Shea, 94 Pike St. (467-9990).

Wild Ginger, 1400 Western Ave. (623-4450).

Palomino Bistro, 1420 Fifth Ave. (623-1300).

Alphabetical Listing

Symbols: AE-American Express; VISA; CB-Carte Blanche; DC-Diners Club; MC-MasterCard.

Expensive, $25 and up each for dinner; Moderate, $15-$25; Inexpensive, under $15 each.

Adriatica, 1107 Dexter Ave. N. (285-5000). This was one of the first homes on the edge of the city to be converted into a restaurant, first as Chez Paul, a French establishment, and now specializing in Mediterranean peasant cuisine. Expensive.

Al Boccalino, 1 Yesler St. (622-7688). This relatively new restaurant is getting raves for its classic Italian dishes served in one of Seattle's oldest buildings on the edge of the Pioneer Square District. Lunch Monday-Friday 11:30 A.M.-2:30 P.M.; dinner Monday-Thursday 5:30-10:00 P.M.; dinner Friday and Saturday 5:30-11:00 P.M. Closed Sundays. Moderate.

Alki Homestead Restaurant, 2717 61st Ave. SW (935-5678). This old log house has been serving chicken dinners for more than fifty years, and regulars say the quality has remained consistently high over the years. Hours: Wednesday–Saturday 5:00–10:00 P.M.; Sunday 3:00–8:30 P.M. Moderate.

Andy's Diner, 2963 4th S. (624-4097). A converted railroad-car restaurant specializing in steaks; a popular lunch spot. Full bar. Monday–Saturday 11:30 A.M.–11:00 P.M.; closed Sunday. Reservations accepted. Moderate.

Atlas Chinese Restaurant, 424 Maynard S. (623-0913). Many insist this cafe serves the best Chinese food in Seattle, and if not the best, it serves certainly one of the best selections. Open 11:00–1:00 A.M. daily for lunch and dinner. No bar. VISA, MC. Reservations. Moderate.

Bahn Thai, 409 Roy St. (283-0444). This has become one of the favorite Thai restaurants in Seattle and has one of the most extensive menus. Hours: Lunch Monday–Friday; dinner seven days a week. Inexpensive.

Beeliner Diner, 2114 N. 45th St. (547-6313). A very busy and very successful small cafe with a crazy atmosphere and unusual offerings, such as hot cabbage salad. Hours: 11:30 A.M.–10:00 P.M. weekdays; 11:30 A.M.–11:00 P.M. Friday; 9:30 A.M.–11:00 P.M. Saturday; 9:30 A.M.–10:00 P.M. Sunday. Beer and wine. No credit cards. Inexpensive.

Benihana of Tokyo Restaurant, 1200 5th (682-4686). Located in the IBM Building Plaza. Japanese cuisine with steaks prepared at your table by flamboyant young cooks who whirl and twirl knives faster than a gunslinger twirls guns. Cocktails and lounge entertainment. Monday–Friday 11:30 A.M.–2:00 P.M.; Monday–Thursday 5:30–10:00 P.M.; Friday–Saturday until 10:30 P.M.; Sunday until 9:30 P.M. Reservations required Friday and Saturday nights. AE, VISA, DC, CB, MC. Expensive.

Boondock's on Broadway, 611 Broadway E. (323-7272). Plants abound in this restaurant, lending an atmosphere of intimacy and warmth. Varied wine list and a thirty-three-page modestly priced menu ranging from snacks to complete dinners. Weekdays 11:00–2:00 A.M.; weekends 9:00–3:00 A.M.; Sunday until 2:00 A.M. Reservations advisable. Moderate.

Bush Garden Sukiyaki, 614 Maynard S. (682-6830). Japanese decor and cuisine. Dining is a pleasant, calm experience at low tables with geisha service. Cocktails. Lunch Monday through Friday 11:30 A.M.–2:00 P.M.; dinner Monday–Sunday 5:00–10:00 P.M. Reservations necessary. Moderate.

Cafe Sophie, 1921 1st Ave. (441-6139). This former funeral parlor has been, thankfully, redecorated into a romantic restaurant with an eclectic menu that includes a wide selection of rich desserts. Hours: Lunch Tuesday–Saturday 11:30 A.M.–3:00 P.M.; dinner Tuesday–Saturday 5:30–10:00 P.M. Sunday brunch 10:00 A.M.–3:00 P.M. Inexpensive.

Cafe Sport, 2020 Western Ave. (443-6000). This is one of Seattle's most popular restaurants, and it serves what some call Northwest Cuisine or Pacific Rim Cuisine. Serves breakfast, lunch, and dinner seven days a week. Reservations. Moderate.

Campagne, Inn at the Market, 86 Pine St. (728-2800). Southern French cooking with Northwest ingredients are this expensive restaurant's specialty. Hours: Lunch, 11:30 A.M.–2:30 P.M.; dinner, 5:30–11:00 P.M. daily. Expensive.

The Canal Restaurant, foot of 24th Ave. NW (783-1964). After decades of having only a tavern and a refreshment stand at the entrance of the Ballard Locks, now we have an explosion of good restaurants. This used to be a boat-building shed and has been turned into a popular restaurant with graphics, weavings, and other bits of tasteful camouflage to conceal the building's past. The menu is mainly beef and chicken plus a good seafood selection. Lunch 11:00 A.M.–4:00 P.M., dinner 4:00–11:00 P.M. daily. Sunday brunch 11:00 A.M.–3:00 P.M. Full bar. Reservations. Expensive.

The Canlis' Restaurant, 2576 Aurora N. (283-3313). One of Seattle's most formal and expensive restaurants. Overlooking Lake Union. Excellent service; seafood and steaks from the charcoal broiler. Of special note are the shish kebabs and Caesar salad prepared at your table. Cocktails at piano bar nightly from 5:00 P.M.–1:00 A.M. Monday–Saturday 5:30–11:30 P.M. Closed Sunday. Reservations recommended. Expensive.

Casa Lupita, 1823 Eastlake E. (325-7350); 437 108th NE, Bellevue (453-9795). Mexican cuisine ranging from Mexican Bean Soup to Steak a la Chicana. Full bar. Lunch and dinner Monday–Thursday 11:00 A.M.–11:00 P.M.; Friday, Saturday, and Sunday dinner until midnight; Sunday brunch 10:00 A.M.–2:00 P.M. Lounge Monday–Saturday 11:00–2:00 A.M., Sunday 11:00 A.M.–midnight. Reservations accepted. Inexpensive.

Charlie's Bar & Grill, 217 Broadway E. (323-2535) A period piece; 1930s-style Hollywood decor with Gary Cooper and Merle Oberon, among others, on the wildly floral walls while songs— most of which are so bad that they're nostalgic and that makes them good—resound throughout the joint. But the menu isn't 1930s at all. It is very up-to-date, with adequate prices (that means they charge enough but don't get carried away with the profit motive). The menu lists more than sixty selections, with six dinner specialties (such as baby rack of lamb) served only after 5:00 P.M. Full bar. Monday–Friday 11:30–2:30 A.M.; Saturday and Sunday 8:00–3:00 A.M. All bank cards. Reservations.

China First, 4237 University Way NE (634-3553); also a restaurant at 6200 196th SW, Lynnwood (775-9800). Hours: 11:00 A.M.–midnight Sunday–Thursday; 11:00 A.M.–10:00 P.M. Friday and Saturday. Inexpensive.

Chinese Gourmet, 364 Roy (282-6616 or 285-9919). Like so many family-operated Chinese restaurants, this one is unpretentious and friendly, and the food is superb and of such generous portions you will almost always take some home. A good place to start or finish a visit to the Seattle Center. Hours: Tuesday–Thursday 11:30 A.M.–11:30 P.M.; Saturday 2:00 P.M.–1:00 A.M.; Sunday 2:00–10:00 P.M. Full bar. Reservations. Inexpensive.

Copacabana Cafe, Pike Place Market (622-6359). Also in Broadway market (323-7554). Founded by a refugee from one of Bolivia's periodic revolutions, the Copacabana has long been an institution at the market. Probably the only place in the area specializing in Bolivian cooking and all at reasonable prices. Monday–Saturday 11:00 A.M.–10:00 P.M.; Sunday 10:00 A.M.–5:00 P.M. Beer and wine. Major credit cards. Reservations. Moderate.

Crepe de Paris, 1333 Rainier Square (623-4111). The old country-French charm of the original Crepe de Paris was lost in the move to new quarters and the intimate atmosphere was replaced with a noisy room, but the menu still is superb and includes onion soup, thirty varieties of crepes, plus eleven dessert crepes, as well as a few noncrepe dishes. Beer and wine. Monday–Friday 11:00 A.M.–11:00 P.M.; Saturday 11:30 A.M.–midnight. Closed Sunday. Reservations for parties of eight or more. Moderate.

Dahlia Lounge, 1904 Fourth Ave. (682-4142). A former Cafe Sport chef went off on his own to open this popular spot and it is making most of the local "best" lists. The menu is international and seafoods are a specialty. Lunch 11:30 A.M.–2:30 P.M. Monday–Friday. Dinner 5:00–10:30 P.M. Monday–Thursday and until 11:00 P.M. Friday and Saturday. Expensive.

Eggs Cetera, 220 Broadway E. (325-3447). Long menu of omelets as well as more standard and well-prepared choices, such as waffles. Monday–Friday 6:30 A.M.–9:00 P.M.; Saturday and Sunday 7:30 A.M.–9:00 P.M.

Emmett Watson's Oyster Bar, behind the Soames-Dunn Building at 1916 Pike Pl. (448-7721). A tiny place in the Pike Place Market with lots of fresh oysters, even if you might have to stand while you eat them. A pleasant courtyard is part of the attraction. Monday–Saturday 11:45 A.M.–6:30 P.M.; closed Sunday. No credit cards. Expensive.

F. X. McRory's Steak, Chop & Oyster House, Occidental S. & S. King (623-4800). A vast restaurant across from the Kingdome named for a restaurant opened in 1915 in New York, McRory's will seat 350 usually noisy patrons, parties, and pro-sports fans in 11,000 square feet of space. It features a well-stocked bar, premium meat, and an oyster bar with marble counters, oysters in the shell on ice, and a condiment bar where patrons can make their own sauce. Cocktails, beer, and wine. Lunch 11:30 A.M.–2:30 P.M. Monday–Friday; dinner 5:00–10:00 P.M. Sunday–Tuesday, 5:00–11:00 P.M. Wednesday–Saturday. Bar opens at 2:00 P.M. with light menu, closes with dining room. Reservations. Expensive.

Franco's Hidden Harbor, 1500 Westlake N. (282-0501). Dining on a Lake Union boat dock amid yachts. Excellent seafood dishes. Casual, friendly service and prices trending up. Hours: Monday–Thursday 11:00 A.M.–10:00 P.M.; Friday–Saturday 11:00 A.M.–11:00 P.M.; Sunday brunch. Full bar. Reservations recommended. Expensive.

The Frederick & Nelson Restaurant, eighth floor, Frederick & Nelson, 5th & Pine (682-5500). One of the few restaurants in Seattle that will bring to mind one of those grand old restaurants in San Francisco, Denver, and New York. It is a vast, high-ceilinged room with table after table, each with sparkling white linen and heavy silver. Even the salad is served in silver bowls on monogrammed silver plates. The lunches are more popular with regulars than dinners, and their chicken and beef pot pies bear no relationship to those that bachelors buy frozen at the supermarket. It formerly was called a tea room, but the addition of a full bar rendered that name obsolete. Monday, Wednesday, Friday 11:00 A.M.–6:00 P.M.; Tuesday, Thursday 11:00 A.M.–3:00 P.M. Reservations. Moderate.

Fuller's, Seattle Sheraton Hotel (447-5544). This place, named for the founder of the Seattle Art Museum (Dr. Richard Fuller) and well stocked with Northwest art, is considered one of Seattle's finest restaurants and one of the best on the West Coast. Be forewarned: it is also one of the most expensive. Lunch Monday–Friday, dinner Monday–Saturday. Expensive.

Gerard's Relais de Lyon, 17121 Bothell Way N.E. (485-7600). A country-house restaurant specializing in lamb, game, and seafood. Hours: 5:30–9:00 P.M. daily. Expensive.

Gretchen's Of Course, 111 3rd Ave. (467-4002), and several other locations. One of the most popular cafeteria chains in Seattle. Cold salads, hot daily specials. Hours: 7:00 A.M.–6:00 P.M. Monday–Friday, no food served after 3:30 P.M. Closed weekends. Catering. Popular deli items. Inexpensive.

Guadalajara Cafe, 1429 4th (622-8722), downstairs at the corner of 4th & Pike (entrance on the 4th Ave. side). One of the best Mexican restaurants in Seattle. Cafe by the same name and same ownership at 1718 N. 45th in the University District (632-7858) and 5923 California SW (932-2803). Beer and wine. Hours downtown: Monday-Saturday 11:00 A.M.-9:00 P.M.; University District Monday-Saturday 11:00 A.M.-10:00 P.M. Reservations not necessary. Inexpensive.

Hiram's at-the-Locks Restaurant, 5300 34th NW (784-1733). A delightfully unpretentious place right on the Ballard Locks, the restaurant is an industrial-architecture building covered with corrugated steel painted factory green. Predominantly seafood menu, small wine list, and a house dressing of honey and lime. Plus that great view over the locks. Lunch 11:00 A.M.-2:30 P.M. Monday-Friday; dinner 4:30-10:00 P.M. daily and a bit later on Friday and Saturday. Sunday brunch 9:00 A.M.-2:30 P.M. Reservations advised. Expensive.

Italian Spaghetti House & Pizzeria, 9824 Lake City Way NE (523-2667). Specialty is stuffed lasagne and cannelloni alla Romano, and of course spaghetti and pizza; beer and wine. Daily 4:30-11:30 P.M. Reservations recommended for parties of six or more. Inexpensive.

Italo's Casa Romana Restaurant & Lounge, 14622 15th NE (362-8934). Some call this the best Italian restaurant in Seattle. Followers of Italian cuisine will find calzone here. Cocktails. Monday-Thursday 11:00 A.M.-10:30 P.M.; Friday-Saturday 7:00 A.M.-11:00 P.M.; Sunday 4:00-10:00 P.M. Reservations suggested for eight or more. Moderate.

Ivar's Restaurant. This seafood group is one of Seattle's most popular under the same ownership. *Acres of Clams*, Pier 54, foot of Madison (624-6852). Weekdays 11:00 A.M.-11:00 P.M.; 11:00 A.M.-midnight weekends. *Captain's Table*, 333 Elliott W. (284-7040). Weekdays 11:00-1:00 A.M. Saturday and Sunday until 11:00 P.M. Cocktails. Lunch reservations only. *Ivar's Indian Salmon House*, 401 NE Northlake, under the freeway bridge on Lake Union (632-0767). Alder-smoked salmon in Indian longhouse decor. No reservations accepted. Lunch 11:30 A.M.-2:00 P.M. Monday-Friday; dinner 5:00-11:00 P.M. Saturday and Sunday open at 4:00 P.M. Salmon House take-out fish bar open Sunday-Thursday 11:00 A.M.-11:00 P.M.; Friday-Saturday until 1:00 A.M. All moderate.

Jake O'Shaughnessey's First Established 1897, 100 Mercer, in the Hansen Baking Company complex near the Seattle Center (285-1897). This is one of the places for people to be "seen," but the food, drinks, and service are superb. Jake's dispenses what must be the most expensive brandy in the land, Ragnaud's: $3,600 a case, $45 a shot. Their bartender also sings opera or Irish, and if you don't see a local celebrity, it will be a surprise. Menu features prime rib roasted in a casing of salt for eight hours, stews, and alder-cooked salmon. 1890s decor. Cocktails, beer, and wine. Tuesday–Friday 5:00–11:00 P.M.; Saturday 4:30–11:00 P.M.; Sunday–Monday 5:00–10:00 P.M. Reservations accepted. Moderate.

Java Restaurant, 8929 Roosevelt Way NE (522-5282). Indonesian dishes range from delicately seasoned pork sate to highly spiced *rijstaffel*. Simple decor. Beer and wine. Dinners only: 5:00–10:00 P.M. Closed Monday. Reservations accepted. No smoking allowed. Moderate.

Kamon on Lake Union, 1177 Fairview Ave. N. (622-4665). This is one of the best Japanese restaurants in Seattle, with three dining rooms: a sushi bar, a tatami room, and a teppanyaki room. Hours: Lunch, 11:00 A.M.–3:00 P.M. Monday–Friday; dinner, 5:00–10:00 P.M. Sunday–Thursday, 5:00–11:00 P.M. Friday and Saturday. Moderate.

Labuznik, 1924 1st Ave. (682-1624). This is one of Seattle's most popular restaurants, and some of us remember when the owner, Peter Cipra, owned another restaurant named The Prague. It has closed, but Labuznik is as good or better than its predecessor. The menu remains intentionally small but has wonderful Czech dishes, such as *svichova* and *palacsinta*. The restaurant in the rear is quiet and elegant; the cafe out front, which opens onto the street in good weather, is more informal and has a larger selection. Dinner: 4:30–10:00 P.M. Tuesday–Thursday; 5:30 P.M.–midnight Friday and Saturday. Closed Sunday and Monday. Expensive.

La Fleur, 5414 Sand Point Way NE (527-3400). This is one of Seattle's more international restaurants and boasts of a waiter who speaks fluent Russian and a menu printed in Russian. The menu leans toward continental with Northwest flourishes. Dinner: 5:00–9:00 P.M. Sunday–Monday; 5:00–10:00 P.M. Tuesday–Saturday. Moderate.

The Lakeside Restaurant, 2501 N. Northlake Way (634-0823). Mirrored trilevel with a view overlooking Lake Union and boat docks. Limited but good menu of steaks, seafoods, eggs, and sandwiches. Cocktails. Lunch 11:30 A.M.–4:00 P.M. Monday–Saturday; dinner 5:00–11:00 P.M. Monday–Saturday, Sunday noon–10:00 P.M. Reservations accepted. Expensive.

Latitude 47°, 1232 Westlake N. (284-1047). Informal restaurant on Lake Union specializing in seafood and prime rib; special salads. Full bar. Entertainment and dancing every day. Monday–Friday 11:00 A.M.–9:45 P.M.; Saturday from 5:00 P.M.; Sunday brunch buffet 10:00 A.M.–12:30 P.M., dinner to 11:00 P.M. Reservations advised. Moderate.

Le Tastevin French Restaurant, 19 W. Harrison (283-0991). One of Seattle's best and least-pretentious French restaurants. Entrees include seafood, veal, steaks, chicken, beef, and lamb ordered with a dinner or a la carte. Complete dinners include soup or salad and a dessert. Excellent wine list and cocktails. Near the Seattle Center and Uptown movie theater. Reservations are recommended. Monday–Friday 11:30 A.M.–11:30 P.M.; Saturday 5:00 P.M.–midnight. Closed Sunday. Expensive.

Matzoh Momma Deli & Restaurant, 509 15th E. (324-6262). A delicatessen-restaurant, complete with rock music and, occasionally, live piano, serving kosher Jewish meals and carry-outs of lox, bagels, chicken soup, herring in sour cream, etc. Wednesday–Saturday 8:00 A.M.–midnight; Sunday–Tuesday 8:00 A.M.–9:00 P.M. No reservations. Inexpensive.

McCormick's Fish House & Bar, 4th & Columbia (682-3900). Menu lists forty-three fish entrees, Northwest salmon, Eastern scallops, New England swordfish, and steaks. Full bar. Open for lunch weekdays, every day for dinner. Monday–Thursday 11:00 A.M.–11:00 P.M., Friday until midnight; Saturday 5:00 P.M.–midnight; Sunday 5:00–10:00 P.M. Reservations advised. Moderate.

Merchants Cafe, 109 Yesler Way (624-1515). A restoration of Seattle's oldest restaurant with the original 30-foot carved backbar. Continental menu in basement level. Monday–Thursday 8:00 A.M.–11:30 P.M.; Friday until 2:00 A.M.; Saturday 9:00–2:00 A.M.; Sunday 11:00 A.M.–11:30 P.M. Cocktails until 2:00 A.M. on weekends. Entertainment 9:30 P.M.–1:30 A.M. Tuesday–Saturday. No reservations required. Moderate.

Mikado Japanese Restaurant, 514 S. Jackson (622-5206). Authentic Japanese cuisine served in an attractive modern dining room; also a bay of tatami rooms for privacy. Menu ranges from an excellent sukiyaki to the formal Kaiseki dinner (twenty-four hours' notice required). Cocktails. Monday–Saturday 5:30–10:00 P.M. Reservations advised. Moderate.

Old Spaghetti Factory, Elliott & Broad (623-3520). Gay nineties feeling in a renovated brick warehouse near the waterfront. Spaghetti dinners with a variety of sauces served in generous portions at unmatched wooden tables or inside a restored streetcar. Full bar. Monday–Thursday 5:00–10:00 P.M.; Friday–Saturday until 11:00 P.M.; Sunday 4:00–10:00 P.M. No reservations or credit cards accepted. Moderate.

Palomino Euro Seattle Bistro, Pacific First Centre (623-1300). Mostly seafoods and some Mediterranean dishes such as spit-roasted meats. One of the newer and highly rated places.

Lunch 11:30 A.M.–2:30 P.M. Monday–Saturday; dinner 5:00–10:00 P.M. Monday–Thursday, 5:00–11:00 P.M. Friday–Saturday, 5:00–9:00 P.M. Sunday.

The Phoenecia Restaurant, 100 Mercer (285-6739). A family-owned Lebanese restaurant that caters to the family trade in an informal dining room with beaten brass and small rugs as wall hangings. They offer at least sixteen dinners and a wide variety of finger foods, pastries, seafood, African curries, and several vegetarian plates. Open 5:00–10:00 P.M. Tuesday–Sunday. Closed Monday. Moderate.

raison d' etre, 113 Virginia St. (728-1113). This small restaurant on the ground floor of the Maritime Building on Virginia just off First Avenue has been winning over new clients for several years with its soups, pastas, entrees, and desserts. Hours: 7:00 A.M.–midnight Wednesday, Thursday, and Sunday; 7:00–1:00 A.M. Friday and Saturday. Beer and wine. Moderate.

Ray's Boathouse, 6049 Seaview Ave. NW (789-3770). This is probably the most popular seafood-with-a-view restaurant in the Puget Sound region. The place burned to the ground in 1987 and came back larger than before, with chicken and beef added to the menu. Hours: lunch, 11:30 A.M.–2:00 P.M. Monday–Saturday, 10:00 A.M.–2:00 P.M. Sunday; dinner, 5:00–10:00 P.M. Sunday–Thursday, 5:00–10:30 P.M. Friday and Saturday. Valet parking. Expensive.

The Red Robin, Eastlake & Fuhrman E. (323-0917); also Northgate Shopping Center (365-0933); 1600 E. Olive Way (323-1600); Pacific Plaza Hotel at 4th & Spring (447-1909). The chain bills itself as the gourmet burger maker, and many former college students remember the original on Eastlake and Fuhrman with special warmth. Also serves fish and chips, pork chops, steaks, and salads. Open daily. Hours vary from place to place, but they're all open late. Moderate.

Saleh Al Lago, 6804 Green Lake Way N. (524-4044). A relatively new Italian restaurant that quickly became a hit. In addition to pasta dishes, their veal, seafood, and beef are popular. Lunch 11:30 A.M.–2:00 P.M. Monday–Friday; dinner 5:30–10:00 P.M. Monday–Thursday, 5:30–10:30 P.M. Friday–Saturday. Expensive.

Skipper's Galley, 2223 California SW (937-7445). Located in the West Seattle area, Skipper's provides you with a choice of four hundred entrees—fresh seafood at its best—as well as beef and veal dishes. During the summer months sidewalk tables and checkers are provided. It is so popular that people coming through Seattle by plane often catch a cab to Skipper's, get their meal, then head back to the airport. No liquor. Wednes-

day–Saturday 10:00 A.M.–10:00 P.M.; Thursday 11:30 A.M.–2:00
P.M. Closed Sunday and Monday. Reservations accepted. No
credit cards. Moderate.

South China, 2714 Beacon Ave. S. (329-5085). One of the best Cantonese restaurants in Seattle, located in a predominantly Oriental neighborhood where the critics would be stern.
Monday–Saturday 11:00–2:00 A.M.; Sunday 3:00 P.M.–midnight. Inexpensive.

Space Needle, Seattle Center grounds (443-2100). A new level has
been added at the 100-foot level in the needle, and it is called
Emerald Suite Restaurant. It is now the seventeenth-busiest
restaurant in the country, according to *Restaurant Hospitality*
magazine. Open Memorial Day to Labor Day, mostly for tourists, and serves more simple fare than the Space Needle Restaurant on top. The top level gives you a 360-degree view of the
region through its once-every-hour complete revolution. Elaborate menu. Lunch daily 11:00 A.M.–3:00 P.M. Dinner every day
5:00 P.M.–midnight. Sunday brunch 10:30 A.M.–3:00 P.M. Reservations. Elevator costs $3.50 for adults, $1.75 for children 5
and up. Major credit cards. Expensive.

Swingside Cafe, 4212 Fremont Ave. N. (633-4057). The chef, Robin
Sanders, is something of a Seattle institution, and she turns
out a limited but impressive menu. Hours: 5:00–10:00 P.M.
Wednesday–Saturday. Inexpensive.

Tai Tung Restaurant, 659 S. King (622-7372). A three-generation
family-operated Chinese restaurant with a long-standing reputation for excellent food. Extensive menu with appeal to both
the Oriental and Occidental palate. Every day 10:00–3:00 A.M.
Reservations. Inexpensive.

Thai Thai Restaurant, 11205 16th Ave. SW (246-2246). This small
place in White Center has one of the largest menus in town and
is a favorite of the local Thai community. Lunch 11:30
A.M.–2:30 P.M. Monday–Friday; dinner 5:00–9:30 P.M. Monday–
Thursday and 5:00–10:00 P.M. Friday and Saturday. Inexpensive.

Thirteen Coins Restaurant, 125 Boren N. (682-2513); also Thirteen
Coins Sea-Tac, 18000 Pacific Hwy. S. (243-9500). A hard-to-find
spot in the Furniture Mart Building. Posh decor but informal
atmosphere and gigantic portions ranging from corned beef
and cabbage to sauteed frog legs. Full bar. Open twenty-four
hours, seven days a week. Reservations for eight or more. Moderate to expensive.

Tien Tsin Restaurant, 1401 N. 45th (634-0223). A description of the
decor of this restaurant in the Wallingford District is not important—but the food is. An extensive menu featuring authen-

tic Peking-style cuisine (no chop suey or egg roll found here) with some Cantonese and Korean dishes. Beer and wine. Lunch 11:45 A.M.–2:00 P.M. Monday–Friday; dinner 5:00–9:45 P.M. Monday–Thursday, 5:00–10:45 P.M. Friday, 4:00–10:45 P.M. Saturday, 4:00–9:45 P.M. Sunday. Reservations for six or more. Inexpensive.

The Top of the Pier, Pier 70, Alaskan Way and Broad St. (441–1867). A waterfront spot with American cuisine. Good view of the sound from the dining room and cocktail lounge. Lunch Monday–Friday 11:30 A.M.–2:30 P.M., Saturday to 3:30 P.M. Dinner Monday–Thursday 5:00–9:30 P.M., Friday–Saturday 5:00–10:00 P.M., Sunday 4:00–9:00 P.M. Sunday brunch 10:00 A.M.–2:00 P.M. Reservations. Moderate.

Trader Vic's, 5th & Westlake, Westin Hotel (728–8520). Very pleasant Polynesian and nautical decor, recorded island music, and a Polynesian menu seem to take you to the islands. The menu is extensive as well as expensive; some meats are roasted and smoked in a Chinese oven. Cocktail bar serving regular as well as exotic-looking drinks. Monday–Saturday 11:30 A.M.–10:45 P.M.; Sunday 5:00–9:30 P.M. Reservations advised. Expensive.

The Unicorn and the Costermonger, 4550 University Way (634–1115). Authentic British cuisine in a rustic Tudor setting. Serving the well-known British specialty, steak and kidney pie, or, with twenty-four-hours' notice, roast pheasant with orange sauce. Imported ale, beer, and wine. Tuesday–Saturday 10:00 A.M.–11:00 P.M. Sunday 11:00 A.M.–9:00 P.M. Reservations for five or more. Moderate.

Vietnams Pearl Restaurant, 914 E. Pike (322–4080). A small, quiet restaurant serving traditional Vietnamese cuisine. Specialty of the house, Imperial Duck, must be ordered a day in advance. No liquor. Monday–Saturday 11:00 A.M.–2:30 P.M., 5:00–10:00 P.M.; closed Sunday. Reservations accepted. Inexpensive.

Wild Ginger, 1400 Western Ave. (623–4450). All the food critics are raving about this place, which specializes in Southeast Asian and hot Chinese dishes. Lunch: 11:15 A.M.–3:00 P.M. Monday–Saturday. Dinner: 5:00–11:00 P.M. Sunday–Thursday, 5:00–midnight Friday–Saturday. Moderate.

Windjammer, 7001 Seaview Ave. NW (784–4070). A view of the yachts bobbing in the marina, plus the sound and mountains. A good seafood selection and steaks. Cocktails, dancing, and entertainment until 2:00 A.M. Lunch 11:00 A.M.–3:00 P.M. Monday–Saturday; dinner 5:00–10:00 P.M. Monday–Saturday, Sunday 4:00–10:00 P.M. Sunday brunch 10:00 A.M.–2:00 P.M. Reservations. Moderate.

Winners Dining and Sporting Establishment, 17401 Southcenter
Parkway (575-8800). The name tells you the atmosphere, and
the food has been described as being as good as the decorations, especially the smoked chicken and prime ribs. Hours:
11:00–2:00 A.M. Monday–Saturday; Sunday buffet brunch 9:00
A.M.–2:00 P.M., regular menu after 2:00 P.M. Expensive.

Entertainment

Gerard Schwarz, Seattle Symphony Conductor

For decades Seattle has had one of the nation's most impressive live theater communities, and only during the past few years has it been getting the attention it deserves. Some insist that Seattle is the best theater town outside New York. Indeed, so many major plays are born in Seattle theaters that we tend to take it more or less for granted when one of our plays makes the big time. For example, the rock-musical comedy, *Angry House-wives*, written by a Seattle playwright and performed here almost forever, went to London and did quite well there. We have almost come to take it for granted that Seattle exports will occasionally win Tonys in their new home back East.

Part of this tradition comes from the two excellent drama schools in Seattle: Cornish and the University of Washington, both of which have a long list of distinguished alumni working regularly in Hollywood and elsewhere.

The number of equity companies continues to grow, but the interest in entertainment isn't limited to live theater; movies do extremely well here, and Seattle has become a favorite place for studios to test the waters with new films before releasing them nationally.

For the first time in a long, long time it appears Seattle has a chance at having an orchestra of international proportions since the Seattle Symphony hired the enormously talented and respected Gerard Schwarz.

All cities have things to grumble about, but it is difficult to complain about Seattle's entertainment situation, especially when compared with most other cities in the country.

Tickets for most events are sold at Fidelity Lane, 1622 4th Ave. (624-4971); the Bon Marche stores; Ticketmaster Northwest (628-0888); University District Ticket Center, 4530 University Way NE (632-7272).

Theaters

STAGE

A Contemporary Theater (ACT), 100 W. Roy, P.O. Box 19400 (box office 285-5110). One of Seattle's most respected equity theaters, ACT tries to produce "the most important plays of our time." Season is May to November with the annual performances of *A Christmas Carol* and the Young ACT Company presenting a full schedule in addition to its annual tour of Washington and Alaska.

Bathhouse Theatre, 7312 W. Green Lake Dr. N. (box office 524-9108). A six-play year-round schedule of contemporary and classical works are presented in the small, 140-seat theater on the northern edge of the lake. Has a resident company of ten to fifteen actors.

Civic Light Opera, P.O. Box 75672 (box office 363-2809). Produces three musicals each year at the Jane Addams Theater, 11051 34th Ave. NE, from October through May.

The Empty Space, 95 S. Jackson (box office 467–6000). An equity theater, the group specializes in producing and developing new plays. In addition to the 225-seat main theater, there's also a 50-seat studio called the 2nd Space.

The Good Companions, P.O. Box 27022 (365–9533). A touring dinner theater company of seven or eight actors who will travel a 300-mile radius from Seattle with a portable stage and complete sound and lighting system.

The Group Theatre, 3940 Brooklyn Ave. NE (box office 543–4327). A multiethnic company that is the resident group at The Ethnic Theatre at the University of Washington. Produces new scripts that deal with social problems in either a humorous or serious manner.

Intiman Theatre Company, Intiman Playhouse, Seattle Center (626–0782 or 628–0888). A professional ensemble that performs six plays each season and emphasizes international dramatic literature, both modern and classic.

Seattle Children's Theater, N. 50th & Fremont N. (box office 633–4567). This professional company produces five shows each year for children, September to June, with a special holiday show in December. Performances are at Poncho Theater at the south entrance of Woodland Park Zoo, N. 50th and Fremont Ave. N.

Seattle Gilbert & Sullivan Society, Bagley Wright Theater (782–5466). Volunteers, who present one Gilbert and Sullivan operetta each year, make up this organization. Totally voluntary with no compensation to anyone, cast or musicians.

Seattle Repertory Theatre, 155 Mercer St., in the Bagley Wright Theater in the Seattle Center (box office 443–2222). This is Seattle's oldest equity theater and is a nonprofit company that produces six plays each year ranging from classic to modern, comedy to drama. Main stage theater seats 860, and the second space, Poncho Forum, seats 170.

MAJOR THEATERS

Many of Seattle's grand old theaters have fallen victim to the wrecker's ball, and I for one was quite disturbed when I moved back to Seattle after a few years' absence to find that both the Orpheum and the Palomar were gone, the former for a hotel and the latter for a parking garage. It is easy to become nostalgic about theaters and railroad stations, and some of my fondest memories of my early years in Seattle were connected with the Palomar, where I worked when soloists, the Little Symphony, and other more intimate concerts were held there.

Seattle has been fortunate, not only because it has always had such good theater, but because it has had such good *theaters* in which to hold plays, concerts, and films. Part of the reason goes back to the turn of the century when Alexander Pantages founded his vaudeville empire here; and another portion of the credit goes to the master theater designer, B. Marcus Priteca, another Seattle native who was kept busy in his hometown building theaters that were both gorgeous and functional.

Not all of the grand old theaters are still grand or even theaters; some, unfortunately, are just old and sort of stand there waiting for someone to do something with them.

In this list, I have selected some of the more interesting theaters. In earlier editions the list was called "Classic Theaters," but so few of those remain that the list would be conspicuous by its brevity. Seattle still has some great theaters, and new ones are being built. But they are more functional than extravagant—as they were during Priteca's heyday.

Coliseum Theatre, 5th & Pike. A Priteca-designed house that was one of the first giant movie houses in the country. It was built in 1915 and for years was the largest theater in the entire West, Los Angeles included.

The Fifth Avenue Theatre, 1308 5th. This gaudy, elaborate, and beloved old cavern of a theater is a fine example of the lost art of building theaters. Fortunately it was taken over by a group of investors who restored it and turned it into a Broadway-style theater with long-run stage shows. However, it has been hurting financially and spends more and more time dark. Its future is uncertain.

Paramount Theatre, 907 Pine St. Also designed by Priteca, the Paramount opened in 1927 and is still recognized as one of the most acoustically perfect theaters on the West Coast. It is now used almost entirely for rock concerts. It is almost as grand as the Fifth Avenue, and its long, winding passageways to rest rooms and sub-lobbies make you wonder if you're going to get there in time. It also has a fabulous Wurlitzer pipe organ, restored to its original condition a few years ago.

SPECIAL INTEREST MOVIE THEATERS

Since Seattle is such a darling with both stage and film producers, who try out their plays and films here, it only follows that the city should have some really nice theaters. Of course the city has a number of shopping-center theaters with four or more small auditoriums in one building, but there are also many pleasant theaters scattered around town with their own personalities. It isn't unusual for one of these houses to run a film for months on end, sometimes one that didn't make a decent showing elsewhere in the country.

Bay Theatre, 2044 NW Market. This was a favorite with my children, and it is still a favorite with a lot of children because the management runs Disney fare in its original state, just the way we parents remember it.

Cinerama Theatre, 4th & Lenora. One of Seattle's finest in a technological sense, with excellent Dolby sound, comfortable seats, and a gigantic curved screen.

Egyptian Theatre, 801 E. Pine. This used to be a Masonic auditorium, so it has acres of space for seating. It hosts the International Film Festival each summer and has all the best equipment.

Grand Illusion Cinema, 1403 NE 50th. A very small art house that runs documentaries and unusual films.

Harvard Exit I and II, 807 E. Roy St. This was one of Seattle's first small houses with personality, and it followed in the tradition established by the Ridgemont of finding films of superior quality, foreign and domestic, and giving them the treatment they deserve. The lobby has a pleasant, living-room quality.

The Market Theater, 1428 Post Alley. This theater is, as the address indicates, in an alley behind the Pike Place Market (turn left under the market sign off Pike St.), but it has a nice auditorium, a pleasant lobby, and good taste in film selection.

Seven Gables Theater, 911 NE 50th. The lobby of this small house is as comfortable as the auditorium, and the special films shown there are almost invariably of high quality.

Toyo Cinema, 5608 Rainier S. For years this small house has specialized in Japanese-language films, and its clientele is international.

IMAX

Seattle has two theaters that show the Imax films on curved, wraparound screens that are actually the theaters' ceilings.

Eames/IMAX Theater, Pacific Science Center.

Omnidome, Pier 59.

Electronics

RADIO STATIONS

The radio market is quite volatile and stations come and go, or stay and change their formats. Here is a recent list of frequencies and formats.

AM

KSEA 100   Adult contemporary
KVI   570   Solid gold rock and roll
KIRO 710   News, sports, talk
KRPM 770   Country
KIXI   880   Middle of road
KJR   950   Classic hits
KOMO 1000 Adult contemporary
KBLE 1050 Religious
KING 1090 News and info
KEZX 1150 Business news
KKFX 1250 Black, urban
KMPS 1300 Country
KZOK 1590 Oldies

FM

KNHC 89.5 Dance music
KCMU 90.3 Alternative music
KUBE 93.3 Contemporary hits
KMPS 94.1 Country
KUOW 94.9 Fine arts, information
KLTX 95.7 Adult contemporary
KXRX 96.5 Adult rock
KING 98.1 Classical
KEZX 98.9 Soft rock, jazz
KISW 99.9 Rock
KPLZ 101.5 Contemporary hits
KZOK 102.5 Classic rock
KBRD 103.7 Beautiful music
KMGI 107.7 Adult contemporary

TELEVISION STATIONS

Nine television stations serve the Seattle area.
Channel 4: KOMO-TV, ABC affiliate, 100 4th Ave. N., Seattle
   98109 (443-4000)
Channel 5: KING-TV, NBC affiliate, 333 Dexter Ave. N., Seattle,
   98109 (448-5555)
Channel 7: KIRO-TV, CBS affiliate, 2807 3rd Ave., Seattle, 98121
   (728-7777)
Channel 9: KCTS-TV, Public Broadcasting affiliate, 401 Mercer St.,
   Seattle 98109 (728-6463)
Channel 11: KSTW-TV, independent, 2320 S. 19th St., Tacoma,
   98411 (572-5789)

Channel 13: KCPQ-TV, Fox Network, 4400 Steilacoom Blvd. SW, Tacoma, 98499 (625-1313)

Channel 20: KTBW-TV, religious, 1909 S. 341st Pl., Federal Way, 98003 (874-7420)

Channel 22: KTZZ-TV, independent, 945 Dexter Ave. N., Seattle, 98109 (282-2202)

Channel 28: KTPS-TV, Public Broadcasting affiliate, 1101 S. Yakima Ave., Tacoma, 98405 (596-1528)

Music

Seattle has such a variety of musical events, ranging from classical to rock, that there is literally something for every taste nearly every week. So well established and mature is Seattle's cultural atmosphere that critics from the East Coast and California are amazed (and envious sometimes).

It is impossible to produce an accurate list of events in the musical category because schedules change, new names are added while others are dropped, and often not even the organizations themselves are certain of concert dates very far in advance. At any rate, here's a list of the major musical organizations. Be sure to watch the newspaper entertainment sections for up-to-date listings.

For University of Washington performances, obtain a copy of *Spectrum*, a listing published quarterly by Continuing Education (543-2300). For Meany Hall performances, call 543-2010. Copies are mailed, free, on request.

A word of warning: Many small groups are listed here under the name and address of the current president. Since organizations hold elections nearly every year (just after this book is published, it seems), some of these addresses and telephone numbers may be out of date.

Not that it makes a lot of difference, but each year KING-FM and *The Weekly* run a survey of their readers/listeners for the most popular pieces of classical music, and Vivaldi's *Four Seasons* wins every year. Also in the top five every year are Beethoven's Ninth Symphony, Pachelbel's *Canon*, Bach's *Brandenburg* Concertos, and Dvořák's Symphony No. 9, the *New World* Symphony.

MAJOR GROUPS

The Philadelphia String Quartet, 4730½ University Way NE, Suite A (527-8839). A few years ago Seattle "stole" the famed quartet from Philadelphia, and it became quartet-in-residence at the university. The group left the university some time ago but still gives some twenty concerts each year.

Seattle Opera Association, Opera House (443-4711). Founded in 1964, the opera made an indelible mark on the international opera scene under the innovative and imaginative management of former general director Glynn Ross. It quickly rose to the top ranks of United States opera and in 1975 went international with the first American performance of the complete Wagnerian *Ring*. The opera kicked off what it calls the Northwest Festival, an annual summer production of the *Ring* in German with English supertitles, which attracts an international following. The English version has been dropped, temporarily at least. In addition, the opera offers five productions each year from September through May, English-language performances, tours, and children's matinees. Performances are always in the Seattle Opera House in the Seattle Center. Speight Jenkens took over as director in 1983.

Seattle Symphony Orchestra, Opera House (443-4747). Founded in 1903, the symphony presents eighteen concerts each year, October through April, on Monday and Tuesday evenings and Sunday afternoons, all in the Opera House. The symphony tries for a balance between the "museum" pieces and modern music, with an occasional premier performance. The SSO offers five pops programs each year and three or four children's programs. Gerard Schwarz is the music director and conductor.

Seattle Youth Symphony, Opera House (362-2300). One of Seattle's favorite musical groups, the Youth Symphony continues to startle and amaze music lovers with the professional quality of the orchestra and soloists. The young (14-22 years of age) symphonists present three major concerts each year, which are usually sold out before the season begins, but blocks of tickets are available for the blind and low-income seniors and youth groups.

OTHER MUSICAL GROUPS

Cascade Symphony Orchestra, 18310 Sunset Way, Edmonds (778-4737). Four concerts each season. Performs at Puget Sound Christian College, Edmonds.

Collegium Musicum, University of Washington School of Music (543-1200). Faculty and student concerts and recitals.

Contemporary Group, University of Washington School of Music (543-1200). Faculty performing group, including members of the Philadelphia String Quartet.

Early Music Guild, 1605 12th Ave. Suite 8 (325-7066). Presents baroque, medieval, and Renaissance music played on authentic instruments.

Gilbert and Sullivan Society, 1500 E. McGraw (322-8682). The group presents an annual major production at the Seattle Center Playhouse as well as children's theater and lecture recitals; maintains a Gilbert and Sullivan library.

Ladies Musical Club, Meany Hall, UW (328-7153). For outstanding women in music who perform in concerts. Sponsors artists in Seattle Concert series, brown bag concerts.

Northwest Chamber Orchestra, 1305 4th Ave. Suite 522 (box office 343-0445). The fifteen-member string group performs music from all periods on the University of Washington campus. Offers children's concerts with Tickle Tune Typhoon.

Norwegian Male Chorus, Norway Center, 300 3rd W. (284-1152). Established in 1889, the performing group is the oldest and largest a capella male chorus in Seattle.

Sea-Chordsmen (Seattle Chapter of the Society for the Preservation and Encouragement of Barbershop Quartet Singing in America, or SCSPEBQSIA!), 3726 147th SE, Bellevue (746-5052). Annual show, frequent sing-outs for schools, banquets, and benefits.

Seattle Classic Guitar Society, 2519 Montavista Pl. W. (283-1710). Sponsors recitals, workshops, lectures, and master classes.

Seattle Community Symphony Orchestra, 939 N. 105th (783-6998). Sponsored by the city parks department, the group usually gives four free concerts a year.

Seattle Symphony Chorale, Opera House (443-4740). Choral group allied with symphony that performs four to six times annually.

Washington Jazz Society, P.O. Box 2813, Seattle, Washington 98111. Promotes live jazz performances, sponsors jazz cruises (see "Guided Tours," chapter 1) and other events.

UNIVERSITY OF WASHINGTON GROUPS

The University of Washington sponsors a number of musical groups composed of students and faculty who give performances throughout the year. In each case, the school of music or the Office of Lectures and Concerts should be contacted for program information. Some of the groups are: Chorale, Concert Band, Madrigal Singers, Opera, Percussion Ensemble, Sinfonietta, Symphony Orchestra, and the Soni Ventorum Wind Quartet.

Dance

Alvfotter, 2456 Alki Ave. SW #304 (938-3405). Specializes in Swedish dances from about three hundred years ago.

Cabata'an Folk Dancers, c/o Filipino Youth Activities, 810 18th (461-4870). Filipino folk dances performed at selected charities and festivals.

Cape Fox Dancers, (784-6369). Tlingit Indian dance group from southeastern Alaska. Performs Northwest Coast Indian dances with traditional songs.

Co-Motion, 1625 Broadway (526-1425), is an ensemble that gives regional tours and workshops and sponsors new works each year by an artist in residence.

Cornish Dance Theater, 710 E. Roy (323-1400). Cornish School's dance company gives performances and supplies dancers for productions in the area.

Madrona Dance Studio, 800 Lake Washington Blvd. (325-4161). Performances, residencies, and master classes in dance; low-fee classes for all ages. Sponsored by the Seattle Parks Department and Dance Advisory Council.

On the Boards, 153 14th Ave. (325-7901). The company is very avant-garde and continues to grow in stature. It sponsors new pieces by both international and local artists.

Pacific Northwest Ballet, Opera House (628-0888). This repertory company has been growing in national stature and gives six performances each year, in addition to the popular Christmas offering of *The Nutcracker* each December, with sets by Maurice Sendak. Kent Stowell and Francia Russell are the artistic directors.

Skandia Folkdance Society, 1810 NW 65th (784-7470). Preserves Scandinavian dances; gives dances, classes, and mixers.

Square and Round Dance Information Center, 1004 SW 4th Pl., Renton (Seattle phone: 722-4747). Promotes square and round dancing, and publishes *Footnotes* magazine.

Music After Dark

Bars and restaurants with live music come and go rapidly as owners search for that magic formula that will create a loyal following. Odd, but some places have the best management, best music, and good food, but the chemistry with customers doesn't work out.

The dance floor is covered with carpet and tables and the bands forgotten.

At any rate, following is a list of places that offered music at this writing, and it is frankly culled from *The Weekly* and *P.I.*'s *What's Happening* magazine, published each Friday.

ROCK

Ballard Firehouse, Russell and Market (784–3516), has a big dance floor, and the management books good rock, reggae, Cajun, and jazz groups.

Central Tavern and Cafe, 207 First Ave. S. (622–0209), calls itself Seattle's only second-class tavern and features both local and touring groups.

Doc Maynard's, 610 First Ave. (682–4649), is a Pioneer Square institution that now attracts the fraternity type of customers who like music too loud to hear; they just feel it.

The Far Side Tavern, 10815 Roosevelt Way NE (362–1480). Local and regional groups in a tavern named for Seattle-native Gary Larsen's comic strip.

JAZZ

Dimitriou's Jazz Alley, 6th & Lenora (441–9729), is Seattle's best jazz club with name performers (including Seattle's *best* performers).

New Orleans Creole Restaurant, 114 1st S. (622–2563), features several local groups, such as Floyd Sandifer and Chuck Metcalf, and brings in national groups.

Patti Summers, 94 Pike (621–8555), is owned by a former touring singer with a voice that still has what it takes to charm a crowd. She brings in locals and touring groups as well.

FOLK

Latona, 643 Latona Ave. NE (525–2238).
New Melody Tavern, 5213 Ballard Ave. NW (782–3480).

ETHNIC CLUBS

China Gate, 516 7th S. (624–1730). Traditional Far Eastern music mixed with traditional American pop. Amateur performers offer Filipino, Korean, and other music.

George's Bar and Grill, 1901 4th Ave. (622–5631). Greek music and belly dancing.

BLUES

The Backstage, 2208 NW Market St. (789-6953). Sometimes features blues in addition to its steady fare of rock.

Merchants Cafe, 109 Yesler Way (624-1515). Occasionally has solo artists.

Owl Cafe, 5140 Ballard Ave. NW (784-3640). A neighborhood tavern that has good blues artists. Dance floor, sandwiches, and beer.

Scarlet Tree Restaurant-Lounge, 6521 Roosevelt Way NE (523-7153). Mostly blues artists.

PIANO BARS

These come and go, according to business and whims of owners, but this selected list is reasonably safe. If you hear a rock group when you walk in, you'll know something has changed.

The Canlis' Restaurant, 2576 Aurora Ave. N.

Henry's Off Broadway, 1705 E. Olive Way.

Lake Union Cafe, 3119 Eastlake Ave. E.

The Ritz Cafe, 429 15th Ave. E.

SINGERS

The Cloud Room, Camlin Hotel, 8th Ave. & Pine St.

The Dog House, 2230 7th Ave.

Red Cabbage Restaurant & Piano Bar, 75 Marion St.

Trade Winds Polynesian Restaurant and Piano Bar, 90 Wall St.

By Dawn's Early Light

Back in the old days when Seattle (and the entire state of Washington) was ruled by the so-called blue laws, hanging out at night was a lot more fun than it is now. The police payoff system, rancid though it was, meant little to the average citizen other than that it permitted people to stay out all night drinking illegally in places where policemen hung around to keep the peace—and, of course, to protect their investments in the payoff system. But things have loosened up on drinking, and late-night sin isn't as much fun anymore.

There are a few places (all legitimate and law-abiding, of course) that stay open all night. Since I don't include roaming the streets in the wee hours as part of my research, I can't vouch for the atmosphere or clientele in most of these places.

Beth's Cafe, 7311 Aurora N.
Cricket, 2947 Eastlake E.
The Dog House, 2230 7th.
Hattie's Hat, 5231 Ballard NW.
Nifty's, 1102 SW Spokane.
Randy's Restaurant, 10016 E. Marginal Way.
Steve's Broiler, 1937 4th.
Thirteen Coins, 125 Boren N. and 18000 Pacific Highway S.

   If you have a thirst late at night that the pop machine down the hall can't satisfy, a Washington State Liquor Control Board store at 6th & Lenora is open until 11:00 P.M. Monday through Saturday.

Lodging

Four Seasons Olympic Hotel

For decades Seattle had only one really luxurious hotel, the Olympic, and a cluster of lesser hostelries. The city seemed to manage very well without getting embarrassed. But gradually Seattle became aware of hotels as a destination in themselves, and when Western International Hotels (now simply Westin) decided to build its own dramatic, luxury hotel in Seattle, things began changing. Westin is a Seattle-based international corporation, yet the best hotel in Seattle then was the Olympic, which it didn't even own; the University of Washington owns the property on which it stands.

During the latter part of the 1970s, a hotel explosion occurred and along with it came a new sophistication within the local hotel community. At last count, six hotels boasted of having a concierge.

The latest coup in the business came in late 1988, when the Zagat U.S. Hotel Survey rated Seattle's hotels the best in the nation in terms of room quality, dining, and personal service. The eight Zagat selected for the best in the entire nation were: The Alexis, Four Seasons Olympic, Inn at the Market, Sorrento, Stouffer Madison, Seattle Sheraton Hotel & Towers, Crowne Plaza, and the Westin.

Here, then, is a brief rundown on the major hotels in Seattle, with no attempt to run a complete directory. Price ranges: Expensive—$100 and up; Moderate—$50-$100; Inexpensive—$50 or less.

Alexis Hotel, 1st & Madison (624-4844). For the wealthy traveler and not the convention-goer, this new and small (fifty-four rooms) hotel is one of Seattle's most intimate and elegant. It features a concierge, whirlpool bathtubs, real fireplaces in some suites, and it is very quiet. Continental breakfasts included in price. Expensive.

Camlin Hotel, 9th & Pine (682-0100). Refurbished in 1988, this smallish, conveniently located hotel has an excellent view across the city's skyline, especially from its top-floor Cloud Room Restaurant. Moderate.

Crowne Plaza Holiday Inn (formerly Park Hilton), 6th & Seneca (464-1980). A tall and slender addition to the skyline with an undistinguished lobby but with spacious and airy lounges on the upper floors. The "real" hotel doesn't begin until beyond the twelfth floor, where the views of the city and sound open up. Concierge service. Expensive.

Edgewater Inn, Pier 67 (728-7000). This waterfront hotel was refurbished in 1989 but is still a good buy for the location, virtually hanging out over Puget Sound. One of the hotel's favorite gimmicks is that it will supply the fishing tackle if you want to drop a line out your window. Expensive.

Four Seasons Olympic Hotel, 4th & University (621-1700). After many years as the city's major hotel, the Olympic was showing its age. A Canadian company took it over, closed it down for refurbishing, and opened it up again with its original splendor. They did away with the ugly sky bridge from the parking garage, and they restored the original curved driveway off University. It is also one of Seattle's most expensive hotels now (nothing less than $140), but out-of-towners don't complain. Expensive.

Hotel Seattle, 315 Seneca (623–5110 or 800–426–2439). A modestly priced and recently remodeled hotel in the heart of the business district. Restaurant and cocktail lounge on the premises. Moderate.

Inn at the Market, 1st & Pine St. (443–4600). One of Seattle's newest hotels, it is billed as a bed-and-breakfast but is much more of a hotel than the traditional B&B and is aimed at the same market as the Alexis and other smaller places. It has sixty-five rooms with a courtyard in the center of the wraparound-styled hotel. Expensive.

Inn at Virginia Mason, 1006 Spring St. (583–6453 or 800–345–7158 in Washington; 800–443–6882 out of state). This small (seventy-nine rooms) European-style hotel is popular with people visiting hospitals and clinics on "Pill Hill," but it is also a good buy for anyone in town who wants a good view of the skyline. Courtyard Cafe on the premises. Moderate.

Mayflower Park Hotel, 405 Olive Way (Seattle, 623–8700; out of state, 800–426–5100; Washington, 800–562–4504). This smallish hotel is sometimes overlooked by visitors and residents suggesting hotels to visitors, but it is right in the heart of the downtown area, across the street from the Bon, and close to just about everything. The rooms are clean, the windows double-paned to cut out street noise. Moderate.

Pacific Plaza Hotel, 4th and Spring (623–3900 or 800–426–1165). A comfortable, heart-of-town hotel with 166 remodeled rooms. A cafe and restaurant off the marble, glass, and brass lobby. Moderate.

Sheraton Hotel & Towers, 6th & Pike (621–9000). Designed primarily for convention business, this midtown hotel is one of the most dramatic additions to the skyline and has done a lot to clean up the tacky stretch of Pike St. above 5th Ave. The top four floors have their own separate lobby and offer a respite from the sometimes noisier lower floors. It has a restaurant named Fullers in honor of the family who supported the Seattle Art Museum for nearly half a century. The restaurant, which gets a steady ration of raves, has many Northwest artists represented on the walls. Expensive.

The Sorrento Hotel, 9th & Madison (622–6400 or 800–426–1265). This charmer on First Hill has long been one of my favorite places in Seattle, and for years the Seattle Freelances, a writers' organization, met in the small restaurant on the top floor. But the hotel was gradually eroding and hardly worth recommending to out-of-towners. Recently new owners took over, cleaned it up, turned many of the rooms into suites by punching out walls, and turned those two upstairs restaurants (sigh) into elegant suites. Now it is one of Seattle's best small hotels with an unmatched view of the skyline, sound, and Olympics. They also serve high tea in the Hunt Room. Expensive.

Stouffer Madison Hotel, 6th & Madison (583-0300). Owned by Stouffers Hotels, it is one of the newest in the luxury class with an unpretentious exterior and a simple, open lobby. But it has handmade cabinets in the rooms, a gym, sauna, two restaurants, a twenty-four-hour espresso bar, concierge service, and many rooms with great views. Expensive.

Warwick Hotel, 4th & Lenora (443-4300). This is a modest but clean and centrally located hotel. It is sometimes used by airlines for the flight crews. Expensive.

Westin Hotel, 5th & Westlake (728-1000). This twin-towered hotel, looking something like two silver mailing tubes side by side, was the first modern luxury hotel in Seattle. It not only ended the Olympic's reign, it also replaced the beautiful old Orpheum Theater where I heard the Seattle Symphony in so many performances. But all is forgiven. The Westin is one of the city's landmarks and as more or less the corporation's flagship, it is a wonderful place to go for lunch in the Market Cafe; dinner in The Palm Court or Trader Vic's; or just for a drink in the lobby or in Fitzgerald's, which looks like bars should look. (I have a feeling I have misplaced a bar in the Westin, but perhaps they either renamed it or replaced it with a gift shop.) Expensive.

THE AIRPORT STRIP

The so-called Airport Strip is mainly along Highway 99, which locally is called Pacific Highway S., both north and south of Sea-Tac Airport. The hotels and motels run the gamut from the distinguished to the tacky and downright dangerous. These are the best of the lot.

Holiday Inn of Sea-Tac, 17338 Pacific Highway S. (248-1000). Almost directly across the street from the airport, the hotel offers most of the amenities. Moderate.

Hyatt Hotel, 17001 Pacific Hwy. S. (244-6000). This has been an airport fixture for nearly three decades now and a popular place for banquets and conferences. Easy access to the airport. Expensive.

Marriott Hotel, S. 176th & 32nd S. (241-2000). One of the most luxurious hotels in Seattle and the nicest in the airport area. It is on a hill overlooking the airport and surrounding area and has a number of dining areas, a spacious lobby, and high-quality rooms. Expensive.

Red Lion Inn, S. 188th & Pacific Hwy. S. (246-8600). A giant among the other large airport hotels with 850 units. It is so large that boxing matches are held in its cavernous hall. Two good restaurants and outside elevators. Expensive.

Obviously there are several dozen others, but after the best are described, the others tend to sound much alike. Inexpensive lodging can be found along Pacific Hwy. S. on either side of the airport and along Aurora Ave. (Hwy. 99) north of Seattle. The bulk of the motels are between downtown and about 80th Ave.

Following are some other categories, bed-and-breakfast lodgings, and places for RV users to stay.

Seattle International AYH, 84 Union St. (622-5443) charges $10 per night for a bunk in the 125-bed facility.

TraveLodge by the Space Needle, 6th N. & John (441-7878). Eighty-nine units: air-conditioning, color TV, radio, music, phones, pool, no pets, no restaurant. Moderate.

Tropics Motor Hotel, 225 Aurora N. (728-7666). One hundred and sixty units: air-conditioning, color TV, many radios, phones, suites, indoor pool, covered parking, dining room 5:30 A.M.-8:30 P.M., cocktails and entertainment. Moderate.

University Motor Inn, 4140 Roosevelt Way NE (University District) (632-5055). Forty-two units: some balconies, color TV, phones, eighteen kitchens (extra), pool, coffee shop 6:00 A.M.-3:00 P.M. Inexpensive.

YMCA, 909 4th (382-5000). Two hundred and forty rooms: for students, youths (25 and under), foreign visitors, men, women, and families. Attractive carpeted rooms, phones, rooms available with color TV/radio, some rooms with private bath. All guests may use physical facilities and participate in resident program activities. Barbershop, tailor, laundry; $23 and up.

Trailer and Tenting Facilities

There are few regular campgrounds in the immediate Seattle area. However, a number of trailer parks with complete hookups welcome overnight guests.

NORTH

National Trailer Park, 912 N. 125th, Seattle, 98133 (362-1408). RVs.

Overland Trailer Court, 1210 N. 152nd, Seattle, 98133 (363-8558). RVs.

Trailer Haven, 11724 Aurora N., Seattle, 98133 (362–4211). RVs.

SOUTH

Burien Gardens Mobile Home Park, 14239 Des Moines Way S., Seattle, 98188 (243–7888). RVs.
Orchard Trailer Park, 4011 S. 146th, Seattle, 98168 (243–1210). RVs.
Skyway Mobile Home Park, 13000 Empire Way S., Seattle, 98178 (772–4777). RVs.

For information concerning state parks, write to State Parks and Recreation Commission, P.O. Box 1128, Olympia, Washington 98504. May 1 through Labor Day call toll free (1–800–562–0990).

Bed and Breakfast

During the past four or five years, the bed-and-breakfast phenomenon has become a major industry in this area, and as the prices of hotel rooms climb, the B&Bs tend to trail along behind, getting more and more expensive. It wasn't long ago that I considered $38 a night for a place to rest my head as outrageous; now you almost have to stay in a trailer park in your own tent to sleep at that rate.

For a brochure on members of the Seattle B&B/Inn Association, write P.O. Box 9583, Seattle, 98111 (547–1020). Following is a sampling of B&Bs:

The Baker Apartments and Guest House, 528 15th Ave. E., Seattle, Washington 98102 (323–5909). An apartment building turned into a B&B with rates upward from $70 for a studio apartment.

Chambered Nautilus, 5005 22nd Ave. NE (522–2536). One of Seattle's first B&Bs, this large old house sits on a steep hillside in the University District. Rates range from $59 to $70 with shared baths, $75 to $89 with private baths.

Chelsea Station, 4915 Linden Ave. N. (547–6077). This is described as a Federal Colonial that reminds you of Grandma's house. It is near the Woodland Park Zoo and Greenlake. Rates are $49 and up.

The College Inn Guest House, 4000 University Way NE, Seattle, Washington 98105 (633–4441). A European-style B&B with shared bathrooms (men and women separate, though) and rates upward from $32 single and $35 double.

The Hotel Alternative, 555 116th NE, Bellevue, Washington (454–2800), is a condominium-rental agency with properties available throughout the Seattle area. Rates begin at $45 for one bedroom and go up to $80 for three bedrooms. Many are in the center of Seattle, as convenient as a hotel.

Pacific Bed & Breakfast, 701 NW 60th St., Seattle, Washington 98107 (784-0539). This is an agency similar to the Travellers' B&B and offers rates from $30 single and $35 double upward. Also has listings in southwest British Columbia.

Prince of Wales, 133 13th Ave. E. (325-9692) is in a turn-of-the-century home with four guest rooms. A block from the Broadway shops. Rates are from $55 to $80.

Seward House, 1717 13th Ave. (322-6537). A Victorian bungalow on Capitol Hill just across the street from the striking Russian Church. It is a brisk walk downtown, or there are three bus lines nearby. Rates are $45 single and $55 double.

Travellers' Bed & Breakfast, P.O. Box 492, Mercer Island, Washington 98040 (232-2345). This is a clearinghouse/booking agency for two hundred listings in southwest British Columbia, all of Washington, and northwest Oregon. A few listings elsewhere in Canada. Rates begin at $45 for two persons.

Bunk and Breakfast

THE M/V Challenger, (340-1201) is a tugboat remodeled into a "bunk and breakfast" with single and double cabins. It is moored on the south end of Lake Union at 809 Fairview Pl. N. on the Henry Pier at Chandler's Cove. Rates begin at $50.

Odds and Ends

Hydroplane, Chinese New Year, Laurelhurst Community Center

Annual Events

Many annual events have a way of coming and going before there's a thing annual about them. Others just seem to hang in there in spite of avowed lukewarm attitudes by the population. Those listed here have, I hope, stood the test of time and should appear again next year and the year after that.

Unfortunately, it is impossible to give precise dates since they change from year to year. Watch the newspapers for more information. You can call the Seattle/King County Convention and Visitors Bureau for more information (447-7273).

JANUARY

Boat Show—Seattle Center, Kingdome
Science Fiction Expo—Seattle Center

FEBRUARY

Chinese New Year—International District
Travel Festival—Seattle Center

MARCH

Seattle Home Show—Kingdome
Seattle Marathon
Public Schools Fine Arts Festival—Seattle Center

APRIL

Cherry Blossom Festival—Seattle Center
African Violet Show—Eames/IMAX Theater, Pacific Science Center
Seattle Art Museum's Architecture Tour—Capitol Hill
Seattle Center Easter Egg Hunt

MAY

Northwest Folklife Festival—Seattle Center
Yachting Season opening day
University District Street Fair
Norwegian Constitution Day
Pike Place Market Festival
Longacres Race Track opens
Mobile Home Show—Kingdome
Seattle International Film Festival—Egyptian Theater
International Children's Festival—Seattle Center

JUNE

Seattle Indian Art Show
Fremont District Street Fair
Seattle Art Museum's Summer Arts Magic Fair
Mercer Island Summer Arts Festival

Out to Lunch free concerts downtown begin, through September
Pioneer Square Fire Festival

JULY

Lake Union Wooden Boat Festival
Bite of Seattle—Seattle Center
Bon Odori—International District
Hispanic Seafair Festival—Seward Park
Gilbert and Sullivan Society Concerts—Seattle Center
Scottish Highland Games—Highline Stadium, Burien
Pacific Northwest Arts and Crafts Fair—Bellevue Square
Seafair Grand and Torchlight parades—downtown and International District
Other Seafair events, more than twenty, occurring throughout city
Seattle Chamber Music Festival—Lakeside School

AUGUST

Seafair Unlimited Hydroplane Races—Lake Washington
Seattle Begonia Society Show—Northgate Mall
Pioneer Days—Lake City
International District Street Fair
Black Community Festival

SEPTEMBER

Bumbershoot Festival—Seattle Center
Seafoodfest—Bergen Place Park, Ballard
Gem and Mineral Show—Seattle Center
Western Washington State Fair—Puyallup
Seattle Symphony season begins—Opera House
Seattle Dahlia Show—Seattle Center
Seafair Salmon Derby—Puget Sound
State Ceramic Show—Seattle Center
Inboard Boat Races—Lake Sammamish

OCTOBER

Issaquah Salmon Festival
Mushroom Show—Science Center
Haunted Houses—KJR Radio and other organizations
Greek Bazaar—Saint Demetrios Greek Orthodox Church, 2100 Boyer E.
Russian Bazaar—Saint Spiridon's Orthodox Cathedral, Yale & Harrison

NOVEMBER

Cat Show—Seattle Center
Boy Scout Show—Kingdome
Harvest Festival—Seattle Center

DECEMBER

Christmas Kaleidoscope—Seattle Center
Christmas Around the World—Museum of History and Industry
Santa Claus Train—Puget Sound Railway Historical Museum near
    Snoqualmie Falls. Rides at reasonable rates.
Science Circus—Pacific Science Center.

For Children

Some social observers with a philosophical turn of mind believe
that one way to judge the quality of a nation or a culture is to
observe the way the very young and the very old are treated. I
believe Seattle can stand comfortably beside any other American
city in its genuine concern for both age groups.

When I first came to Seattle in 1959 and worked in the old (and
heartbreakingly beautiful) Palomar Theater, we staged the old Seattle Junior Theater performances, which were professional, kid-
friendly, and already such a tradition that everyone took it for
granted that children deserved quality in theater.

This has been a common theme in Seattle, and I know of only
one other place where children are treated which such courtesy and
respect, and that is New Zealand, where they think it odd that we
are impressed at how well children are treated, and how well man-
nered children are as a result.

Seattle isn't overloaded with places where children can go and
be unruly, but there are a few places especially for kids where they
can go and not have to act like short British diplomats, either.

RESTAURANTS

Farrell's Ice Cream Parlour Restaurants, Northgate Mall and 930 N.
    130th just off Aurora Ave, and at several other locations in the
    Seattle area. These are friendly, clownish places with Gay
    Nineties decorations, lots of drum-banging and noisemakers
    for birthday celebrants, funny hats, etc. Kids love them, and
    few parents leave without a smile.
Pizza & Pipes, 100 N. 85th and other locations. These are fun
    places, too, with gigantic pipe organs, silent movie clips, and

other activities to keep your spirits up and make the wait for the pizza easier for the kids to tolerate.

Shakey's Pizza Parlors, located all over the region. While people of all ages are found in them, they offer a birthday club for kids under 12, who receive free pizza and soft drinks on their birthday, along with balloons, trinkets, etc.

Other kid-friendly restaurants are the Old Spaghetti Factory and Ivar's waterfront restaurants (see Restaurants chapter).

ENTERTAINMENT

The Seattle Children's Museum, Seattle Center House (441–1768). The museum relocated to the center from Pioneer Square in the spring of 1986 and should become even more popular with kids and parents. It has a miniature neighborhood, including a grocery store, a doctor's office, a restaurant, and a play center. It is very much a hands-on place and is designed for toddlers to 10-year-olds. Hours: Wednesday, Thursday, and Saturday 10:00 A.M.–5:00 P.M.; Friday 10:00 A.M.–8:00 P.M.; Sunday noon–5:00 P.M. Closed Monday. Admission: $3, toddlers under 12 months old free.

The Seattle International Children's Festival, 305 Harrison St., Seattle 98109 (684–7338) is a six-day performing arts festival with performers from all over the world. It is designed to teach children about other cultures in an enjoyable way.

Since Seattle's natural setting is so conducive to outdoor recreation, many things children can do are the same things their parents are likely to be doing with their spare time.

Boating. Children can learn all kinds of boating—rowing, sailing, motorboating, etc.—through a variety of programs offered by private and public agencies.

Coast Guard (442–7390). The Coast Guard Auxiliary sponsors water safety classes for kids in the spring and fall. Call for information.

Corinthian Yacht Club (322-7877). Sailing classes for ages 10–20. Call for information.

Mount Baker Rowing and Sailing Center (625-5767). New facility operated by the Seattle Parks Department. Offers many classes in all kinds of boating: sailing, rowing, canoeing, etc.

THEATER

A variety of stage shows are available for children, including: *Piccoli Big Theater for Little Folk*, 1932 2nd Ave. (441-5080). The organization produces stage shows for preschoolers and elementary-school children at the Seattle Center House Theater July through September and is available throughout the rest of the year for touring-show engagements.

Seattle Mime Theater, 915 Pine St. (324-8788). Although it is listed as an adult theater, the group also offers a range of children's programs throughout each year. Has its own theater on Capitol Hill.

Seattle Puppetory Theater, 13002 10th Ave. NW (365-0100). Hand-puppet shows for all ages are presented with puppets made by Joan King and scripts written by Jean Mattson.

Tickle Tune Typhoon, P.O. Box 15153, Wedgewood Station (524-9767). A musical theater revue that presents original music for children and parents. It focuses on positive self-image, human relationships, and mutual respect.

World Mother Goose, Seattle Center (441-7469). A nonprofit professional theatrical group that performs primarily for preschool children. Uses mime, improvisation, and children's literature.

OF SPECIAL NOTE

One of the most useful tools for parents of younger children is the tabloid newspaper, *Seattle's Child*, which has become something of a bible for area parents. The monthly publication lists all manner of activities for children. It also has in-depth stories on subjects of great interest to parents, such as private schools and special programs available through the public school system. Address: P.O. Box 22578, E. Union Station, Seattle, Washington 98122 or phone 322-2594. A good guidebook for parents is *Places to Go with Children Around Puget Sound* by Elton Welke, published by Chronicle Books.

KidsPlace, 158 Thomas (441-0848). This is a community project founded by Metrocenter YMCA, the City of Seattle, and the Junior League. It sponsors the annual KidsDay in April and gives children their own special day and several free events. For example, on a recent KidsDay, children and parents were given free admission to Woodland Park Zoo, Pacific Science Center, Children's Museum, Seattle Aquarium, Monorail, Museum of Flight, Space Needle Elevator, and concerts at Westlake Mall.

More and more agencies and events are adding children's events or giving emphasis to them. The Pacific Science Center and both the YMCA and YWCA have special programs. Seattle Parks and Recreation offers programs, and so do several other organizations, such as the Seattle Audubon Society and most museums.

King County Library System. Similar to programs offered by the Seattle system (see below). Monthly bulletins available at check-out desks of all branches and listed in newspapers.

Seattle Public Libraries, main lobby at 1000 4th (625-4952). The main library and all branches have children's programs year-round, which include picture-book time, puppet shows, story-telling, films, poetry clubs, talks by authors of children's books, creative dramatics for 4- to 5-year-olds, and a summer reading club. Also available (main branch only) are children's records, 16mm films, and pictures. Sometimes special tours for children are offered. Call libraries for programs and watch for listings in newspapers, particularly the *P.I.*'s *What's Happening* on Friday and the *Seattle Times' Tempo Magazine* on Friday.

Senior Citizens

Seattle supports one of the most progressive city-funded programs to make life more pleasant and useful for persons 65 and over in the United States. The city established the Senior Information Center within the Department of Human Resources primarily to reduce the cost of necessities for senior citizens, and the program was met with enthusiasm by the business community. A special savings brochure is available from this office at no charge; call 386-1274.

Following are some of the savings available to senior citizens age 65 and older residing in Seattle or King County:

Chore Services. Call 721-4000; 322-3637; or 324-4834.

Free Appliance Parts. Free replacement parts for range, water heater, or permanently connected electric heating owned by a senior citizen are available by calling 448-9297 for an application.

Free Tuition. Seattle Pacific University offers free tuition to senior citizens working toward a degree. The student must sign up for classes that are not filled by regular students. Call Admissions for information (281-2021). University of Washington and other state schools have a $5 fee for courses on a space-available basis.

Mayor's Office for Senior Citizens, 315 Jones Building, 1331 3rd (386-1274). Possible discounts on water, sewer, and garbage bills; City Light surcharge exemption; reduced bus fare passes; etc.

Metro Buses. Ride anywhere in the county for $.20 or $3 a month. Passes available at 821 2nd. Call 447-4800 or 386-1274.

Older Workers Employment Program. Under the Seattle Department of Human Resources, this program for workers 55 years of age and up provides training, support groups, placement counseling, and a job hot line. For information, call 386-1274.

Pacific Science Center. Admission is $1.

Pet Licenses and Taxi Discounts. If your income is less than $11,087 for a single person, or $14,498 for couples, you can get a 50 percent discount on taxi fares and a 50 percent discount on pet licenses. Call 386-1274 for information.

Tax Exemptions, King County Assessor's Office (County Administration Building, 500 4th (296-3920). Possible deferment and exemptions of property taxes.

Restaurant Discounts. About two hundred restaurants give a discount on meals. Call 284-1139 and ask about Golden American program, 2142 8th Ave. Membership costs $16 a year.

Other Discounts. Some pharmacies, food co-ops, tours, and theaters. Call 386-1234 or the individual business and inquire.

FOOD

Low-Cost Meals—Several local centers offer low-cost meals. Call 448-3110 for information.

Meals and low-cost staples for the home-bound are available from Meals on Wheels (448-3110).

Seattle-King County Nutrition Program for the Elderly (448-5767). Hot meals every weekday for persons aged 60 or older in neighborhood centers. Usually open from 10:00 A.M.–2:00 P.M., providing recreation, escort service, volunteers. Call for nearby location.

S.P.I.C.E., Administration office: 3311 NE 60th (281-6298). Lunch, recreation, and health clinic in eight Seattle Public Schools. Free health checkups; call for location.

MEDICAL SERVICES

Community Home Health Care, 190 Queen Anne N. (282-5048). Health-care services; also sells a directory of services for handicapped and elderly.

Hospice of Seattle, 230 Fairview N. (326-5969). Offers home care for terminally ill.

Seattle-King County Department of Public Health Geriatric Clinics. Free services for those 60 and over at activity centers and SPICE locations. City, central region (587-2755); north of Ship Canal (363-4765); county, southwest area (344-7474); southeast (344-6700); east of Lake Washington (344-6882).

PROGRAMS

Day Care Centers: Call Community Information Line for locations (447-3200). Personal care, health screening, social activities.

The Lifetime Learning Center at Sacred Heart Catholic Church, 202 John (283-5523), offers low-cost continuing education.

Seattle Department of Parks and Recreation, 8061 Densmore N. (684-4951). Offers a program of lawn bowling, field trips, concerts, etc.

Senior Centers. King County Senior Services and Centers, 800 Jefferson (448-5757), operates most of these, which provide daytime social activities, arts and crafts, bus trips, etc. Centers are located: Central area, 500 30th S.; Jefferson House, 800 Jefferson; Northwest, 5249 32nd NW; Wallingford, 4649 Sunnyside N.; Greenwood, 525 N. 85th; Lee House, 7515 39th S.; West Seattle, 4217 SW Oregon; Tallmadge Hamilton House, 5525 15th NE; Shoreline, 835 NE 155th. Also Central Openhouse at Central Lutheran Church, 1710 11th (322-7500); The Columbia Club, 424 Columbia (622-6460); The North Shore Senior Center, 9929 180th NE, Bothell (487-2441).

VOLUNTEER OPPORTUNITIES

Foster Grandparent Program, 15230 15th NE (364-0300). Work with day-care and retarded youngsters four hours daily, five days a week. Paid mileage, hourly wage, and meals.

King County Retired Senior Volunteer Program (323-2345). Finds work opportunities in private and nonprofit agencies.

Volunteer Service Office of Seattle Public Schools (281-6342). Puts persons 55 or older at work directly with students in tutoring or classroom assistance or in libraries.

Volunteer opportunities also exist in a number of museums (Seattle Art Museum and Museum of Flight in particular) and theater and music groups. Theater groups include: Bathhouse Theater (524-3608), New City Theater (323-6800), and Seattle Children's Theater (633-4567). Music groups include Early Music Guild (325-7066), Friends of the Philadelphia String Quartet (527-8839), Seattle Chamber Music Festival (282-1807), and Seattle Youth Symphony (362-5606).

REASSURANCE SERVICES

Postal Alert (625-4834). Mailmen alert to oldsters living alone.

Reassurance Telephone Call Service: Providence Hospital (326-5711). A free call to seniors living alone to make sure they're all right.

ORGANIZATIONS

Citizens for Improvement of Nursing Homes, 3530 Stone Way N. (461-4553). Statewide organization attempting to improve quality of care in nursing homes; some patient advocacy.

Gray Panthers, Good Shepherd Center, 4649 Sunnyside N. (632-4759). Part of a national group working for social change, such as fighting against mandatory retirement, decent housing at reasonable rent, etc.

Homesharing Programs for Seniors, 1601 2nd, Suite 800 (448-5725). Matches homeowners with compatible tenants for mutual economic and social benefit.

Japanese American Citizens' League, 316 S. Maynard (623-5088). Represents rights of Japanese-Americans, with the Issei group dealing with the needs of the elderly.

Northwest Senior Craftsmen, Pier 70 (728-0967). Handmade items made by senior citizens sold on consignment.

Seattle-King County Division on Aging, 400 Yesler Building: (city 684-0660). Plans delivery of services to elderly.

Senior Rights Assistance, 1601 2nd, Suite 800 (448-5720). Trained senior citizens offer legal information and assistance in social security, medicare, health insurance, wills, etc.

Senior Services and Centers, Home Repair Division, 500 30th Ave. S. (447-7802). Provides free labor for minor home repairs: plumbing, carpentry, electrical work, ramps, and railings. Clients furnish the materials.

Social Security Administration (800-234-5772). Telephone service for those over 65.

INFORMATION

Red Cross Aid to Aging, 1900 25th S. (323-2345). Similar services as below.

Senior Information Center, room 315 on the third floor of the Jones Building at 1331 3rd (448-3110). A place to go just to relax in the lounge and visit or obtain help and information on all services available to senior citizens. Among the things available at the center are: combined Metro ID card (with picture) and Senior Citizen ID card for discounts, property tax exemption applications, applications for utility credit, and more. Call or visit the center for any information concerning senior citizens.

Senior Services Information & Assistance, 1601 2nd Ave., Suite 800 (447-5720). Counseling for those over 60 with problems in health care, housing, home maintenance. Workers will visit homes to give information on services and help fill out applications. Can arrange transportation for medical appointments and grocery shopping with ten days' notice (small fee for transportation).

Climate

Someday a climatological genius, perhaps the same one who wanted to set off an atomic bomb in the Van Allen Belt, is going to suggest a way to give Seattle more clear weather, and when he does, somebody is going to throw him, charts and graphs and all, into Puget Sound. If there is anything Seattleites don't want, it's someone messing around with the thing they complain the most about.

In the winter it rains a lot, and when it isn't raining, it looks like it just did or is going to in a few minutes. In the summer it rains less, but not enough less to satisfy the constant complainers.

True, true. It does rain a lot, and there are weeks when the sun is only a dim memory; something somebody saw last month in Las Vegas or Wenatchee. Yet it seldom gets very cold in Seattle—perhaps a week out of the year with freezing temperatures—and it rarely gets unbearably hot, even in August.

The weather is one of the favorite, but least effective, tools of that grumpy group that calls itself Lesser Seattle, whose purpose is to discourage immigrants to Seattle. They insist it rains all the time, but the ski buffs know that means yards of snow in the winter. Lesser Seattle says the sun never shines, but to a desert rat that is more soothing than Coppertone. Lesser Seattle says there is so little difference between the seasons one has to watch the calendar to know the month, but who needs blizzards, droughts, and tornadoes? They'd as well give up and admit it: Seattle isn't perfect, but nobody or nothing is. Some places are better than others, and Seattle is one of them.

So here are the statistics, courtesy of the National Oceanic and Atmospheric Administration, compiled from its station at Seattle-Tacoma International Airport. Please bear in mind that these statistics are for the airport only; it does get both colder and hotter in downtown Seattle on occasion.

AVERAGE TEMPERATURE BY MONTH

Month	Temperature		Precipitation	Wind	
	Daily Max.	Daily Min.	Normal Total	Mean Hourly Speed	Prevailing Direction
January	43.4	33.0	5.79	10.5	S
February	48.5	36.0	4.19	10.1	S
March	51.5	36.6	3.61	10.4	S
April	57.0	40.3	2.46	10.1	S
May	64.1	45.6	1.70	9.3	S
June	69.0	50.6	1.53	9.1	SW
July	75.1	53.8	0.71	8.6	NNW
August	73.8	53.7	1.08	8.2	NNW
September	68.7	50.4	1.99	8.4	SSE
October	59.4	44.9	3.91	9.1	SSE
November	50.4	38.8	5.88	9.4	SSE
December	45.4	35.5	5.94	10.2	SSE

Source: U.S. National Oceanic and Atmospheric Administration, *Local Climatological Data*. Airport data based on thirty-year period.

Additional statistics, compiled and published by KIRO Radio-TV and KSEA, address the matter of clear versus overcast days. They say that Seattle has:

56 clear days,
81 partly cloudy days, and
228 cloudy days per year.

Health

MAJOR HOSPITALS

Cabrini Hospital, Terry & Madison (682-0500): 150 beds.
Children's Hospital and Medical Center, 4800 Sand Point Way NE (526-2000): 196 beds, burn center.
Group Health Hospital, 201 16th E. (326-3000): 260 beds. Also other locations.

Harborview Medical Center, 325 9th (223-3000): 250 beds, emergency trauma center.
Northwest Hospital, 1550 N. 115th (364-0500): 262 beds, communicative disorders, stroke unit.
Overlake Memorial Hospital, 1035 116th NE, Bellevue (454-4011): 160 beds.
Providence Medical Center, 500 17th (320-2000): 333 beds, cardiac center, rehabilitative center.
Swedish Hospital and Medical Center, 747 Summit (386-6000): 422 beds, Northwest Kidney Center, Tumor Institute, and Fred Hutchison Cancer Research Center.
University of Washington Hospital, 1959 NE Pacific (548-3300): 298 beds, teaching, research, neonatal intensive care, spinal cord injury center.
U.S. Government Veterans Hospital, 1660 S. Columbian Way (762-1010): 354 beds.
Virginia Mason Hospital, 925 Seneca (624-1144): 290 beds.

LOW-COST MEDICAL CLINICS

Country Doctor, 402 15th E. (322-6698). General medical and physician referral.
45th Street Community Health Clinic, 1629 N. 45th (633-3350).
High Point Community Health Center, 6554 32nd SW. (935-8150). All services but major surgery and X-ray. Fee is $2 for low-income patients.
International District Community Health Center, 416 Maynard S. (622-9650).
Pioneer Square Neighborhood Health Station, 206 3rd (223-3540). Geared to elderly but will accept persons in area or those with low income. Access to Language Bank.
Seattle Indian Health Board, 1122 12th Ave. S. (324-9360). Medical, dental, mental, and eye care. Alcohol program. Sliding fee scale.
Seattle-King County Health Department, Public Safety Building, 3rd & James (587-4600). Family planning, adult and child health, immunizations, VD clinic. Free or according to ability to pay.
Senior Services and Centers (448-5757), various locations in the city. Provide foot care, health education and nutrition counseling, and recreational activities for the elderly.
S.P.I.C.E., Administration office: 3311 NE 60th (281-6298). Health clinic, meals, and recreation for elderly in various Seattle Public Schools. Noon meals.

University of Washington Dental School (543-5830). Long waiting period but low-cost orthodontics and dental care.

FREE LEGAL CLINICS

The Young Lawyers Section of the local bar association has set up free legal clinics, four thus far with more under consideration. They operate one night each week. They are open 7:00-9:00 P.M.: Freemont Public Association (632-1285), Country Doctor (322-6698), Central Legal Clinic (625-5273), and Lake City Legal Clinic (625-2223). See "Low-Cost Medical Clinics" for addresses and telephone numbers. If you are a lawyer and want to help, call 622-3150.

MISCELLANEOUS

Alcohol and Drug 24-Hour Helpline (722-3700).
Alcoholics Anonymous (587-2838).
Cancer Lifeline (461-4542). Twenty-four-hour telephone counseling service.
Community Services Officers, Seattle Police Department, 1810 E. Yesler Way (625-4661). Emergency food, shelter, and clothing available to city residents.
Crisis Clinic, 1530 E. Eastlake (461-3222). Counseling, shelter, and financial aid for stranded individuals and others.
Millionaire Club (728-5600). Free breakfasts and dinners, day-work referrals.
Northwest Center for the Retarded (285-9140). Training school for retarded children and adults.
Tel-Med (621-9450). Health information in layman's language, 175 three- to five-minute tape recordings.

Schools

COLLEGES AND UNIVERSITIES

Seattle Pacific University, 3rd W. & W. Nickerson (281-2000).
Seattle University, Broadway & Madison (626-6200).
University of Washington, 15th NE & NE 45th (543-2100).

COMMUNITY COLLEGES

Bellevue Community College, 3000 Landerholm Circle SE, Bellevue (641-0111).

Edmonds Community College, 2000 68th W., Lynnwood (771–1500).
Highline Community College, S. 240th & Pacific Hwy. S. (878–3710).
Seattle Community College: North, 9600 College Way N. (634-4507); Central, 1701 Broadway (587–3800); South, 6000 16th SW (764-5300).
Shoreline Community College, 16101 Greenwood N. (546–4101).

OTHER SCHOOLS

Antioch University Seattle, 1165 Eastlake E. (323–9150).
The Art Institute of Seattle, 2323 Elliott (448–6600).
City University, 16661 Northrup Way, Bellevue (624–1688); 20000 68th Ave. W., Lynnwood (771–2233).
Cornish School of Allied Arts, 710 E. Roy (323–1400).
Golden Gate University, 310 Skinner Building, 5th & Union (622-9996).

ADULT EDUCATION

Seattle has gone on an adult-education boom during the past few years. All colleges and universities in the city offer a staggering number of courses, from belly dancing to some of the more obscure folk dances to the classics. Public schools and community centers also offer evening adult education classes for noncredit. For information, call each of the schools listed above or your neighborhood high school or community center.

Foreign Visitors

As Seattle's role in international business and tourism expands—and it is expanding more rapidly than many of us comprehend—the need to comunicate with people from all over the world increases dramatically. We have polar flights bringing in Europeans, and many daily flights between Seattle and the Orient—Tokyo, Hong Kong, Singapore, Manila, and Bangkok, to name a few. Seattle has some programs already under way that are helping enormously.

LANGUAGE SCHOOLS

Here are some schools for foreign languages so you can understand the people of the country you visit or the people who come here to visit.
Berlitz Language Centers, 1525 4th Ave. (682–0312). Any language.

Foreign Consulates. Austria, 4131 11th NE (633-3606); Belgium, 1415 5th Ave. (623-5005); Bolivia, Box 58241 (244-6696); Finland, Box 40598, Bellevue (451-3983); Great Britain, First Interstate Center (622-9253); Canada, Plaza 600 Building (433-1777); Chile, Joshua Green Bldg. (624-3772); Costa Rica, 227 8th Ave. W., Kirkland (822-3054); France, 400 E. Pine (323-6870); Germany, IBM Building (682-4312); Guatemala, 2100 5th Ave. Bldg (728-5920); Honduras, 1402 3rd Ave. Suite 1019 (623-6485); Iceland, 5610 20th NW (783-4100); Japan, 3110 Rainier Bank Tower (682-9107); Mexico, 2132 3rd Ave. (448-3536); The Netherlands (827-0584); Norway, Joseph Vance Bldg. (623-3957); Peru, 7209 NE 149th Pl, Bothell (488-4705); Philippines, 2033 6th Ave. (441-1640); South Korea, 2033 6th Ave. (441-1011); Sweden, Joseph Vance Bldg. (622-5640); Switzerland, (762-1223); Taiwan, Westin Bldg. (441-4586).

Language Bank. This is probably the city's oldest effort, started in the early 1960s by the Altrusa Club. It grew so rapidly that the club couldn't do justice to it, so the American Red Cross "adopted" the organization. Now some 450 persons volunteer their services and are on call twenty-four hours a day. They speak approximately seventy languages, and the number of calls is soaring. At last count, some fifteen hundred calls were being logged each year, and with Seattle becoming so popular with Oriental tourists, the number is bound to continue upward. For help, or to volunteer your services, call 323-2345.

Seattle Public Library, 1000 4th Ave. (625-2665). Publishes a booklet listing all sources of language instruction in Seattle.

Washington Academy of Languages, 98 Yesler Way (682-4463). German, French, Japanese, Mandarin Chinese, Italian, and Spanish.

Seattle's Sister Cities

Seattle has fifteen sister cities scattered around the world. In the mid-1970s it had one more civic sister, Dawson City, Yukon. The Yukoners, an independent lot, showed so little interest in the arrangement that the relationship died from disuse. Seattle's current sister cities are: Kobe, Japan: October 7, 1957; Bergen, Norway: May 22, 1967; Tashkent, U.S.S.R.: January 22, 1973; Beer Sheva, Israel: April 18, 1977; Mazatlan, Mexico: November 19, 1979; Nantes, France: April 21, 1980; Christchurch, New Zealand: January 26, 1981; Mombasa, Kenya: April 6, 1981; Chongging, China: June 3, 1983; Nimbe, Cameroon: April 2, 1984; Managua,

Nicaragua: November 19, 1984; Galway, Ireland: March 10, 1986; Reykjavik, Iceland: May 5, 1986; Taejon, Korea: October 4, 1989; Kaohsiung, Taiwan: September 24, 1990.

Baby-Sitters and Day Care

Best Sitters (682-2556). Twenty-four-hour service, children and elderly. Motels-hotels.
Day Care Referral (461-3207).
Downtown Seattle. Call individual department stores for more information regarding their services.

Home Repairs

Home Owners Club of Seattle, 1202 Harrison (622-3500). One of the few such clubs that have been a success, it was organized to give homeowners more time to enjoy themselves with less time spent fiddling around the house making repairs. For $25 a year a homeowner can call to report a problem, from yard work to new construction, and the club will see that the work is done at a fair price. They keep a list of fully investigated contractors, and a representative of the club may visit your home to consult with you on the work needed and possible cost.

Libraries

SEATTLE PUBLIC LIBRARY

Main Library, 1000 4th (386-4683); quick information on any subject (386-4636). The Main Library offers a wide variety of research materials for scholars, including rare manuscripts, historical photographs, and rare books. Meeting rooms are available for groups, and the library maintains an extensive music and film rental library. Call for information on tours of the bindery and other behind-the-scenes activities.
Municipal Reference Library, 307 Municipal Building, 600 4th Ave. (684-8031). Open weekdays as a reference service to city and county employees as well as persons interested in local government.

Other libraries are housed in the colleges and universities, all of which may be used by the public. Of particular interest to historians is the University of Washington Library and its Special Collections section, with one of the best libraries on the Pacific Northwest, Alaska, and the Arctic.

KING COUNTY LIBRARY SYSTEM

Headquarters, 300 8th N. (684-9000). The system conducts a wide variety of programs countywide for the public of all ages. A sample month's program for various branches would include films, a wine-making workshop, visits by the Seattle Repertory Theater's Rep 'n Rap troupe talking about a new play and performing excerpts from it, a talk by a policeman on home security, autograph parties for authors, and a talk on home canning and freezing by a county extension officer. The system also offers numerous children's programs (see "For Children" in this chapter). The modern-architecture branches are located in Algona, Bellevue, Black Diamond, Bothell, Boulevard Park, Burien, Burton, Carnation, Des Moines, Duvall, Fall City, Federal Way, Forest Park, Foster, Issaquah, Kenmore, Kent, Kirkland, Lake Hills, Lester, Maple Valley, McMicken, Mercer Island, Newport Way, North Bend, Pacific, Park Lane, Preston, Redmond, Redondo, Richmond Beach, Shoreline, Skykomish, Skyway, Snoqualmie, South Park Courts, Valley Ridge, Vashon, Vista, and White Center. Bookmobiles run on a scheduled basis to smaller communities and rural areas.

Singles Groups

There are more than fifty organizations sponsoring activities, lecture series, and consultation services available for single adults. These are in addition to—and separate from—the computer dating firms, escort services, and other businesses that capitalize on loneliness. Most in this partial listing are sponsored by churches or similarly legitimate and serious organizations.

All City Jewish Singles (232-7115). Largest Jewish group in area. Recreational and cultural.

Association of Formerly Married Catholics (767-6372). Meetings Sunday at 7:30 P.M. in the Roanoke House, Broadway E. & E. Roanoke.

Chancellor Club of Seattle, 6727 Greenwood N. (782-6281). For single Catholics 21-40.

Chareso Club (242-9903). For unmarried Catholics over 35.

Cornerstone Fellowship, NE 47th & 16th NE (524-7300). For singles 21-35. *Genesis* is for singles 35 and up. Meetings each Sunday in the Inn of University Presbyterian Church.

162   Odds and Ends

Divorce Lifeline, 1013 8th (624-2959). Group counseling for adults and children.

FOCAS (Fellowship of Christian Adult Singles) (672-9058). Chapters throughout the greater Seattle area meeting Sunday morning at 8:45 A.M. FOCAS sponsors Pacific Northwest Christian Singles Convention each spring, retreats, tours, banquets, and various seminars. Call for information.

Parents Without Partners (361-2060). Activities for single parents and their children. Call for information on chapters in Seattle area.

University Unitarian Church, 6556 35th NE (525-8400). This church sponsors two groups. The Solo Series meets Sunday nights at 7:00 P.M. The Discovery Program meets Friday nights at 8:00 P.M.

Widow's Information and Consultation Service (246-6142). Group counseling, group discussions.

Publications

Seattle is one of the few large cities with two major daily newspapers under different ownership, but due to a recent Joint Operating Agreement entered into by the papers and approved by a series of courts, it really doesn't make much difference who owns them. The feisty, independent *Post-Intelligencer* had a few teeth pulled by the JOA, some of its talent has either left or been watered down, and it hardly exists at all in the combined Sunday paper. Shortly after the two merged into the Sunday mixer, a *Seattle Times* columnist wrote about a man (real) who injured himself reading the Sunday paper: he fell asleep reading and fell out of his chair.

For most purposes, the papers still exist separately and have newsrooms in different buildings. The *Times* handles the money (the *PI* needed a bit of help in that department), meaning it handles advertising and circulation for both papers.

Daily Journal of Commerce, 83 Columbia (622-8272). The *Wall Street Journal* of Seattle, minus the feature stories and interviews. The *Journal* reports on all important contracts, bond sales, and other business news.

Fishermen's News, Fishermen's Terminal (282-7545). A widely respected publication that covers the entire West Coast commercial fishing industry, from Alaska to South America.

Fishing & Hunting News, 511 Eastlake E. (624-3845). Exactly what the name indicates, a weekly covering both sports in depth.

Marple's Business Newsletter, Colman Building, 911 Western (622-

0155). A biweekly report on Pacific Northwest business. Subscription only.

Nor'westing Boating Magazine, 180 W. Dayton, Edmonds, Washington 98020 (776–3138). A pleasure-boating magazine covering most of the Inside Passage, from Puget Sound to Alaska.

Pacific Northwest, 222 Dexter Ave. N. (682–2704). Formerly *Pacific Search,* it is a regional magazine covering events and issues in Seattle, Portland, the two Northwest states, British Columbia, and Alaska. Some California coverage.

Puget Sound Business Journal, 101 Yelster Way (583–0701). A business tabloid that, in addition to hard business news, contains travel stories, restaurant reviews, and profiles of business professionals.

Seattle Guide, Pioneer Building, 600 1st Ave. (682–5960). A free weekly color magazine listing entertainment, sightseeing, and restaurant information. Available in hotels, restaurants, and information centers around town.

The Seattle Post-Intelligencer, 101 Elliott Ave. W. (448–8000). Owned by the Hearst Corporation, its advantages are the *New York Times* News Service, two daily crosswords, a lively sports section, an occasional battle against someone who can fight back (as opposed to attacking only public servants who cannot fight back), and some good columnists, such as John Owen, John Hahn, and Susan Paynter.

The Seattle Times, Fariview & John (464–2111). The dominant paper, it is owned by the Blethen family of Seattle, with 49.5 percent of voting stock owned by Knight-Ridder Newspapers. Several good columnists (Rick Anderson, Emmett Watson, Jean Godden, John Hinterberger, et al.) and good cartoons ("Peanuts," for example). The combined Sunday paper has a *Times*-produced rotogravure section called *Pacific,* the national weekly *Parade,* and a hefty advertising-editorial ratio.

Soundings Northwest, (682–9277). A guide to FM radio and an arts calendar. Available by subscription or at record, radio, and bookstores.

Sunset Magazine, Logan Building (682–3993). Publishes a Northwest edition with travel and gardening information for the regional audience.

The Seattle Weekly, 1931 2nd (441–5555). Founded by David Brewster, alumnus of *Seattle Magazine* and *Argus,* this tabloid offers in-depth coverage of local and regional politics, arts, and some business. Complete guide to entertainment and recreation with a great deal of space devoted to restaurants and shopping.

Up the Down Sidewalks

Some of the sidewalks are so steep between 1st and 3rd that cleats were cast in the concrete. Actually, steps would have been better. And if you're going downhill, you're in danger of getting started on a trot that won't stop until you're teetering precariously on the curb with taxis whipping past. But there's a way around this, so simple that most people never think of it. You use elevators and escalators.

To get from the ferry dock to 6th Avenue, cross Alaskan Way Viaduct on the pedestrian overpass to 1st; then go into the Federal Building between Madison and Marion streets, take the elevator marked Floors 2, 4 and 14-26, and get off at the fourth floor, which lands at 2nd Avenue. Cross 2nd into the First Interstate Center and take the escalator to 3rd Avenue. Enter the Seafirst building at 3rd and Madison and take the escalators to 4th Avenue, or take the elevator to the fifth floor. Then cross 4th to the Seattle Public Library and take the escalator or elevator to the 5th Avenue lobby. Cross 5th at Spring to the first floor of the U.S. Courthouse and take the elevator to 6th Avenue.

The same technique can be used to traverse the hills all the way from Pioneer Square north to the Denny Regrade area, although the only way I've found to avoid that lung-stretcher from Pike Place Market to 1st Avenue is simply to go around it to Pike Street.

Public Rest Rooms

Hardly any. It takes imagination, gall, desperation, and determination to find public rest rooms in Seattle. Apparently the only truly public ones are in the Pike Place Market and Freeway Park, although there is frequent talk about building them in some of the mall areas, such as Westlake Mall. There is also talk of restoring the elegant one in Pioneer Square beneath the pergola. Some of the large department stores have them for the convenience of their customers, but unless you've been there before you've got to waste frantic moments asking a clerk where they are cloistered. But don't blame the city government or the stores; security, both personal and for the fixtures, is difficult with the high incidence of vandalism, today's equivalent of the old KILROY WAS HERE signs. Tips: Stroll into a bar or restaurant that doesn't have a maitre d'. Walk into a good hotel. But never betray what you're there for. After a few such trips, you'll have the best places spotted, and you might even become friends with the owners of the establishments.

The most spectacular rest room in Seattle is on the 75th (and top) floor of the Columbia Seafirst Center. It is for women only, and since it is higher than the tops of other buildings, it has a picture window with no curtains or blinds. Its wash basin has gold fixtures, and each stall has louvered doors. It is a popular place for the curious to visit, and men are permitted in when accompanied by the appropriate officials or when it is vacant.

City and County

BEATING CITY HALL

First, call the Citizens Service Bureau (684-8811), which will take your complaint and send a copy to the appropriate department head, who must report back within twenty working days with either a resolution or a good excuse why the problem is impossible to solve.

If that doesn't work, try the King County Ombudsman in the county courthouse (296-3452). The office has the staff to investigate corruption and governmental abuse and is an independent agency answering to no politicians.

If your problem is only a little one or you need advice not available at those two offices, try the "little city halls" (community service centers). These offices provide information, accept utility bill payments, issue pet licenses, register voters, and assist in neighborhood programs. They are located at: Ballard, 2309 NW Market (684-4060); Capitol Hill, 506 19th E. (684-4574); Central, 1825 S. Jackson (684-4767); Fremont, 708 N. 34th (684-4054); Greenwood, 7209 Greenwood N. (684-4096); Lake City, 12707 30th NE (684-7526); Queen Anne/Magnolia, 3054 15th W. (386-4207); Southwest, 9407 16th SW (684-7416); South Park, 8201 10th S. (767-3650); Southeast, 4859 Rainier S. (386-1931); University, 4710 University Way NE (684-7542).

GOING TO COURT

Some people make a hobby of attending trials in the various courts in Seattle, which isn't a bad way to spend a slow afternoon. One way to participate within the safety of numbers is to call the various courts for information on cases being tried: municipal courts (684-5600); superior court (296-9100); and U.S. District Court (442-5598).

CITY AND COUNTY COUNCIL COMMITTEE MEETINGS

For information on these, call Seattle City Council (684-8888); County Council (344-7445).

Private Clubs

There are numerous private and fraternal clubs, including the Elks, Moose, American Legion, and other national organizations, and country clubs. Some of those listed below have reciprocal guest arrangements with other clubs across the country. The major ones are:

College Club, 5th & Madison (622-0624).
Rainier Club, 4th & Marion (296-6848).
University Club, 1004 Boren (622-1132).
Washington Athletic Club, 1325 6th (622-7900).

BREAKING IN

Breaking into Seattle's social scene is supposedly a bit different from most other cities, in part because long-time residents are so reluctant to call attention to themselves. Be prepared to hear people apologize for being extravagant; according to Susan Phinney, the *P-I*'s society reporter, women freely admit it when they rent a dress for a special occasion. (It is an exaggeration that men and women rely on Recreational Equipment Inc. for their evening wear.)

Susan also warns that you may feel out of place at the Pacific Northwest ballet benefits if you're larger than a size 8, since its supporters tend to be "thin and very well dressed."

She notes that being fashionably late at Seattle functions is not "in" here. Things tend to start right on time, and you can expect to miss the best food and best buys at auctions if you arrive late.

The most popular benefits include Symphoneve for the Seattle Symphony; PONCHO (Patrons of Northwest Civic, Charitable and Cultural Organizations); the Kids Auction for boys' and girls' clubs; and Tuxes and Tails, a benefit for the Humane Society that attracts local celebrities. Others are the Hutchinson Center, Cancer Society, and Children's Hospital benefits.

Few events are sell-outs, according to Susan—an exception is PONCHO, which is sold out months in advance. The only very private, very selective guest list is that of the Seattle Art Museum.

Some Things Newcomers Should Know

Voting. You must be at least 18 years old and a U.S. citizen. There are no residency requirements, but you must have registered to vote at least thirty days before any election. Information: King County Voter Registration Department, 553 King County Building, 5th & James (344-5282).

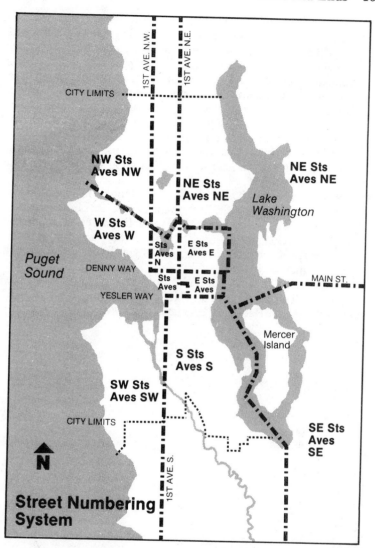

1ST AVE. N.W.

1ST AVE. N.E.

CITY LIMITS

NW Sts
Aves NW

NE Sts
Aves NE

NE Sts
Aves NE

Lake
Washington

W Sts
Aves W

Sts
Aves
N

E Sts
Aves E

Puget
Sound

DENNY WAY

Sts
Aves

E Sts
Aves

MAIN ST.

YESLER WAY

Mercer
Island

S Sts
Aves S

SW Sts
Aves SW

CITY LIMITS

SE Sts
Aves
SE

N

1ST AVE. S.

**Street Numbering
System**

Taxes. There is no state personal income tax; rather, it is taken
impersonally when you buy any nonfood item, at the rate of
7.9 percent. State law limits property taxes to 1 percent of the
true and fair value, but special levies for schools, cities, coun-
ties, road districts, etc. can be tacked onto this—and are.

Business and occupation (B & O) taxes are levied on gross
income or receipts; state taxes range from .079 percent plus
the local rate. Gasoline tax is $.18 a gallon for state and $.09
federal. Motor vehicle taxes are $13.50 for a new-car purchase

plus a 2 percent excise tax, and each following year the basic
fee is $10 plus 2.3 percent of the vehicle's depreciated value.

When bringing a car into the state, you must have a car
inspection ($10) and a $4 transfer fee plus a 2 percent excise
tax on the depreciated value of the car. License plates expire on
a staggered basis now. Be warned, however, that the wheels of
the Department of Motor Vehicles turn slowly and that it
takes up to three months for titles on cars to be transferred.
Also, getting information from the department is usually an
exercise in futility. A driver's license costs $3 for the examina-
tion plus $7 for the license, which is good for four years and
costs $14 to renew.

Utilities. You will most likely have to pay a deposit when you start a
new service with Pacific Northwest Bell, City Light, Washington Natural Gas Company, the Water Department, and a garbage collection company. The rates vary according to the
service you want and arrangements you had with utilities at
your former address.

Seattle's streets. The lettering and numbering system for Seattle's
streets is confusing, to say the least. The map (on page 167)
shows Seattle, Bellevue, Kirkland, and Mercer Island.

A Handy Telephone Guide

Abortion-Birth Control
Referral Service, 634-3460
Alcohol and Drug Help Line,
722-3700
Alcoholics Anonymous,
587-2838
American Cancer Society,
283-1152
American Civil Liberties
Union, 624-2180
Animal Control Service,
386-4254
Audubon Society, 523-4483
Auto. Club of Wash. (AAA),
448-5353
Auto Impound, 684-5444
Auto Licenses, 296-4000
Auto Recall, 800-424-9393

Better Business Bureau,
448-8888
Bicycle Hot Line, 522-BIKE
Birth & Death Records,
296-4768
Boat Numbering Info.,
442-7355

Canadian Govt. Office of
Tourism, 443-1777
Cancer Lifeline, 461-4542
Carpool, 625-4500
Cascade Ski Report, 634-0200
Census Bureau, 728-5300
Chamber of Commerce,
389-7200
Charitable Sales Permits,
684-8484
Child and Family Referral,
461-3207
CIA, 382-1527
Citizen's Serv. Bur. (info. &
complaints), 684-8811

City Council Info., 684-8888
City Light, 625-3000
City Parks Info., 684-4075
Coast Guard, 442-5295
Community Crime Prevention
Program, 684-7555
Community Information Line,
461-3200
Composting Hotline, 633-0224
Consumer Complaints &
Inquiries, 684-8811
Consumer Credit Counseling
Serv., 441-3290
Consumer Products Safety
Com., 442-5276
Consumer Protection (state),
464-6684
Cooperative Extension Service,
296-3900
County Council Info.,
296-1000
Crisis Clinic, 461-3222
Crystal Mt. Report, 634-3771
Customs Service, 442-4676

Daughters of the American
Revolution, 323-0600
Day Care Referral Serv.,
461-3207
Dial-A-Prayer, 282-4545
Dial-A-Story, 386-4656
Divorce Lifeline, 624-2959
Doctor, 24-hr. answering serv.,
622-6900
Domestic Abused Women's
Network (DAWN),
854-STOP
Driver's License
Central, 464-7331
Federal Way, 931-3934
Greenwood, 545-6755
North, 364-2830

Renton, 277-7230
West Seattle, 764-4137
Drug Abuse
   Alcohol and Drug Help Line,
   722-3700
   Drug Enforcement Adm.,
   442-5443
DWI Hot Line, 682-7437

Elder Citizen's Coalition,
   322-6188
Employment Security Dept.,
   464-6449
English Speaking Union,
   362-8330
Environmental Protection
   Agency, 442-1200
Evergreen Legal Services,
   464-5911
Evergreen Safety Council,
   526-1670

FBI, 622-0460
FCC, 764-3324
Federal Information Center,
   800-726-4995
Federal Job Information
   Center, 442-4365
Ferries, Sched. Info., 464-6400
Fire, 911
Flood Control, 296-8100
Food Stamps, 1-455-7058
Forest Fire Reports,
   800-562-6010
Friends of the Earth,
   633-1661

Garbage Dump Info.,
   684-7600
Govt. Printing Office
   Bookstore, 442-4270
Gray Line Tours, 624-5077
Grief Support Group Referral,
   326-4265
Gun Permits, 684-5500

Herpes Hot Line, 223-3272
Highway Conditions Report,
   1-976-ROAD (winter only)
Highway Dept. Info.,
   562-4009
Historic Preservation,
   622-6952
Human Rights Com.,
   464-6500

Immigration, 442-5956
Insurance Com., Consumer
   Info., 464-6262
IRS, 442-1040

Keep Washington Green
   Assoc., 543-2750
King County
   County Executive, 296-4040
   Elections Div., 296-1565
   Parks, 296-4232
   Veterans Aid, 296-7656
   Youth Service Dept.,
   296-5229
King County Medical Society,
   621-9393

Language Bank, 323-2345
League of Women Voters,
   329-4848
Liquor Control Bd., 464-6860
Lost Pets Hot Line, 283-7387

Marriage Licenses, 296-3933
Medic One, 911
Medicare, 800-234-5772
Metro Info., 447-4800
Metro Lost & Found,
   684-1585
Municipal League, 622-8333

Nat. Forest & Nat. Park Info.,
   442-0180
Newcomers Service, 622-6348

Northwest Road Report,
448-8611
Northwest Ski Report,
634-0071
Nursefinders, 328-1760

Organ Donor Assoc.,
800-422-3310

Pacific Science Center,
443-2001
Parking Meters (defective),
684-8763
Passports, 442-7941
Peace Corps, 442-5490
Pet Licenses, 386-4262
Phenomena Research,
722-3000
Pioneer Assoc., 325-0888
Planned Parenthood, 328-7700
Poaching Hot Line,
800-477-6224
Poison Information Center,
526-2121
Police, 911
Postal Info., 285-1650
Pothole Hotline, 684-7508 or
386-1218
Public Defender, 447-3900

Rape Relief, 632-7273
Recycling Info., 800-732-9253
Red Tide, 800-562-5632
Rubber Tree-ZPG, 633-4750

SCORE-Small Business Adm.,
442-8403
Seattle Arts Com., 684-7171
Seattle Center, 684-7200
Seattle Design Com., 684-0434
Seattle Div. on Aging,
684-0500
Seattle Harbor Tours,
623-1445

Seattle/King Co. Convention &
Visitors Bureau, 461-5840
Seattle Public Library Quick
Check, 386-4636
Senior Citizen's Info.,
448-3110
Sex Info. Line, 328-7711
Sexual Assault Center,
223-3047
Sierra Club, 621-1696
Small Bus. Adm., 442-5534
Soc. Sec. Adm., 800-234-5772
Space Needle, 443-2100
State Dept. of Ecology
Hotline, 800-732-9253
State Parks Info.,
800-562-0900 (summer only)
State Patrol (Seattle, Bellevue,
Mercer Is.)
Emergency, 911
Hero Hot Line, 764-4376
Other, 455-7700
Road Info, 455-7900
Steelheaders Hot Line,
526-8530

Tax Information
Bus. Tax, 684-8484
Employment Sec. Tax
(state), 545-6518 or
764-4290
Internal Rev., 442-1040
Real Estate Tax Statement,
296-3850
Sales Tax (excise), 464-6827
Social Security tax (federal),
800-234-5772
Tel-Med, 621-9450
Tel-Time, 1-976-1616
Transit Info., 447-4800
Travel Immunization,
296-4759
Traveler's Aid Soc., 461-3888
"Twin Peaks" Hotline
(KLSY-FM), 455-KLSY, ext. 222

Unemployment Ins., 545-6629

VD National Hot Line,
   800-227-8922
Veterans Adm., 624-7200
Veterans Hosp., 762-1010
Veterinary, 24-hr. answering
   serv., 284-9500
Visiting Nurse Assoc.,
   548-8100
VISTA, 721-2980
Voters Reg. Info., 344-5282

Wash. Advocates for the
   Mentally Ill, 783-9264 or
   800-782-9264
Wash. Pass Report,
   1-976-7623
Wash. State Employment
   Office, 464-5886

Wash. State Health Facilities
   (complaint info.),
   800-525-0127
Water, Sewer & Garbage Bills,
   684-5800
Whale Hotline, 800-562-8832
Widow Info. & Consultation,
   246-6142
Wild Animal Clinic,
   1-794-WILD
Wildlife Dept., State, 775-1311
Wood Burning Hotline,
   296-5100
Woodland Park Zoo (recording),
   684-4800

Youth Serv. Center, 323-9500

Zero Pop. Growth, 633-4750
Zip Code Info., 442-6200

Beyond the Yellow Pages

HEALTH

*If your child says there's a shark in the Ballard pool and he hasn't
   seen* Jaws:
   Animal Control, 386-4254.
If the raisins in your cereal are doing the Australian crawl:
   Consumer Products Safety, 442-5276.
For thrifty medical shopping:
   Tel-Med, 621-9450; ask to hear tape no. 19.
For the shot that is felt around the world:
   Travel Immunization, 296-4759.
If your doctor prescribes snake's eyes or bat wings:
   King County Medical Society, 621-9393.
To defuse the population bomb:
   Rubber Tree-ZPG, 633-4750.
If your frame is getting bottom heavy:
   TOPS, 772-4525.
Need help from above?
   Dial-A-Prayer, 282-4545.
If you have a crick in your sacroiliac:
   Washington Chiropractors Association, 1-235-4428.

SAFETY

If Snoopy and the Red Baron buzz your house:
Aircraft Accidents & Low Flying Complaints, 431-1300.
If you're lost in the people-mover at Sea-Tac:
Traveler's Aid Society, 461-3888.
If your safety razor wasn't:
Consumer Products Safety Commission, 442-5276.

ENVIRONMENT

To find out if Chicken Little is right:
Weather Service Forecast, 526-6087.
If you want to save a wild river:
Friends of the Earth, 633-1661.
When you can't see the Columbia Center Building at high noon:
Environmental Protection Agency, 442-1200.
If your neighbor's furniture is floating past your window:
Flood Control, 296-8100.
Was it a pileated woodpecker or a tommy gun?
Audubon Society, 523-4483.
To find out what's dining on your azaleas:
Arboretum Foundation, 325-4510.

PUBLIC SERVICES

If the last elevator ride gave you a nose bleed:
Elevator Permits & Inspections, 296-6600.
If you lost your VW bug in a chuckhole:
Street Maintenance, 386-1218.
If your neighbor is raising hogs:
Zone Code Information, 684-7899.
If your boat becomes a submarine:
Coast Guard, 442-7070.
The lifetime guarantee just died:
Consumer Complaints & Inquiries, 684-8811.
To set up your own sweatshop:
Minor's Work Permits, 281-5505.
To report WW III:
Civil Defense Emergency Services, 296-3830.
To prove you exist . . . or did:
Birth & Death Records, 296-4768.
For a list of jobs for somebody else:
Employment Security Department, 464-6449.
To create a ripple in the airwaves:
FCC, 764-3324.

If you've perfected perpetual motion:
   Department of Energy, 1-586-5000.
If you want to reroute the Columbia River alongside I-90:
   Army Corps of Engineers, 764-3742.
If your dog went out to make a mess on the neighbor's lawn and didn't come back:
   Animal Control Service, 386-4254.
To zip up your mail:
   Zip Code Information, 442-6200.
To find out how long it will take a Christmas card to get across town:
   Postal Information, 442-6255.
To find out if Rough Riders are eligible for VA loans:
   Veterans Administration, 624-7200.
To find out how much vacation you have left:
   Unemployment Insurance, 464-6449.
If you find Bigfoot:
   State Wildlife Department, 775-1311.
If your neighbor's plant just ate your fence:
   State Department of Ecology, 1-885-1900.
If you're sleeping alone and something nibbles your ear:
   Seattle Health Department, 296-4600.
If your spouse—and bank account—are missing:
   Missing Persons, 684-5582.
If you lost your seat on the bus:
   Metro Lost & Found, 684-1585.
If your beer tastes like water:
   Liquor Control Board Enforcement Office, 464-6094.
If you really can't get there from here:
   Highway Department Information, 455-7900.

MONEY

Does 83 percent compounded monthly sound a mite steep?
   Consumer Protection, 464-6684.
To find out how rich you'll be when you retire:
   Social Security Administration, 800-234-5772.
If even the loan sharks turn you down:
   Creditors Consulting Services, 223-1464.

CARS

To get rid of your neighbor's junk heap:
   Auto Impounds, 625-2061.

If your neighbor got yours first:
   Auto Theft, 911.
To hit the road to Lilliwaup:
   AAA Automobile Club of Washington, 448-5310.

HOMES

If you don't want your outhouse torn down:
   Historic Preservation, 296-4858.
If your gas range develops reverse thrusters:
   Washington Natural Gas, 464-1999.

THE LAW

If you want to make it legal and end a friendship:
   Marriage Licenses, 296-3933.
When a fellow really needs a friend:
   Public Defender, 447-3900.
To learn if your mother-in-law is deductible:
   Internal Revenue Service, 442-1040.

IF YOU'RE CURIOUS

To see the city from above:
   Space Needle, 443-2100.
To see the city from below:
   Underground Tour, 682-1511.
But if you don't want to burn your bridges or draft cards:
   Passports, 442-7941.
For the business boys in the white hats:
   Better Business Bureau, 448-8888.
If little green men land on your patio and it isn't Halloween:
   Phenomena Research, 722-3000.

Almanac

How Many Hills?

Seattle's hills have been the cause of much profanity and anxiety over the years. Although optimists praise them for their contributions to physical stamina and character development, most weary pedestrians have trouble believing that engineers slaved for decades with hydraulic pumps and conveyors to remove some hills entirely and to reduce sharply the grades on others. These ungrateful folks are inclined to dismiss the remarkable, expensive engineering achievements as token efforts and to condemn the founding fathers for failure to find a better townsite.

Over the years residents occasionally found satisfaction in noting that Seattle, like Rome, was built on seven hills. But cosmopolitans smile at the comparison, knowing how puny and ill-defined are the hills of the Holy City. And what neither ardent boosters nor complacent engineers can defend is the increase in number of the city's hills.

Originally the seven hills were Capitol, First, Magnolia, Queen Anne, Beacon, West Seattle, and Denny.

Then in 1950, city engineers determined that there were twelve after adding Renton, Sunset, Crown, Yesler, and Phinney Ridge.

Regarding comparative heights, West Seattle Hill leads with an elevation of 512 feet near 35th Ave. SW and W. Myrtle.

Magnolia Bluff and Sunset Hill are the most abrupt. In a distance of 500 feet, Magnolia ascends from the bay to a 200-foot elevation. Near W. 85th, Sunset Hill peaks at 305 feet after rising sharply from the sound.

Beacon Hill's highest point is 336 feet at Beacon Ave. and Holgate St.

Yesler, formerly "Profanity Hill" because of the cursing from people struggling up it, has two summits: 234 feet at 7th Ave. and Spruce St., and 256 feet near Broadway and 10th Ave.

First Hill rises steeply to 322 feet at Boren Ave. and Madison St., then more gradually for a few blocks to reach a peak of 339 feet.

Capitol Hill stands at 450 feet at the Volunteer Park water tower.

Before regrades, Denny Hill's summits at 2nd Ave. and Stewart St. and just north of Lenora St. were 212 feet and 225 feet. Now those levels are 143 feet and 142 feet.

Queen Anne Hill reaches a towering 456 feet near 1st Ave. N. and Lee St.

CITY OF SEATTLE—1900-1980

	1900	1910	1920	1930	1940	1950	1960	1970	1980
Total Population	80,671	237,194	315,312	365,583	368,302	467,591	557,087	530,831	493,846
White	76,815	227,753	302,580	350,639	354,101	440,424	510,559	463,870	396,275
Non-White	3,856	9,441	12,732	14,944	14,201	27,167	46,528	66,961	97,571
Black	406	2,296	2,894	3,303	3,789	15,666	26,901	37,868	46,565
Japanese	2,990	6,127	7,874	8,448	6,975	5,778	9,351	9,986	10,427
Chinese	438	924	1,351	1,347	1,781	2,650	4,076	6,261	9,430
Filipino	—	19	458	1,614	1,392	2,357	3,755	5,830	9,591
American Indian	22	24	106	172	222	666	1,729	4,123	6,158
Other	—	70	49	60	42	50	716	2,893	15,400

Percent Distribution

	1900	1910	1920	1930	1940	1950	1960	1970	1980
Total Population	100.00	100.00	100.00	100.00	100.00	100.00	100.00	100.00	100.00
White	95.22	96.02	95.96	95.91	96.14	94.19	91.65	87.39	80.24
Non-White	4.78	3.98	4.04	4.09	3.86	5.81	8.35	12.61	19.76
Black	0.50	0.97	0.92	0.90	1.03	3.35	4.83	7.13	9.43
Japanese	3.71	2.58	2.50	2.31	1.89	1.24	1.68	1.88	2.11
Chinese	0.54	0.39	0.43	0.37	0.48	0.57	0.73	1.18	1.91
Filipino	—		0.14	0.44	0.38	0.50	0.67	1.10	1.94
American Indian	0.03	0.01	0.03	0.05	0.06	0.14	0.31	0.78	1.25
Other	—	0.03	0.02	0.02	0.01	0.01	0.13	0.54	3.11

Source: U.S. Decennial Censuses of Population.

Crown Hill runs along at an even 335 feet on W. 85th St. from 11th to 15th Ave. NW.

Phinney Ridge, along Phinney and Greenwood avenues, reaches an elevation of 340 feet at N. 55th St. and 350 feet at N. 60th St.

The Department of Engineering's figures are street levels, measured on the "Seattle datum," which uses a longtime average of high tides as zero. Other methods of measurement, including that of the Coast and Geodetic Survey, start from a mean low-tide level. If you prefer this method, add about 13 feet to all the above figures.

1990 Census

The final count won't be in until well after press time, but the unofficial population for Seattle in the summer of 1990 was 512,094.

Seattle's Flag

Seattle is one of the few major cities without a flag. Many efforts have been made to gain official acceptance of a design, but officials have failed to act. Their reluctance has stemmed variously from artistic insecurity ("How do we know what good art is?") and arrogance, ("I don't know anything about art, but . . .").

Proposals for a flag made in the 1940s came to nothing. In 1964 designer William Werrbach submitted a flag to the City Council and Arts Council, but officials avoided the potentially disruptive issue.

Dr. William Goff, a surgeon and flag collector, offered Mayor Dorm Braman a flag in 1968 that featured alternating horizontal stripes of blue, green, and blue; a jet aircraft; the Space Needle; and the word *Seattle*. Braman complained that the flag's pictorial symbols might not survive the test of time. He favored the city seal on a plain background. He rejected the suggestion that the Arts Council choose a design because it was said that the council members liked abstract art.

The David Strong Design Group offered a flag in 1976, but it was not accepted.

It may be that officials are right to resist a flag, since any decision would provoke controversy and derision, thus threatening the very unity and loyalty a flag is supposed to encourage.

Seattle's Streets

The origin of names given to many Seattle streets is veiled in obscurity. Who was the Abelia of Abelia Court South? Was the Abraham of S. Abraham Place the biblical man or a lesser descendant?

Eventually all mysteries may be solved, including the city fathers' reason for using a double alphabet system to name major downtown streets: Jefferson, James; Cherry, Columbia; Marion, Madison; Spring, Seneca; University, Union; Pike, Pine. And who was the wag who coined an easy way of remembering the alphabetical sequence of JCMSUP while deriding the city: "Jesus Christ made Seattle under protest"?

STREET NAMES

Alder, Cherry, and Pine named for trees.

Alki Point was originally called Point Roberts after a crewman by Charles Wilkes, then New York-Alki by the original pioneers. *Alki* in Chinook jargon meant "by and by."

Bagley Avenue named for pioneer Dr. H. B. Bagley.

Ballard named in 1890 for W. R. Ballard, shingle manufacturer.

Ballinger Way named for Judge Richard A. Ballinger, early Seattle mayor and secretary of interior under Taft; or, like Lake Ballinger (Snohomish County), for Ballinger's father, Col. R. H. Ballinger. Richard owned the land around Lake Ballinger and named the lake for his father.

Battery Street may have been named because of the high bluff above the bay, which existed before regrading. The bluff suggested a battery placement point.

Bay Street so named because it ran to the waterfront.

Bell Street and Bellevue Avenue named for pioneer William N. Bell.

Blaine Street named for pioneer Rev. David Blaine.

Boren Avenue named for pioneer Carson D. Boren.

Bothell Way named for David C. Bothell, who established a shingle mill at Bothell in 1886.

Broad Street so named because it was intended to be unusually wide.

Bryn Mawr named after the Pennsylvania town and recalling a Welsh phrase meaning "big hill."

Burien Way named for Gottlieb Burian [sic] who settled Lake Burien in 1884.

Burke Street named for Judge Thomas Burke.

Capitol Hill named by realty promoters, who offered the site for the
state capitol.

Carkeek Drive S. named for Morgan J. Carkeek, who donated the
land, which later became the Sand Point Naval Air Station, to
the city.

Charles Street named for pioneer Charles Plummer.

Cherry Street perhaps named for Cherry Grove, Illinois, where the
pioneer Denny family lived before starting west, or for the fruit
tree.

Clay Street named for Henry Clay, U.S. senator.

Dearborn Street named for H. H. Dearborn and his brother, realty
promoters.

Decatur Place named for the U.S. Navy sloop that participated in
Seattle's Indian War.

Denny Way named for pioneer David T. Denny.

Duwamish River derived from Indian *dewampsh* meaning "the
people living on the river."

Elliott Bay (and Avenue) named by Capt. Charles Wilkes in 1841,
probably for Midshipman Samuel Elliott rather than for the
Reverend J. L. Elliott, chaplain of the U.S. Navy's Wilkes Expedition, who was in disfavor at the time.

Fauntleroy Cove named in 1857 by George Davidson of the U.S.
Coastal Survey for his girlfriend's father, Robert H. Fauntleroy, or (more likely) for his sweetheart, Elinor Fauntleroy.

Fortson Place named for Capt. George H. Fortson, killed in the
Philippines in 1899.

Fremont named for Fremont, Nebraska, by the Blewitt family and
L. H. Griffith.

Frink Boulevard named for pioneer J. M. Frink.

Hanford Street named for pioneer Edward Hanford.

Harrison, Jackson, Jefferson, Madison, and Washington streets
named for the presidents.

Holgate Street named for pioneer John Holgate.

Howell Street perhaps named for Capt. Jefferson D. Howell, captain of the coastal side-wheeler, the *Pacific*.

Inverness Drive named for the shape of the district, which resembles the Scottish Inverness cape favored by Sherlock Holmes
and others.

James Street named for James Marion Denny, brother of Arthur
and David Denny.

John Street named for pioneer John B. Denny.

Judkins Street named for Norman B. Judkins, developer of south
Seattle.

King County and King Street named for William Rufus King, thir-
teenth vice-president of the United States.

Kinnear Place named for pioneer George Kinnear.

Lake Union and Union Bay named by Thomas Mercer in 1854.

Lane Street named for James L. Lane, Oregon's territorial delegate to congress.

Lenora Street named for the daughter of Arthur Denny.

Leschi District and Park named for an Indian leader who fought the settlers and was convicted and hung for the murder of an army officer at Steilacoom.

Magnolia Bluff named by George Davidson of the U.S. Coastal Survey, who mistook native madrona trees for magnolia trees.

Main Street, the name traditionally given to what is expected to be the leading business street.

Marion Street named for James Marion Denny, brother of Arthur and David Denny, whose middle name recalled Francis Marion, the Swamp Fox of American Revolution fame.

Maynard Avenue named for pioneer Dr. David Maynard.

McGilvra Boulevard named for Judge John McGilvra.

Mercer Street named for Thomas Mercer.

Minor Avenue named for pioneer T. T. Minor.

Mount Rainier named by George Vancouver for Adm. Peter Rainier. The Indian name was Tah-ho-ma, and efforts to rename the mountain, usually by Tacoma residents, occur from time to time.

Occidental Street named for the Occidental Hotel, which was located on it.

Olive Way named for Olive Bell, wife of James A. Stewart and daughter of pioneer William N. Bell.

Phinney Avenue named for Guy C. Phinney, who laid out 286 acres later sold to the city for Woodland Park.

Pike Street named for John Pike, pioneer builder.

Piper's Road named for pioneer A. W. Piper.

Post Street named for pioneer J. J. Post, a millman.

Prefontaine Place named for pioneer Catholic priest, the Reverend F. X. Prefontaine.

Puget Sound named for an officer with Capt. George Vancouver.

Queen Anne Avenue and district named for the style of residential architecture favored in the early development of the area.

Renton Place named for Capt. William Renton, pioneer sawmill man.

Royal Brougham Way named for the longtime *PI* sports editor.

Salmon Bay named by Edward Carr and John Ross, the first white men on the bay who made claims there.

Seattle named for Chief Sealth.

Seneca Street named for Rev. David Blaine's hometown, Seneca Falls, New York, or for the Roman philosopher.

Skid Road named for log skid used when Yesler's Mill operated on the central waterfront.

Smith Cove named for Dr. Henry A. Smith, pioneer who lived there.

Spokane Street named for the Washington city, which in turn was named for an Indian tribe.

Spring Street named for nearby springs used by the original pioneers for water.

Stewart Street named for Joseph A. Stewart.

Summit Avenue perhaps named for its high location on Capitol Hill.

Surber Drive named for William H. Surber, the city's first sheriff, who homesteaded in Laurelhurst.

Terry Avenue named for pioneer Charles Terry.

Thomas Street named for pioneer D. Thomas Denny.

Union Street commemorates Civil War patriotism.

University Street so named because it ran directly to original university grounds.

Virginia Street named for the daughter of pioneer William N. Bell.

Volunteer Park named for First Washington Infantry in 1901 after the soldiers returned from the Philippines.

Weller Street named for John Weller, governor of California, by Dr. David Maynard.

West Seattle was originally named Lam's Point, Freeport, and Milton.

Yesler Way named for Henry S. Yesler.

Seattle's Nickname or Motto

For decades the city motto was "The Queen City of the Pacific Northwest." Recently the promotional tone of this motto has become suspect. In an age of ecumenicalism, anticolonialism, and humility, the "Queen City" boast seemed out of place. Then in 1981 a public contest determined a new motto: "The Emerald City." Some complaints have been noted, but the new nickname has caught on.

The Three Great Makers of Seattle

James R. Ellis, a champion of Metro, Forward Thrust (1950s–1970s), and the 1980 Convention Center, whose services to the city have been commemorated with a plaque in Freeway Park.

J. D. Ross, superintendent of the Department of Lighting (City

Light) from 1911 to 1937 and promoter of the Skagit dams and other means to provide cheap power.

Reginald H. Thomson, city engineer 1882–86, 1892–1911, 1930–31; the driving force behind the regrades and other improvements.

Projects Unrealized

Although the face of the city has changed remarkably over the years, there have been a number of planning and individual construction schemes that have not been carried out. Some of these have focused on particular problems like public transit or the rupture between downtown and the waterfront, and their completion might have improved the city. Here are some of the more notable unrealized projects. Most of the information is taken from the fascinating Ph.D. dissertation of Steven Cecil, University of Washington, *A Forgotten Future: One Possible Seattle*, 1981.

*   *   *

A Seattle Opera House Building, including a theater and apartment block, was planned in 1890 for 2nd Ave. and University Street by Alder and Sullivan after the great fire. Louis Sullivan, the famed Chicago architect, visited Seattle to present his design of a towered complex that would undoubtedly have become an architectural landmark, but the project was not realized. The building, resembling the Auditorium Theatre and Hotel in Chicago, would have been Seattle's first skyscraper.

*   *   *

The Olmsted Brothers' Park and Parkway Plan of 1903 included a 20-mile pleasure drive from Seward Park to Fort Lawton (now Discovery Park). Boulevards would connect landscaped residential areas along Lake Washington Blvd., Greenlake, Woodland Park, around north Queen Anne to Magnolia Bluff. Much of this naturalistic concept in transportation and city planning was eventually completed.

*   *   *

Mass Transit–Subway and Elevated Systems: 1906, 1907, 1918, 1920, 1926, 1968, 1970.

In the 1970 plan defeated by voters, there would have been 46.5 miles of track with termini in Ballard, Lake City, Bellevue, and

Renton, and the main line would have run under 3rd Ave. with a branch at Westlake to Capitol Hill.

All the earlier plans and arguments in support of them were similar. In 1925 the Seattle Rapid Transit *Report to the City Planning Commission* pointed out the loss in transit riders due to the fare increase in 1924 and the congestion and slow service downtown, caused by the increased numbers of automobiles. The report recommended elevated transit lines between South and West Seattle and downtown; and a subsurface line from 1st and Pike over Westlake and Eastlake to the University District. The elevated and subsurface lines would be supported by some surface lines but would eliminate many others. Other versions of the plan included subsurface lines up Pike Street to Lake Washington; a connection between the Ship Canal and Green Lake; and a line from 5th and Pike Street to Yesler Way.

The report stressed the time passengers would save and the comfort they could enjoy in covered waiting stations on elevated and subsurface lines.

*   *   *

A scheme was proposed in 1908 for the University's Metropolitan tract on 10 acres between Seneca and Union, and 4th and 5th avenues. It was conceived as a unifying core for the commercial district, similar to Rockefeller Center in New York. A hotel, department store, and apartment and office buildings were planned, all conforming to an eleven-story height and utilizing common building materials and design features. The Cobb Building and White-Henry-Stuart Building were built by Howells and Stokes following this plan, but the latter was razed for Rainier Square in 1975.

*   *   *

A 1908 master plan by A. Warren Gould for the southern part of downtown featured a broad esplanade along 5th Ave. from Seneca to King St., lined with trees and terraces. Tunnels would have carried the intersecting streets to First Hill. The City Beautiful scheme would have given Seattle an impressive entry from the railroad stations.

*   *   *

The Central Building proposed in 1906 featured a fifteen-story block capped with a clock tower. Arthur L. Hawley and Judge W. D. Wood promoted the project, but their association could only raise enough capital to build the eight-story building that exists today.

* * *

A 1911 civic center plan by Myers and Henley called for nine buildings, including the city hall and library between 3rd and 6th avenues and Columbia and Spring streets. Slope problems were overcome by a network of subsurface passages leading to elevators in the nine buildings.

* * *

Graham and Myers proposed Union St. and dock improvements in 1910. The plan called for a series of street bridges from 1st Ave. to a huge dock with buildings on Elliott Bay. Traffic would have been carried over Alaskan Way, Western Ave., and Post Alley; and two giant loops would have provided tramways to deck level.

* * *

Another 1910 plan for a civic center by Gould and Champney had some similarities to Gould's 1908 plan for the same southern section of downtown. New streets and buildings would be built in the vicinity of city hall, the train stations, and the waterfront.

* * *

The Bogue Plan of 1911 envisioned a city possibly as magnificent as London. Downtown there would be a grand civic center, new highways and boulevards, a subway system, and several waterfront projects, including an imposing water gate entry to the city. The civic center would extend from 4th Ave. and Blanchard and be reached by a grand boulevard from downtown. There would be a new rail terminal on Lake Union. Rapid transit would be provided by a 3rd Ave. subway.

* * *

A 1913 Waterfront Terminal designed by Howells and Stokes planned five piers from Lenora to Pike St. and included huge factories. Beneath the factories there was a railroad terminal; above them there was a park and beer garden. Pike Place and Western Ave. would have become tunnels to the east of the railroad depot's waiting room. An office and hotel complex would have towered over the complex along 1st Ave. Under 1st Ave. there would have been three levels of subways. A staggering cost of $20 million may have deterred investors.

*   *   *

In 1932 J. Lister Holmes designed an office tower for the triangle formed by 2nd Ave., James St., and Yesler Way (formerly occupied by the Occidental Hotel until the 1889 fire, and then by the Hotel Seattle). The new tower of thirty-eight stories might have led to the early "Manhattanization" of Seattle had it been built. Instead the hotel was eventually razed and replaced by a parking lot.

*   *   *

A 1944 Pioneer Square plan by the chamber of commerce would have razed most buidings from King to Yesler between 1st and 2nd avenues and along the north side of Yesler Way to the waterfront. Most of the buildings would not have been replaced. Also included was a waterfront elevated highway, wide boulevards, trees, and a new ferry terminal. The main idea seemed to have been the elimination of Pioneer Square transients under the guise of civic improvement. The ugly waterfront viaduct was built later as a result of another plan.

*   *   *

Paul Thiry's 1961 freeway lid proposal between Marion and Pike streets was a bold answer to the new highway's severing of the city. All existing streets would cross over the freeway lid, and a broad new boulevard would run north-south along the lid. At each end of the tree-lined esplanade tall pylons would mark the entry to the city. A modification of Thiry's splendid plan (the projected cost was only $1.7 million) eventually resulted in Freeway Park, a modest but lovely contribution to the city.

*   *   *

Paul Thiry had another scheme in 1962 for a lid between Pike and Madison streets. Second Ave. and Elliott Bay offered a platform at 2nd Ave. level extending unbroken to the waterfront, reaching the bay level with a series of terraces. The Alaska Way Viaduct could have fit nicely within a tunnel under the platform. Parking for all the new buildings within the fifteen-block area would also be found on levels beneath the platform.

*   *   *

The 1963 Monson Plan for downtown Seattle was on the scale of the Bogue Plan and featured a road circling downtown and major reconstruction within the area, particularly on the waterfront and in the new Federal Building neighborhood. The plan would answer transportation needs and leave the central commercial core intact but destroy Pioneer Square and the Pike Place Market.

*   *   *

The 1968 Better City Plan for the Westlake area was one of several that have stirred controversy over that part of downtown for several years. More recent schemes, including one supported by the city that includes space for the Seattle Art Museum, have not been acted upon.

*   *   *

Fred Bassetti and Company designed a World Trade Center in 1969, which featured three high tower blocks housing offices, apartments, and a hotel. The entire area of Piers 50 and 51 would be decked at 30 feet above Alaskan Way. Pedestrians could reach the towers across landscaped open spaces or from tiers holding parking areas and shops below the deck's surface.

*   *   *

Pike Plaza, designed in 1971 by Brady and Johanson, would have retained the Public Market but otherwise reconstructed the area with a hotel and housing complex just west of 1st Ave. Three modular units would have accommodated five thousand residents with a parking area provided below the surface.

*   *   *

The Rockwise Waterfront Plan of 1972 for Piers 48 through 66 arose out of the Forward Thrust proposal for a waterfront park. While the park was the plan's core, it was also designed to accommodate Bassetti's World Trade Center plan (1969) and the Pike Plaza plan (1971). Features included a public marina, marine entertainment center, hotel, restaurants, and thirteen hundred residential units. The plan would have tied the waterfront to the city with a funicular and terraced housing. Only the park has been built.

Seattle Symphony Conductors

Harry West	1903–7
Michael Kegrize	1907–9
Henry Hadley	1909–11
John Spargur	1911–21
Mme. Davenport-Engberg	1921–24
Karl Krueger	1926–32
Basil Cameron	1932–38
Nikolai Sokoloff	1938–41
Sir Thomas Beecham	1941–44
Carl Brichen	1944–48
Eugene Linden	1948–50
Manuel Rosenthal	1950–51
Milton Katims	1954–76
Rainer Miedel	1976–83
Gerard Schwarz	1984–

Seattle's Mayors

Henry A. Atkins	1869–70, 1870–71
John T. Jordan	1871–72
Corliss P. Stone	1872–73
Moses R. Maddocks	1873
John Collins	1873–74
Henry L. Yesler	1874–75, 1885–86
Bailey Gatzert	1875–76
Dr. Gideon A. Weed	1876–77, 1877–78
Beriah Brown	1878–79
Orange Jacobs	1879–80
L. P. Smith	1880–81, 1881–82
Henry G. Struve	1882–83, 1883–84
John Leary	1884–85
William H. Shoudy	1886–87
Thomas J. Minor	1887–88
Robert Moran	1888–89, 1889–90
Harry W. White	1890, 1890–91
George W. Hall	1891–92
James T. Ronald	1892–94
Byron Phelps	1894–96
Frank D. Black	1896
W. D. Wood	1896–97
Thomas I. Humes	1897–1904 (four terms)
Richard A. Ballinger	1904–6

William Hickman Moore	1906–8
John F. Miller	1908–10
Hiram C. Gill	1910–11, 1914–18
George W. Dilling	1911–12
George F. Cotterill	1912–14
Ole Hanson	1918–19
C. B. Fitzgerald	1919–20
Hugh Caldwell	1920–22
Edwin J. Brown	1922–24, 1924–26
Bertha K. Landes	1926–28
Frank E. Edwards	1928–30, 1930–31
Robert H. Harlin	1931–32
John F. Dore	1932–34, 1936–38
Charles L. Smith	1934–36
Arthur B. Langlie	1938–40, 1940–41
John E. Carroll	1941
Earl Millikin	1941–42
William F. Devin	1942–51
Allan Pomeroy	1952–56
Gordon S. Clinton	1956–64
James D. Braman	1964–69
Floyd C. Miller	1969
Wesley C. Uhlman	1969–77
Charles Royer	1978–90
Norm Rice	1990–

Chiefs of Police

Thomas S. Russell	1865–67
William H. Surber	1867
Hillary, Butler, Prosch	1868
John L. Jordan	1869–70
L. V. Wycoff	1871–72
F. A. Minnick	1872–73
D. H. Webster	1873–74
L. V. Wycoff	1874–75
R. H. Turnbull	1875–76
E. A. Thorndike	1876–77
F. A. Minnick	1877–78
E. A. Thorndike	1878–79
J. J. McGraw	1879–80
J. H. Woolery	1881–86
W. M. Murphy	1886–88
H. G. Thornton	1889–90

George C. Munroe	1890
Bolton Rogers	1890–92
Andrew Jackson	1892–94
D. F. Willard	1894
Bolton Rogers	1894–98
C. S. Reed	1898–1900
William Meredith	1900–02
John Sullivan	1903
Thomas R. Delaney	1904–6
Charles Wappenstein	1906–8
Irving Ward	1908–10
Charles Wappenstein	1910–11
Michael T. Powers	1911
Claude G. Bannick	1911–14
Austin Griffiths	1914–16
Louis Lang	1916
C. L. Beckingham	1916–18
J. F. Warren	1918–20
W. H. Searing	1920–22
W. B. Severyns	1922–24
W. B. Severyns	1924–25
Claude G. Bannick	1926
W. B. Severyns	1926
W. H. Searing	1926–28
Louis J. Forbes	1928–31
William B. Kent	1931–32
L. L. Norton	1932–34
G. H. Comstock (Acting)	1935
George F. Howard	1935–36
Charles L. Smith	1936
William H. Sears	1936–41
Walter B. Kirtley	1942
Herbert D. Kimsey	1942–46
George D. Eastman	1946–52
H. J. Lawrence	1952–61
Frank Ramon	1961–69
M. E. Cook	1969
Frank Moore	1969
Charles R. Gain (Acting)	1970
Edward M. Toothman	1970
George P. Tielsch	1970–74
Robert L. Hanson	1974–78
H. A. (Bud) Vanden Wyer	1978–79
Patrick S. Fitzsimons	1979–

Fire Chiefs

Garner Kellog	1889–92, 1896–1901
A. B. Hunt	1892–94
Alex Allen, Jr.	1895
William H. Clark	1895, 1911
Ralph Cook	1895–96, 1901–6
Henry Bringhurst	1906–10
John H. Bayle	1910–11
Frank L. Stetson	1911–20
George M. Manton	1920–31
Robert L. Laing	1931–32
Claude W. Corning	1932–38
William Fitzgerald	1938–63
G. F. Vickery	1963–72
J. N. Richards	1972–74
G. A. Shelton	1974
Frank R. Hansen	1974–80
Robert L. Swartout	1980–

Seattle Has Worried Most About . . .

Paving Lake Washington.
The R. H. Thomson Freeway.
Wobblies.
Destruction of the Pike Place Market.
Boeing unemployment.
A declining school population (down 41 percent in the last decade).
Invidious comparisons with San Francisco.
Failures of the Mariners and Seahawks.
Rain.
Reckless growth.
Lack of recognition.
New Hoovervilles.

Seattle Is Most Proud Of . . .

Pike Place Market.
Nordstrom's.
Boeing Airplanes.
Waterfronts.
Group Health Cooperative.

Mount Rainier and other natural surroundings.
Burke-Gilman Trail.
Fire Department.
Seattle Opera Company and the Wagner Festival.
Children's Hospital.
Arboretum.
Forward Thrust bond program for parks.
Magic Carpet (free downtown bus service).
Low power rates.
Floating bridges.
Houseboats.
Smith Tower, Olympic Hotel, Washington Mutual Tower, and Chinatown (International District).

Seattle's Skyline

City skylines are always changing, and Seattle's is no exception. Older buildings are added on to, and new ones continually rise up to tower over their predecessors.

Responsible for much of Seattle's skyline is John Skilling, who has been a structural engineer for forty years. His firm has engineered 140 building projects here, as well as the steel and concrete skeletons of more than one thousand buildings worldwide.

Building heights are given for number of stories and feet from street level. A story is usually about 10 feet but can be less than 9 feet to more than 12 feet. The year given is when the major construction was completed or when construction was expected to be finished.

Bank of California Center, 4th Ave. & Madison St.
    42 stories, 536 feet, 1973
Bay Vista, 2nd Ave. & Broad St.
    24 stories, 250 feet, 1982
1600 Bell Plaza, 7th Ave. & Pine St.
    33 stories, 456 feet, 1976
Century Square, 4th Ave. & Pike St.
    29 stories, 336 feet, 1985
Columbia Seafirst Center, 4th Ave. & Cherry St.
    76 stories, 943 feet, 1985
Continental Place, 1st Ave. & Blanchard St.
    34 stories, 320 feet, 1981
Crowne Plaza Hotel (Park Hilton), 6th Ave. & Seneca St.
    33 stories, 352 feet, 1979
Exchange Building, 2nd Ave. & Marion St.
    23 stories, 275 feet, 1929

First Hill Plaza, Summit Ave. & Madison St.
    33 stories, 344 feet, 1982
First Interstate Center, 3rd Ave. & Marion St.
    48 stories, 574 feet, 1983
Fourth and Blanchard Building
    24 stories, 360 feet, 1979
Grandview Condominium, 3rd Ave. & Blanchard St.
    27 stories, 235 feet, 1979
Henry M. Jackson Federal Building, 2nd Ave. & Madison St.
    37 stories, 487 feet, 1973
Hilton Hotel Downtown, 6th Ave. & University St.
    25 stories, 260 feet, 1971
IBM Building, 5th Ave. & Seneca St.
    20 stories, 272 feet, 1963
Kingdome, 201 S. King St.
    250 feet, 1973
Madison Hotel, 6th Ave. & Madison St.
    27 stories, 296 feet, 1983
Marsh and McLennan Building, 8th Ave. & Olive Way
    19 stories, 273 feet, 1981
Metropolitan Park Plaza, Minor Ave. & Olive Way
    20 stories, 260 feet, 1980
Norton Building, 2nd Ave. & Columbia St.
    21 stories, 310 feet, 1959
One Union Square, 6th Ave. & University St.
    38 stories, 456 feet, 1980
Pacific Building, 3rd Ave. & Columbia St.
    22 stories, 298 feet, 1969
Pacific Science Center, 200 2nd Ave.
    100 feet, 1962
Park Place, 6th Ave. & University St.
    21 stories, 270 feet, 1971
Peoples Bank Building, 1414 4th Ave.
    20 stories, 266 feet, 1973
Plaza 600 Building, 6th Ave. & Stewart
    20 stories, 270 feet, 1969
Rainier Bank Tower, 5th Ave. & University St.
    42 stories, 514 feet, 1977
Royal Crest Condominium, 3rd Ave. & Lenora St.
    26 stories, 230 feet, 1973
Royal Manor Condominium, 8th Ave. & Seneca St.
    21 stories, 181 feet, 1970
Safeco Plaza, Brooklyn Ave. NE & NE 45th St.
    22 stories, 325 feet, 1973
Seafirst Building, 4th Ave. & Madison St.
    50 stories, 609 feet, 1969

Seafirst Fifth Avenue Plaza, 5th Ave. & Marion St.
    42 stories, 543 feet, 1981
Seattle Tower, 3rd Ave. & University St.
    27 stories, 314 feet, 1929
Sheraton Seattle Hotel, 7th Ave. & Pike St.
    34 stories, 371 feet, 1982
Sixth and Pike Building
    29 stories, 360 feet, 1983
Smith Tower, 2nd Ave. & Yesler Way
    42 stories, 500 feet, 1914
Space Needle, Seattle Center
    605 feet, 1962
1111 Third Avenue Building
    35 stories, 454 feet, 1980
Tower 801, 8th Ave. & Pine St.
    24 stories, 237 feet, 1970
Two Union Square Building, 6th & Union
    58 stories
Unigard Financial Center, 4th Ave. & University St.
    30 stories, 389 feet, 1972
Washington Athletic Club, 6th Ave. & Union St.
    22 stories, 232 feet, 1930–72
Washington Building, 4th Ave. & Union St.
    21 stories, 293 feet, 1960
Washington Mutual Tower, 1201 Third Ave.
    55 stories, 730 feet, 1988
Washington Park Tower, 43rd Ave. E. & E. Blaine St.
    21 stories, 289 feet, 1969
Washington State Convention and Trade Center, 8th Ave. & I-5
    under construction
Watermark, 1st Ave. & Spring St.
    22 stories, 244 feet, 1983
Westin Building, 6th Ave. & Virginia St.
    34 stories, 410 feet, 1981
Westin Hotel, 5th Ave. & Stewart St.
    40 stories, 397 feet, 1969
    second tower
    44 stories, 448 feet, 1982

Sources: *Seattle Times/Seattle Post-Intelligencer, Pacific* magazine, January 5, 1986; *Seattle Times/Seattle Post-Intelligencer*, May 20, 1984.

1980 CENSUS NEIGHBORHOOD STATISTICS

Neighborhood	Estimated Population	Generalized Boundaries (Precise census data boundaries may vary somewhat but with only slight impact on population)
Bitter Lake	3,500	City limits, Aurora, 130th, Puget Sound
North Haller Lake	3,600	City limits, I-5, 130th, Aurora
Pinehurst	5,300	City limits, 15th, 107th, Roosevelt, 115th, I-5
Olympic Hills	6,000	City limits, 30th, 125th, 19th, 130th, 15th, Jackson Golf Course
Cedar Park	4,000	City limits, Lake Washington, 125th, Sand Point Way, 120th, Hiram, 125th, 30th
Matthews Heights	6,700	120th, Sand Point Way, 125th, Lake Washington, 95th, 43rd, 98th, 35th, 110th, 30th, 105th, Lake City Way
Victory Heights	4,100	125th, Hiram, Lake City Way, 100th, 15th
South Haller Lake	3,100	130th, 5th, 115th, Roosevelt Way, Northgate Way, 110th, Aurora
Broadview	7,300	130th, Aurora, 110th, Carkeek Park, Puget Sound
North Beach	4,400	Puget Sound, 100th, 24th, 96th, 20th, 85th, Golden Gardens
Viewlands/Crown Hill	6,600	Puget Sound, Carkeek Park, 1st, Holman Rd., 15th, 85th, 20th, 96th, 24th, 100th
North Greenwood	4,100	Holman Rd., Greenwood Ave., 85th, 15th
Oaklake	9,500	110th, Meridian, 85th, Greenwood
Olympic View	3,600	Northgate Way, Roosevelt Way, 85th, Meridian
Sacajawea	3,900	106th, 15th, 100th, Lake City Way, 85th, Roosevelt Way

West Wedgewood	6,800	105th, 30th, 110th, 35th, 80th, 32nd, 75th
East Wedgewood	4,400	98th, 44th, 95th, Lake Washington, 85th, 45th, 75th, 35th
View Ridge	6,700	75th, 45th, 85th, Lake Washington, 65th, 35th
Hawthorne Hills/ Windermere	5,600	65th, Lake Washington, NE 50th, 50th NE, Sand Point Way
Bryant	9,000	75th, 35th, 65th, 40th, Sand Point Way, 25th
Roosevelt/Ravenna	6,900	85th, 20th, 75th, 25th, Ravenna Park, 60th, Roosevelt Way
East Greenlake	9,900	85th, Roosevelt Way, 60th, Greenlake, Aurora
West Greenlake	6,700	85th, Aurora, 50th, Greenwood
Phinney Ridge	9,500	85th, Greenwood, 50th, 3rd, 65th, 8th
Whittier Heights	9,300	85th, 8th, 65th, 24th
Loyal Heights/Sunset Hills	8,000	Golden Gardens, 85th, 24th, 65th, 32nd, Ship Canal, Puget Sound
Adams	6,800	65th, 15th, Ship Canal, 32nd
West Woodland	6,500	65th, 3rd, 46th, 8th, Ship Canal, 15th
Fremont	6,900	50th, Aurora, Ship Canal, 8th, 46th, 3rd
Wallingford (North)	8,500	65th, I-5, 44th, Aurora, Green Lake
Wallingford (South)	9,200	44th, I-5, Ship Canal, Aurora
University Heights	14,600	60th, Ravenna Park, 25th, 45th, 15th, 40th, I-5
University Campus	4,400	45th, Union Bay Pl., 41st, 38th, Union Bay, Ship Canal, I-5, 40th, 15th
Laurelhurst	5,400	45th, Sand Point Way, 50th, 50th, Lake Washington, 38th, 41st, Union Bay Pl.
Lawton	8,400	Puget Sound, Ship Canal, 15th, Dravus, 30th, Barrett, 36th, Emerson

Briarcliff/Carleton Park	5,300	Emerson, 36th, Barrett, 34th, Puget Sound
Southeast Magnolia	5,600	Barrett, 30th, Dravus, 17th, Puget Sound, 34th
Mount Pleasant	8,700	Dravus, 6th, Roy, 3rd, McGraw, 1st, Howe, 4th, Galer, 3rd, Kinnear, 5th, Elliott Bay, 14th, McGraw, 14th
North Queen Anne	6,400	Ship Canal, Aurora, Queen Anne Dr., Smith, 1st, McGraw, 3rd, Roy, 6th, Dravus, 14th
East Queen Anne	6,000	Lake Union, Crockett, Aurora, Comstock, 6th, Galer, Taylor, Garfield, 4th, Prospect, Queen Anne, McGraw, 1st, Smith, Queen Anne Dr.
South Queen Anne	9,000	Howe, Queen Anne, Prospect, 4th, Garfield, Taylor, Galer, 6th, Comstock, Aurora, Denny Way, Elliott Bay, Mercer, 5th, Kinnear, 3rd, Galer, 4th
Eastlake	3,300	Lake Union, I-5, Howe
North Broadway	3,300	Ship Canal, Evergreen Point Freeway, Hwy. 520, Interlaken, Boren Park, Howe, I-5
Montlake	3,600	Ship Canal, Arboretum, Interlaken Blvd., Roanoke cutoff, Hwy. 520, Portage Bay
Madison Park	5,300	Ship Canal, Lake Washington, Mercer, Arboretum
Stevens	10,400	Interlaken Blvd., Arboretum, Madison, 15th, Boren Park
Broadway	8,300	Howe, 15th, Madison, Union, Broadway, Roy, I-5
Southwest Capitol Hill	7,100	Roy, Broadway, Pike, I-5
Cascade	2,200	Howe, I-5, Olive, Westlake, Denny, Aurora, Crockett, Lake Union
Denny Regrade/Pike Place	3,400	Denny Way, Westlake, Stewart, 2nd, Blanchard, Elliott Bay
Downtown	900	Blanchard, 2nd, Stewart, 5th, Cherry, 1st, Columbia, Elliott Bay

Pioneer Square	1,200	Columbia, 1st, Cherry, 5th, Yesler, 4th, Jackson, Elliott Bay
First Hill	7,400	Olive, Melrose, Pike, Broadway, Union, 12th, Jefferson, 9th, James, I-5, Cherry, 5th
Yesler Terrace	2,000	Cherry, I-5, James, 9th, Jefferson, 12th, Jackson, I-5, Yesler, 5th
International District	1,600	Yesler, I-5, Dearborn, 5th, Jackson, 4th
Mann/Minor	10,100	Madison, Empire Way, Yesler, 12th
Harrison	2,300	Mercer, Lake Washington, Madrona Dr., Denny, Empire
Madrona	4,500	Denny, Madrona Dr., Lake Washington, Cherry, Empire
Leschi	5,500	Cherry, Lake Washington, Norman, Empire
Atlantic	4,700	Yesler, Empire, Rainier, 12th
Alki	5,000	Puget Sound, Bronson Way, California Way, Hillside, 56th, Charleston, 52nd, Oregon, Puget Sound
North Admiral	11,500	Hillside, California Way, Harbor Ave., Charleston, 55th
Genesee	7,900	Charleston, Avalon Way, Fauntleroy Way, Edmunds, 52nd
North Beacon	10,900	Dearborn, Corwin Pl., I-90, Rainier, Columbia Way, Snoqualmie, I-5
Mount Baker	10,000	Norman, Lake Washington, 50th, Snoqualmie, Rainier, Empire
Seward Park	4,000	Lake Washington, Kenyon, Seward Park Ave., Graham, 51st, Wilson, 50th
Columbia	9,800	Rainier, Alaska, Snoqualmie, 50th, Wilson, 51st, Graham, Empire
Dearborn Park	6,900	Snoqualmie, Columbian Way, Empire Way, Holly, 32nd, Morgan, Graham, I-5
Georgetown/Industrial	2,200	Jackson, 5th, Dearborn, I-5, city

		limits, Duwamish River, 1st, Marginal Way, Waterway, Elliott Bay
North Delridge	3,200	Avalon Way, Spokane, Marginal, Brandon, 35th
Fairmount Park	5,100	Edmunds, Fauntleroy, 35th, Graham, California
Seaview	4,900	Oregon, 52nd, Edmunds, California, Fauntleroy, Holly, 48th, Puget Sound
Gatewood	6,400	48th, Holly, Fauntleroy, Graham, 35th, Thistle, Lincoln Park, Puget Sound
High Point	4,300	Brandon, Delridge, Othello, 35th
Riverview	2,000	Brandon, Marginal, Highland Pk. Way, Holden, Dumar Dr., Delridge Way
Fauntleroy	4,800	Lincoln Park, Thistle, 35th, Roxhill, Marine View Dr., Puget Sound
Arbor Heights	6,500	Roxbury, city limits, Marine View Dr.
Roxhill	2,700	Othello, 26th, Roxbury, 35th
South Delridge	3,100	Orchard, Dumar Way, 16th, Roxbury, 26th
Highland Park	4,800	Holden, Highland Park Way, SR509, city limits, 16th
South Park	2,800	Duwamish River, 96th, SR509, 1st
South Beacon	5,300	Graham, 31st, Morgan, 28th, Myrtle, Holden, Norfolk, I-5
Holly Park	2,500	Morgan, 32nd, Holly, Empire, Holden, Myrtle, 28th
Brighton	6,600	Graham, Seward Park, Kenyon, Empire
Dunlap	4,000	Kenyon, Lake Washington, Rainier, 51st, Fletcher, Empire
Emerson	7,700	Fletcher, 51st, Rainier, Lake Washington, city limits, I-5, Norfolk, Empire Way
TOTAL	502,200	

A Chronology
of Seattle's History

1792
Captain George Vancouver lands near Everett.

1841
Lieutenant Charles Wilkes surveys Puget Sound and names Elliott Bay.

1851
John C. Holgate explores Puget Sound from Olympia to the Snoqualmie River in July and August and decides the Duwamish area is the best. He stakes a claim and goes back to Oregon to recruit some neighbors. When he comes back, Luther Collins has covered his claim with his own, so Holgate moves farther south. His brother-in-law, Edward Hanford, files just south of his claim.

On September 15, a party consisting of Luther M. Collins and his wife and daughter; Henry Van Asselt; and Jacob Maple and his wife and son arrive by land and stake claims on the bank of the Duwamish River near the site of Georgetown. They immediately plant a garden, and when the more famous Denny party arrives, they sell them potatoes.

On September 28, David Denny, John Low, and Lee Terry reach Alki Point and build the first cabin in the area. Arthur Denny and twenty-one others land at Alki Point from the schooner *Exact* from Portland on November 13 in the rain and are greeted by the advance party. The pioneers had migrated over the Oregon Trail to Portland earlier in the year.

The members of the so-called Denny party were Mr. and Mrs. Arthur Denny, Mr. and Mrs. John Low, Mr. and Mrs. Carson Boren, Mr. and Mrs. William Bell, Mr. David Denny, Miss Louisa Boren, Mr. Charles Terry, and Mr. Lee Terry. The Dennys had three children, the Lows had four, the Borens had one daughter, and the Bells had four daughters.

The Hudson Bay side-wheeler, the *Beaver*, arrives and is the first steamer on Puget Sound.

1852
Arthur Denny, Carson Boren, and William Bell relocate to the east side of Elliott Bay on February 15. The settlement is called Duwamps because of its proximity to the Duwamish River. Later

the settlement is renamed Seattle at the suggestion of a newcomer, Dr. David S. Maynard, who made friends with the Indian leader named Sealth.

Seattle becomes the seat of King County, which was created on December 22.

Robert W. Moxlie is hired to make a twice-weekly canoe trip to Olympia for mail. He charges $.25 for each letter sent or received.

The first vessel to load at Seattle is the brig *John David*, skippered by Capt. George Plummer, which arrives in April.

The first white female child born in Seattle, on September 18, is the daughter of George McConaha.

First divorce in King County is Dr. David S. Maynard by power of the Oregon legislature, December 2, from the wife he left behind in Ohio.

First religious service is conducted by Catholic Bishop Modeste Demers.

1853

First marriage certificate is issued in King County, on January 23, attested by Dr. David S. Maynard, justice of the peace, who performed the ceremony uniting David T. Denny and Louisa Boren, both members of the settlers' party.

First schoolteacher is Catherine Blaine, wife of the Reverend David Blaine. She starts teaching in January 1854.

Yesler's cookhouse for sawmill workers is the city's first restaurant.

Felker House opens; Seattle's first hotel, which survives until the fire of 1889.

On July 23, Dr. Maynard sells the northeast corner of 1st S. and Washington St. to Franklin Matthias for $20, which is the first real-estate transaction in Seattle.

Washington Territory is formed on April 25.

Plan of Seattle is filed with territorial government on May 23.

First post office is established in August with Arthur A. Denny as postmaster.

First white male child born in Seattle is Orion O. Denny, son of Arthur A. and Mary A. Denny, on July 17.

Henry Yesler arrives in Seattle in October.

First schoolhouse in King County is opened on Van Asselt's land claim.

First American steamboat to arrive on Puget Sound is the *Fairy*.

First election in Seattle, for a delegate to the Oregon territorial legislature. Arthur A. Denny is elected.

Luther Collins takes in the first fruit crop in Seattle. His apple trees bear a bumper crop he estimates is worth $5,000.

1854

Washington Territory is formed by taking the area north of the Columbia River from Oregon Territory.

The city's first trial occurs when a ship captain is charged with the unlawful dumping of his rock ballast into Elliott Bay.

1855

The first public relief case in King County is that of Charlie Hanson.

Seattle's first church is constructed, a Methodist church at 2nd and Columbia. The Reverend David Blaine is pastor.

Henry Yesler builds Seattle's first water system connected to a spring by wooden troughs.

1856

In January, Klickitat Indians cross Snoqualmie Pass and Lake Washington to join a group of local Indians for an attack on Seattle. The battle occurs on January 26 at 1st Ave. S. near Main, where a howitzer shell lands from the USS *Decatur* and small-arms fire of the sailors and marines drives off the attackers. Two white men and several Indians are killed before the battle ends.

1857

Dr. Maynard trades his 260 acres south of Yesler Way for 320 acres at Alki Point, which he sells in 1868 for $460.

Population is 250.

1861

Territorial University opens with thirty-one students.

Temperature down to 4 degrees below zero, 2 feet of snow falls, and 6-inch-thick ice forms on lakes.

1862

Population is 350.

University of Washington is incorporated, with Daniel Bagley, Paul K. Hubbs, J. P. Keller, John Webster, Frank Clark, George A. Meigs, Calvin H. Hale, and Columbia Lancaster named first Board of Regents. Thomas M. Gatch is elected president, but he refuses to come because of a salary dispute. But twenty-five years later he comes as president and serves until 1897.

Transcontinental Telegraph reaches Seattle.

In June, Luther M. Collins, one of Seattle's founders, drowns in the Snake River.

1863

Newspaper, *Washington Gazette*, is first published on August 15, although it is printed in Olympia until December 10.

1864

Coal mines are opened across Lake Washington at Coal Creek.

The eleven Mercer Girls (Civil War widows and orphans from back East recruited by Asa Mercer) arrive on May 16 to be greeted joyously by bachelors in search of brides. Only one—Lizzie Ordway—remained single.

1865

City is incorporated on January 18.

1866

Chief Sealth dies on June 7 and is buried at Suquamish, across the sound from his namesake city.

In June the temperature reaches 114 degrees in the shade.

After much travail and recriminations, Asa Mercer arrives in Seattle with the second batch of Mercer Girls.

Telegraph line is strung between Seattle and Victoria by way of Lopez and San Juan islands.

1867

The *Weekly Intelligencer* begins publishing on August 5.

First Catholic church is opened by Father F. X. Prefontaine for the ten Catholics in town.

Founder Charles C. Terry dies on February 17 at the age of 49.

1868

First wagon road is pushed through Snoqualmie Pass. Seattle residents help raise money for it, but the road is poorly built and hardly maintained, so it isn't used for many years.

No rain between July 1 and October 30, and forest fires threaten the city.

Library Association is founded.

Founder John C. Holgate is murdered near Silver City, Idaho, in mining dispute. He was 39 years old.

Henry Yesler builds new sawmill.

Dexter Horton builds city's first building of a material (stone) other than wood. The one-story 28 × 72-foot house stands on the west side of First Avenue S. near Washington.

1869

New city charter is promulgated on December 2 and Seattle is incorporated.

City's first ordinance prohibits public drunkenness.

First circus appears in Seattle, "The Great Eastern & Royal European." A local newspaper critic says it is "tame and insipid, and almost entirely devoid of merit."

The last elk killed in the city limits is brought down by David T. Denny and weighs 630 pounds.

1870

Population is 1,107.

Central school opens at 3rd and Marion with one hundred pupils.

Dexter Horton Bank is established on June 16.

Strawberries ripen on Thanksgiving Day due to an unusually hot autumn.

Fire department is organized, but when first fire occurs at the corner of Fifth and Cherry—in the most costly home in the territory, owned by James R. Robbins—there isn't enough hose to reach the slowly burning mansion, and there isn't any water in the system anyway.

Steamboat fares from Seattle are: Mukeltio, $1.50; Tulalip, $2; Coupeville, $2.50; Utsalady, $3; LaConner, $3.50; and Whatdcom, $4.

1871

First horse-drawn stage in Seattle goes from Seattle to Lake Washington along what is now Yesler Way.

A telegraph line is strung to Port Townsend after a Seattle boat captain, H. H. Hyde, pulls a scam by getting the election results of Sen. Seleucinus Garfielde's race while in Seattle. Then he steams over to Port Townsend, where nobody knows the results because there is no telegraph system, and bets on the outcome with several local citizens. They find him out, take him to court, and make him refund $100 to one man and pay the court costs. It isn't long before a telegraph line is strung.

1872

Population is 2,000.

On November 25, residents enjoy free rides on the coal train operating from Pike St. bunkers to Lake Union wharves.

First brick building in Seattle, Schwabacher Brothers.

Seattle's first baseball club, the Dolly Varden, is formed.

1873

Mayor Corliss P. Stone gives up his office and his business reputation when he goes to San Francisco to buy supplies for his firm and disappears. His partner absorbs the $15,000 loss, settles outstanding bills, and closes down—reflecting on Stone's treachery. Friends say Stone was considered an honest man but suffered from domestic problems. The *Washington Standard* of Olympia speculates that Stone's woes "had driven him to sacrifice his reputation as a dread alternative for ills that had become insupportable."

Seattle becomes the first grain shipping port in the territory.

First gas plant is built, with a capacity of 10,000 cubic feet of gas. Pipes are logs with holes bored in them.

1875

Lake Union freezes over in January, and so much ice comes down the Duwamish into Elliott Bay that Yesler's Wharf is blocked for several days.

Steamship service to San Francisco begins.

1876

University of Washington graduates its first college students.

James Colman buys Yesler's Wharf and completes Seattle and Walla Walla Railroad out to the Renton coal mines.

YMCA is established.

The ordinance of June 8 provides for the city's first regrade, which is 1st Ave. from Yesler Way to Pike St. and Yesler Way from 5th to 8th avenues.

City is $9,066 in debt.

First daily mail service starts from Tacoma.

1878

First phonograph is displayed at Yesler's Hall.

Twenty-four people die of diphtheria.

A vote for a new courthouse is defeated 435 to 157.

1879

Yesler Way is improved with a plank roadway.

First theater in Seattle is Squire's Opera House at Washington and 1st Ave. S.

Andrew Chilberg, representing Sweden and Norway, is the first consul of a foreign government in Seattle.

1880

Population is 3,553.

First hack is owned by John Hildebrand.

Elizabeth Holgate, a pioneer, dies on January 22 at age 84.

1882

Three men accused of murdering George B. Reynolds are taken from the courthouse by a lynch mob. On James St. the mob throws up a scaffold and hangs the suspected murderers. Judge Roger Greene of the state supreme court, who witnessed the lynching, summons a grand jury to consider evidence against the lynchers, but no indictments are returned.

On July 20, a Committee of Safety appoints twenty special policemen, who round up undesirables and order them out of town.

The first steamer to cross the Pacific from Seattle is the *Madras*, a British vessel of twenty-five hundred tons.

The first King County–owned courthouse opens at 3rd and Jefferson.

The first city hall also opens, on 2nd Ave. S. between Yesler Way and Washington St.

The city's first pipe organ is installed in the Church of Our Lady of Good Hope.

Seattle Chamber of Commerce is organized on April 17.

1883

Mary Kenworthy and other suffragettes secure voting rights for women.

First transcontinental rail connection via Tacoma is established, then stopped when the president of Northern Pacific Railroad, Henry Villard, a friend to Seattle, is replaced.

Denny Park becomes city's first.

1884

Telephone exchange is opened on March 7.

First horsecars go into service: Seattle Street Railway built about three miles of track, 2nd Ave. to Pike St. to 1st Ave. to Battery St., with a branch from Pike St. to Lake Union.

1885

Thomas Burke and Daniel Gilman organize the Seattle, Lake Shore, and Eastern Railroad. Although intended to tie Seattle with the Canadian Pacific to the north and Spokane to the east, the eastern line ends at Snoqualmie and the northern at Arlington.

Seattle General Hospital opens at 4th and Jefferson.

Regrading is done on twenty-eight streets, including 2nd, 3rd, 4th, and 9th avenues S.

1886

A mob charges into Chinatown on February 7 and 8, rounds up the Chinese, and marches them to the waterfront for boarding onto the *Queen of the Pacific*, bound for San Francisco. Thomas Burke, John J. McGraw, and other law-and-order advocates protest, and Governor Squire declares martial law. Five rioters are shot, one fatally, while resisting the army.

A small steam plant is built by Sidney Z. Mitchell and Fred H. Sparling to produce the city's first electricity. The first lights go on on March 22.

General William T. Sherman visits Seattle.

1887

George Kinnear donates land to the city for the park named in his honor.

To promote tourism, the steamer *Olympia* is put into service to run between Seattle and Alaska, but on the first run only three passengers show up, and the trip is cancelled. The ship loses $20,000 on the season.

1888

The Ladies Library Association is instrumental in establishing a permanent public library.

The first ferry in Seattle, the *City of Seattle*, begins operations to West Seattle.

The first cable railway, built by Fred E. Sander and associates, runs from Yesler Way and Occidental to Lake Washington with a return via Jackson St.

1889

The first electric streetcar goes into operation in April along Queen Anne Ave.

Stone and Webster acquires Union Electric Company.

Cataract Power Company receives the first electricity from the Snoqualmie Falls generating plant to Seattle.

Fire caused by overturned glue pot tended by John E. Back, in the cabinet shop owned by James McGough, levels the entire business district on June 6. The fire, which burns 64 acres—everything south of Union and west of Second—occurs just after the Johnstown Flood in Pennsylvania, and few people in America hear of it. Seattleites had collected $558 to send to Johnstown, and at a town meeting while the city is still smoldering, George B. Adair, in charge of the collection, tells the crowd that he still has the money and questions whether Seattle should keep it or send it on to Johnstown as originally planned. The choice is unanimous: Send it to Johnstown. The crowd also decides against asking for help but determines that it will accept it if it is offered. This makes a good impression on the Americans who hear of the fire, and soon $104,150 comes in as gifts: $22,049 from San Francisco, $13,024 from Portland, $9,958 from Spokane, $7,631 from Tacoma, etc.

First fish are planted in Lakes Union, Washington, and Sammamish—a total of 350,000 whitefish.

Seattle Post Office becomes second first-class post office north of San Francisco, Portland being the first.

1890

Population is 44,748.

Freeholders Charter is prepared by a convention.

A cougar is seen between Fourth and Fifth on Pike, and soon it kills a chicken. A local businessman, Eugene Chapin, shoots it.

1891

Seattle Pacific College is chartered.

President Benjamin Harrison visits on May 6.

On July 1, Fremont, Edgewater, Latona, Ross, Green Lake, and Boulevard are annexed to the city.

1892

Seattle College is founded.

R. H. Thomson becomes city engineer.

Population is 57,542.

Henry Yesler dies on December 16 at the age of 82.

1893

Great Northern Railroad reaches Seattle from Everett on June 18.

The present University of Washington campus is established.

The worst depression of the late nineteenth century strikes.

A massive snowstorm buries the city.

1894

Seattle becomes the first city in the nation with a municipally owned utility when it buys the Spring Hill water supply system.

Cornerstone is laid for Denny Hall on the University of Washington campus.

Many of Seattle's unemployed join Gen. Jacob Coxey's "army" to march on Washington, D.C.

A blue catfish weighing 6 pounds is caught in Lake Union.

1895

The American Protective Association, a politically ambitious organization made up primarily of British-born residents, campaigns against Catholic influences. After gaining successes in school-board elections, the APA candidates fail to win the county offices they sought, and the group fades away.

In June a project of filling tide flats south of Yesler begins and continues until July 1897.

Seattle and Lake Washington Waterway Company begins dredging the Duwamish River and uses the dredge spoils to begin building Harbor Island.

Street naming abolishes seven hundred old names and establishes an orderly naming system.

1896

On August 31, the *Miike Maru* arrives from Japan to establish the first contracted shipping route between Asia and the West Coast of America.

The first naval vessel, a torpedo boat, is built at the Moran shipyard.

1897

Fort Lawton (now Discovery Park) is established on 640 acres donated by the county, state, and private citizens.

The coastal steamer *Portland* arrives in Seattle on July 17 with triumphant Klondike miners carrying fortunes in gold. Hundreds of enterprising men and women quit their jobs to head north. Mayor W. D. Wood, who is in San Francisco when the news arrives, does not bother returning to Seattle. He wires his resignation, forms a mining company, leases a ship, and heads for the goldfields. To the comfort of moralists, Wood's abandonment of his fair city does not bring success; in fact, it brings great discomfort and financial loss.

1898

First Eagles Club organized by John Cort, John Considine, et al.

Cedar River pipeline right-of-way, 60 feet wide and 28 miles long, is acquired by the city in August for $25,000.

Police Chief Bolton Rogers and his men swoop down on the Skid Road district on a lively night to arrest every hustler working on King and Jackson streets between 3rd and 7th avenues. The police estimate that three hundred prostitutes were working in that area. Women of all races are represented, but Japanese are in the majority. The larger number of Japanese women indicates that the "slave" traffic, which arouses some concern later in 1908, had been well established earlier. Chief Rogers lets white women off with a lecture and no bail; Japanese women have to post $25 bail.

1898

First Ave. regrade from Pine to Denny Way is completed on January 6, and the dirt is used to fill Western and Railroad avenues.

United States government opens a gold assay office on July 1 because of the city's importance as a Klondike gold-rush terminal. The Nome gold rush has ensured the city's continued prosperity for a while.

In August, the Third U.S. Cavalry, after bivouacing in Woodland Park, sails for the Spanish American War in the Philippines.

1900

Population is 80,671. Seattle is now the forty-eighth largest city in the nation.

Seattle buys Woodland Park from the estate of Guy C. Phinney for $100,000.

Ralph Hopkins drives the first automobile, an electric, along 2nd Ave.

Several miles of wooden sidewalk is replaced with concrete.

1901

Whiteford Rapid Vehicle and Motor Launch Company is the first automobile dealer in Seattle.

First Cedar River water reaches the city. Lake Washington water had been used since 1884, and various other sources were used before that.

Work begins on a canal cut through Beacon Hill to Lake Washington. It is later abandoned in favor of the present ship canal.

Chief of Detectives Charles Wappenstein and Chief of Police W. L. Meredith are forced to resign after the city council accepts charges of corruption. Wappenstein goes on to head the police at the Alaska-Yukon-Pacific Exposition and serves as police chief twice until his final fall from grace in 1911.

Ex-Chief W. L. Meredith is killed by John W. Considine in Guy's Drugstore at 2nd and Yesler Way. Meredith had been forced to resign his position because of bribery charges brought by Considine, a gambler and theater operator. A coroner's jury finds murder, but a King County jury frees Considine.

Charles W. Nordstrom is hanged for the murder of Willy Mason. Although the murder was near Issaquah, Nordstrom occupied a King County jail cell for ten years while a determined lawyer, James Hamilton Lewis, fights vigorously to save his life.

1902

The Reverend Mark A. Matthews becomes minister at First Presbyterian Church.

Keel of the battleship *Nebraska* is laid on July 4 at Moran Brothers Shipyard.

Pike St. regrade from 5th to Broadway is completed February 4. Pike St. regrade from 2nd Ave. to Broadway is completed on April 11.

Harry Tracy and David Merrill escape from Oregon State Penitentiary in Salem after killing four men. On July 2 Tracy lands in Ballard on a tug he had forced to carry him from Olympia after he killed Merrill. Tracy hangs around Seattle four days, then kills two policemen in Bothell and wounds two others. He goes into a house near Woodland Park and kills one pursuer and wounds another. Early in August he is finally cornered in a field west of Spokane, and after he is wounded he kills himself to become the ninth victim of his escape.

1903

Seattle Symphony Orchestra is founded.

Olmstead Brothers, landscape architects, present a plan for A Comprehensive System of Parks and Parkways for Seattle which, when adopted, will make Seattle much more beautiful.

President Theodore Roosevelt visits Seattle and Bremerton Navy Yard on May 23.

1904

Battleship *Nebraska* is launched.

Rainier Club building is completed.

First steel manufactured in Seattle is by the Seattle Steel Company, which is owned by William Piggott.

First steel vessel is built by the Moran brothers.

1905

Alaska Building, the city's first "skyscraper" at fifteen stories, is completed.

South Seattle is annexed on October 16.

1906

Seattle Public Library, on 4th Ave., opens.

Seattle Board of Health condemns its own building as unsanitary and orders building closed.

Waldorf Hotel, the first concrete-reinforced building in the city, is completed.

West Seattle operates the first municipally owned street railway system in the nation.

212 A Chronology of Seattle's History

George Mitchell shoots Joshua Creffield, "The Prophet," dead at 1st and Cherry. In July jurors free Mitchell on a temporary insanity plea. All Seattle rejoices because Creffield's unsavory cult of Holy Rollers in Corvalis, Oregon, received lots of unfavorable publicity. Creffield's success with women got him run out of one town and a two- to seven-year jail term in another city. After Mitchell is freed, he is shot dead in King Street Station by his own sister, Esther, who is a follower of Creffield. A jury finds Esther insane, and she is committed.

Seattle Mountaineers hiking club is organized after Dr. Frederick Cook lectures in Seattle about his "ascent" of Mount McKinley. Later Cook, who claims he reached the North Pole in 1908, is discredited on both the mountain and polar records. But the Mountaineers thrive to become one of the world's largest mountaineering organizations.

1907
Catholic Diocese of Seattle is created and Saint James Cathedral dedicated.

New First Presbyterian Church is completed at 7th and Spring with the Reverend Mark A. Matthews as pastor.

Alexander Pantages opens the Crystal Theater.

Pike Place Public Market opens.

Moore Hotel and Theater are built at 2nd and Virginia, and theater opens with *The Alaskan*.

West Seattle is annexed; also South Park, Columbia, Ballard, Dunlap, and Rainier Beach.

1909
Lake Washington Ship Canal construction begins.

Alaska-Yukon-Pacific Exposition opens on the University of Washington campus. It has 3,740,551 paid admissions for $1,096,475.64 and earns a profit.

Seattle Post-Intelligencer editor Erastus Brainerd calls for removal of billboards along city streets.

President Taft visits the A.Y.P. Exposition in September.

Chicago, Milwaukee, and Saint Paul Railroad comes to Seattle.

City engineer R. H. Thomson forecasts continuous sidewalks from Everett to Tacoma to join a single city within thirty-five years.

Jackson Street is regraded (1907-9). Grade is reduced from 15 degrees to 5 degrees. The greatest cut, at 9th Ave., is 85 feet. Dearborn St.'s grade is reduced from 19 percent to 3 percent. The greatest cut, at 12th Ave. S, is 112 feet.

Financier Sam Hill builds a mansion at 814 Highland Dr. to

house his friend, Crown Prince Albert of Belgium, on a visit to the A.Y.P. Exposition, but the prince is a no-show. However, another royal friend, Queen Marie of Romania, comes to visit in 1926.

Former Washington State Adjutant General Otis Hamilton is indicted on charges of embezzlement, forgery, and perjury. His downfall was his love for Hazel Moore, a lovely Seattle prostitute whose brown eyes suggested occult mysteries.

Sixty-one people are injured on May 7 when a gallery rail breaks at the Armory during a track meet.

1910

Population is 237,174.

Municipal League is formed.

Alexander Pantages opens another new theater, the Palomar, at 3rd and University.

First airplane flight is in May by Charles K. Hamilton, an itinerant pioneer barnstormer, in a Curtiss pusher biplane.

Westlane Ave. is opened.

Georgetown is annexed.

1911

Mayor Hi Gill is recalled from office in March after an intense reform surge. Gill wins the office back in elections in both 1914 and 1916.

Ex-Chief of Police Charles Wappenstein is tried for taking bribes to protect gamblers. Despite the support of the *Seattle Times* publisher, Alden Blethen, Wappenstein is convicted. He enters Walla Walla state prison to begin his three-year term.

Virgil Bogue submits a city plan on August 24, which preaches against skyscrapers because they are breeding grounds for diseases such as malaria.

Fairview Ave. is opened.

Port of Seattle is established.

The first nonpartisan election of mayor and city councilmen is held.

Union Station is completed.

New Providence Hospital location is established at 17th and Jefferson.

Swedish Hospital is founded.

The main portion of Denny Regrade is completed on October 31, with 5 million cubic yards of earth removed between 2nd and 5th avenues from Pike to Cedar streets. Fourth Ave. at Blanchard has been lowered 107 feet.

The Metropolitan Theater opens on October 2.

The first Potlatch civic festival occurs.

1912

Controversy erupts over a privately developed terminal on Harbor Island.

Voters reject the Bogue plan for city development.

United States Congressional subcommittee hears testimony on Judge Cornelius Hanford's performance in Seattle.

Hoge Building is constructed.

Dearborn Street Bridge opened. It is 66 feet wide and 420 feet long.

Linda Hazzard, the "Starvation Specialist," begins her monitored thirty-day fast at the Lincoln Hotel. The event is the inspiration of the *Seattle Star* and Mrs. Hazzard's answer to the Kitsap County jury that convicted her of manslaughter in her starving treatment of a patient in her Olallah clinic.

1913

Violence directed at political radicals erupts during Potlatch festivities.

A.F.L. convention comes to Seattle.

Construction begins on the County-City Building.

A mob of mostly servicemen, incited by the fulminations of the *Seattle Times* against radicals and Wobblies, wrecks their meeting places on June 18. Mayor Cotterill orders censorship of the *Times*, but a superior court judge overrules the mayor.

1914

Saloons are banished.

Cornish School is founded.

L. C. Smith Building (Smith Tower), at forty-two stories the tallest west of the Mississippi, is opened on June 1.

Yesler Regrade is completed between Main and Judkins streets, and 4th and 12th avenues. Excavations of 5 million cubic yards of earth fill the tidelands to create the South Industrial area.

1915

Jefferson Park golf course, the first public golf course in the nation, opens on May 12.

1916

Wobblies involved in the Everett "massacre" are jailed in Seattle.

Ballard and Fremont bridges across the ship canal are completed.

The Boeing Company is established as Aero Products on Lake Union.

1917

Lake Washington Ship Canal and Government Locks open.

Vice drive stirs city as the army commander of Fort Lewis puts Seattle off-limits to his troops.

Mayor Hi Gill is again threatened with a recall election. He fires the police chief. Some citizens call for military control of the city, although their concern is more with political radicals than prostitutes.

1918

Judge Thomas Burke and other minutemen investigate high school German teachers because of World War I sentiments.

Hulet Wells is convicted for opposing conscription.

Anne Louise Strong is recalled from the school board in a March election for anticonscription sentiments.

Ole Hanson is elected mayor after vigorous "Americanism" campaign.

Port of Seattle's tonnage is second nationally only to New York's.

1919

A general strike of all blue-collar workers is held February 6 to 11.

President Woodrow Wilson visits Seattle on September 13.

A riot occurs in Centralia involving Wobblies, and the American Legion leads the roundup of Wobblies in Seattle and the attacks on the *Seattle Union Record*.

Ole Hanson resigns as mayor to seek lecture fees and a possible national office.

Ruth Garrison, 18, poisons Grace Starrs, 28, at the Bon Marche Tearoom because Grace refused to give up her husband, Dudley. Pretty, outgoing Ruth wins the hearts of police and journalists when she confesses her love and crime so candidly. Some folks are outraged, though, when the sheriff houses Ruth at the House of Good Shepherd because the county jail is "unfit for a girl of Ruth's tender years." Ruth's jury finds her not guilty by reason of insanity. She is committed to the ward for the criminally insane at Walla Walla until 1931.

1920

Population is 315,312.

A.C.L.U. committee is formed in the city.

"Americanism" is an issue in local elections.

Sand Point Naval Air Station construction begins on 270 acres, which is later increased to 400 acres.

KJR broadcasts its first program. It is the second radio station in the nation.

University of Washington Husky Stadium is completed.

Lieutenant Roy Olmstead of the Seattle Police Department is arrested for rum-running. His dismissal from the force frees him for full-time operation in the booze trade.

1921

Kate Mahoney is missing. Her ex-con husband, James Mahoney, is not concerned, but police are interested after someone sees James row out into Lake Washington with a trunk. On August 8, after a long search, police find a trunk in Lake Washington containing Kate's body. Mahoney insists that Kate was visiting friends in Saint Paul, but he had been disposing of her property and preparing for a departure. Seattle friends of Kate had received postcards from Saint Paul with her signature. It turns out that Mahoney's sister actually sent the cards after registering in a hotel using Kate's name and posing as Kate to execute a fake power of attorney. Jurors agreed that Mahoney needs hanging.

1922

On Saint Patrick's Day the body of a Skid Road police officer, Charles O. Legate, is discovered in his car. Three bullets killed him. Officers determine that Legate shot himself. Three months later the new police chief, William Severyns, and Mayor Edwin Brown declare that Legate was murdered because he threatened to reveal police corruption. Criminologist Luke May's ballistic examination shows that two guns fired the fatal bullets. A grand jury reverses the suicide determination, but no one is ever indicted for the murder.

1923

President Warren Harding visits the city on July 27 after his Alaska tour.

The city's first zoning ordinance is adopted.

Prohibition corruption causes the *Argus* to decide that "Seattle has become ... so rotten that it stinks."

1924

Olympic Hotel opens.

United States Army around-the-world fliers begin and end their flight at Sand Point.

1925

Bootlegger (and former policeman) Ray Olmstead is indicted.

The Reverend Ambrose M. Bailey leads a vice crusade in the city.

1926

Fifth Avenue Theater opens with Cecil B. DeMille's *Young April*.

Ray Olmstead's trial opens in January. Despite protests of famed defense attorney George Vanderveer over the admission of wiretaps, Olmstead and his associates are convicted in federal court. Later, although it doesn't help Olmstead, congress bans wiretaps.

1927

First "talkie" movie opens in the Blue Mouse Theater on March 18.

1928

Second Denny Regrade (1928–31) begins. Power shovels and movable belts replace the earlier giant hydraulic methods, and 4,233,000 cubic yards of earth are dumped in deep waters off the waterfront. The maximum cut is 89 feet.

Last issue of *Seattle Daily Union-Record* is published on February 18.

1929

Boeing Field opens.

The city contracts with famed sculptor Alonzo Victor Lewis for a World War I memorial honoring our doughboys. In 1931 times are not prosperous, and critics object to the smile on the huge bronze soldier's face as he strides back from battle bearing Hun trophies. "Bestial," cries a local architect. "The statue would be repugnant to German tourists," says a councilman. After much controversy the city finally pays Lewis and sets the dedication of the *Doughboy* for Memorial Day, 1932. But the critics take their revenge by decreeing that the statue should have no inscription identifying it as a war memorial. The *Doughboy* still stands in an obscure corner of the Seattle Center without a war-memorial inscription.

1930

Population is 365,583.

Denny Regrade completed, 5th to Westlake and Virginia to Harrison, on December 10.

1931

Federal Office Building and Hotel Edmund Meany are completed.

Mayor Frank Edwards fires J. D. Ross, the popular head of City Light.

Mayor Frank Edwards is recalled and Ross is reinstated.

King County Hospital is dedicated on February 27.

1932

Population is 366,000.

George Washington Memorial Bridge (Aurora) is opened on February 22. Cost was $2,918,584.

Unemployed Citizens League helps elect Mayor John Dore.

Presidential candidate Franklin Roosevelt speaks at the Civic Auditorium.

1933

Cincinnatus Party is established.

University Bridge reconstruction is completed on April 7.

The New Seattle Art Museum opens in Volunteer Park in June.

Film *Tugboat Annie* premiers on July 28. The film is based on the popular *Saturday Evening Post* stories by Norman Reilly Raine.

1934

United States Marine Hospital is completed.

Police use tear gas against waterfront strikers who are picketing the docks. An offensive is launched by three hundred police after gas bombs are thrown from the Garfield Street Bridge. The two thousand strikers give way, some fleeing up Queen Anne Hill.

1935

Dave Beck, Teamster leader, is appointed to the state parole board.

Robert Driscoll is caught setting fire to Saint Spiridon, the Russian church on Lakeview Ave. Eventually Driscoll confesses to 115 arson fires in Seattle and 25 others outside the city between 1931 and 1935. They include the Dugdale Baseball Park, the A. A. Ghiclione and Sons macaroni factory, and Albers Milling Company. He insists he has been blackballed by capitalists since World War I. His obvious deranged mental condition precludes any prosecution beyond that of the church, for which he receives a five- to ten-year term in Walla Walla.

1936

Seattle Post-Intelligencer staff goes on strike.

Anna Louise Strong is denied the use of a Seattle hall for her lecture visit.

Police arrest twenty-eight in Hooverville (a shanty town) after seizing communist literature. The downtown "Red College" is smashed by American Legionnaires as the police look on.

AV, a businessmen's antiradical organization, targets liberal candidates, particularly those of the Washington Commonwealth Federation.

1937

Trackless trolleys are demonstrated on March 18.

1938

Arthur B. Langlie is elected mayor, leading a reform ticket.

The city deficit in January is $6.5 million. City employees have difficulty cashing their pay warrants.

Controversy rages over the decision to install parking meters downtown.

1939

The maiden flight of Boeing's new Stratoliner is held in January. Pan-American Airways orders three of the first passenger planes designed to fly in the substratosphere.

The city faces an acute rental-housing shortage.

Dr. J. Warren Hastings, pastor of the University Christian Church, forms a committee to crusade for the cleanup of vice.

1940

Population is 368,302.

Mercer Island Floating Bridge (formally the Lacey B. Murrow bridge, named for a prominent civil engineer and brother of the commentator, Edward R. Murrow) is dedicated on July 2.

Queen Anne Hill's counterbalance cable car is replaced by trackless trolleys.

City shanty towns are razed as unemployment eases.

1941

Seattle-Tacoma Shipbuilding Corporation receives a $76 million contract to build thirty C-3 cargo ships. Work is under way on twenty-five destroyers.

United States government announces a plan to build a huge new Boeing plant at Renton.

1942
Army asks New Year's Eve celebrants to keep the noise to a minimum and to stay indoors.

Fifty young women answer the call for female taxi drivers.

Longacres Racetrack and Puyallup Fairgrounds are used as reception centers for Japanese-Americans who are being evacuated from the West Coast.

1943
Mayor William F. Devin orders a vice cleanup.

Some 10,500 tons of streetcar rails are removed from city streets.

A four-engine experimental Boeing bomber crashes into the Frye Packing Plant on Airport Way, killing thirty-two people.

1944
Mayor William F. Devin appoints Seattle Civic Unity Committee to promote racial accord.

Seattle gamblers are getting rich riding ferries carrying Winslow shipyard workers.

Black Ball ferry fleet is augmented by the purchase of *City of Sacramento* from San Francisco owners.

1945
Boeing payroll in January is 44,754. On April 10 the last B-17 of the 6,981 built in Seattle is completed (others were built elsewhere) as the B-29 production starts.

1946
School board grants married teachers the right to regular teaching contracts.

Colman Ferry Terminal is remodeled to increase capacity.

Waste of navy surplus supplies at Sand Point is investigated.

1947
Three-day ferry strike is held in March.

Fund-raising begins for the long-projected Museum of History and Industry.

Cases of venereal diseases are sharply reduced.

Group Health Cooperative opens at old Saint Luke's Hospital on Capitol Hill.

1948
Group Health Cooperative sues King County Medical Association for blacklisting its doctors and loses the case.

1949
Bow Lake (Seattle-Tacoma International Airport) is dedicated July 9.
Tolls are lifted on the Mercer Island bridge in July.
University of Washington president recommends firing two avowed communists on the faculty.
Earthquake on April 13 registers 7.1 on Richter scale, causing eight deaths, four by heart attacks.

1950
Population is 467,591.
Police department vacates its old triangular building.

1951
Public Safety Building is dedicated on January 19.
City Light takes over Puget Sound Power and Light facilities on March 5.
First annual Seafair is held.
Manual Rosenthal, conductor of the Seattle Symphony Orchestra, is fired when the board discovers he is living with a mistress and passing her off as his wife.

1952
Alaska Way Viaduct is completed.
Seattle Art Museum receives gifts from Kress Foundation and plans a special Kress Gallery.
Panty raids at University of Washington spark riots on Greek Row.

1953
New Children's Orthopedic Hospital opens in April. Cost is $5 million.
Five men are charged with subversion and get five-year terms.
University of Washington poet Theodore Roethke wins Pulitzer Prize for his collection *The Waking*.

1954
First details on Boeing's new 707 jetliner are revealed in March.
Hundreds of Seattle motorists discover pits on their wind-

shields. Hysteria grows as acid rain, spacemen firing cosmic ray guns, and boys shooting BB guns are blamed. After some days motorists lose interest in examining their windshields, and the excitement dies down.

The battle over the site of a second Lake Washington bridge continues. Sand Point is the latest possibility.

1955

University of Washington faculty protests loyalty-oath requirement.

University of Washington president provokes national controversy by prohibiting J. Robert Oppenheimer's lectures.

Metropolitan Theater is razed in favor of a new motor entrance to the Olympic Hotel.

Seattle Art Commission is formed in May.

Seattle passes New York as pleasure-craft capital of the world, with sixty thousand boats.

1956

University of Washington students protest ban against political speakers.

Civic Center Advisory Committee studies development problems.

1957

Dave Beck is convicted in federal court of misuse of Teamster funds.

Boeing announces it expects to get contracts for supersonic bomber and guided missiles.

Seattle is listed as one of the cities with significant air-pollution problems.

1958

City begins program of street tree planting.

Seattle Garden Club takes lead in fight to eliminate billboards along the new north-south freeway.

In March voters reject James Ellis's Metro Plan for rapid transit, sewers, and the establishment of areawide planning. But at another election in September, voters approve a revised plan for an area sewer system that will clean up Lake Washington.

First Boeing 707 commercial flight.

1959

Washington, Norton, and Logan buildings are under construction.

1960

Van Gogh exhibition at the Seattle Art Museum draws large crowds.

Debate goes on over replacing trolleys with smelly, noisy diesel buses.

Residential construction is off $53 million from 1959.

1961

Estimates indicate some ten thousand city women have alcohol problem.

The *Argus* helps promote state legislation restricting billboards.

Antique dealer Guy Rockwell is found guilty in October of grand larceny for keeping money given to him for an antique purchase. But the trial does not bear on the mysterious disappearance of Rockwell's wife and her daughter in March 1960. Suspicions of foul play, Rockwell's own disappearance in August 1960, and his arrest in New York in December keeps the Rockwell story in the news for months. With no *corpus delecti*, he is never charged with murder. After receiving a suspended sentence for the grand larceny conviction, Rockwell is never heard from again. The two missing women are never found.

Architect Paul Thiry calls Alaska Way Viaduct a "monstrosity" and "an ugly bunch of junk."

1962

August Werner's 16-foot bronze statue of Leif Erikson is unveiled at Shilshole Bay. This commemoration of the discoverer of America makes everyone happy until September 1967, when the generous artist offers the use of the plaster cast to Rogaland Province, Norway. The Norwegians reject it, calling Erikson an Icelander and "shameful murderer." Werner is indignant. He argues that Erikson may have been the first missionary from Norway to Greenland. Supporters of Columbus are pleased by the controversy discrediting a rival explorer, but Erikson stands firmly at Shilshole Bay.

Campaign to preserve historic character of the Pike Place Market is launched.

Century 21 Exposition from April through October is a financial success and gives the city permanent gains of the Opera House, Playhouse, Pacific Science Center, the Arena, and many other buildings.

City Transit begins metro-area planning. Hearings in November on replacing trolleys with obnoxious diesel buses.

1963

Transit orders ninety diesel buses in January. In September a petition with ten thousand signatures is filed against diesel buses.

1964

IBM Building is constructed.

Transit officials contest trolley fans, argue for economy and dependability of buses. "Bring back trolleys" bid is defeated 2-to-1 in March election.

Sea-Land container shipping company moves to Port of Seattle's Terminal 5 to begin weekly van service to Alaska.

1965

Palomar Theater's last performance is on April 25. The theater is one of many commissioned by Alexander Pantages, famed vaudeville impresario. Theater is razed so a parking lot can be built in its place.

James Ellis introduces his Forward Thrust scheme for metro-wide rapid transit, parks expansion, highways, flood control, sewer separation, and domed stadium.

Port of Seattle tonnage, which has been increasing dramatically since 1963, exceeds the level reached in 1918 for the first time.

An earthquake, on April 29, registers 6.5 on the Richter Scale, causing slight damage. This leads some to say April is "earthquake weather" for Seattle, since the previous one also struck in April.

The first section of Interstate 5 through Seattle is opened on February 3.

1966

Boeing payroll increased by 24,800; total employed now is 88,400.

Plans are announced for a third Lake Washington bridge.

In court battle over constitutionality of the billboard prohibition laws, the distinguished attorney Alfred Schweppe argues that billboards keep drivers alert.

1967

Citizen protest induces state and city to shelve the R. H. Thomson Expressway planned for the Arboretum. The protest had been voiced since 1963.

Boeing adds 12,500 employees; total employed is 100,900.

Soaring crime rate attracts attention. Murders are up 146 percent over 1960. Burglaries are up 1,300 percent.

1968

Forward Thurst program for new parks, highways, sewer separation, and domed stadium is approved in the February election, but rapid transit is defeated.

Boeing is working on an SST.

Debate continues over metro-area rapid transit.

Seven police officers are injured in the Central Area disturbances featuring gunfire, fire bombs, and rock throwing. The riot follows the arrest of two Black Panther leaders on July 29.

Boeing's payroll is down by 5,400 employees.

1969

Boeing's payroll is reduced by 34,100.

United States Navy commissions the supply ship USS *Seattle* in April.

1970

Seattle-born rock star James M. "Jimi" Hendrix dies in Europe and is buried in Greenwood Memorial Park in Renton.

Several Seattle police officers are charged with accepting payoffs.

City votes to remove R. H. Thomson Expressway from the city's Comprehensive Plan.

Port of Seattle's new grain terminal is completed at Pier 86 at a cost of $13 million. Composed of 68 silos, each 130 feet high with a diameter of 28 feet, its 4.2-million-bushel capacity could be expanded to 12 million bushels. Loading rate into ships is 3,000 tons per hour, more than twice the rate of the old Hanford Street Terminal (Pier 25). Vessels up to 73-foot draft can be served. Unfortunately, many Queen Anne Hill residents are surprised when the elevators block part of their view, because the plans as presented to the neighborhood were aerial views rather than ground-level.

Arson fire at the Ozark Hotel at Westlake and Lenora kills twenty-one. A year later twelve die in a fire at the Seventh Avenue Apartments. City council responds with the Ozark Ordinance, which sets stricter fire codes for hotels and apartment buildings.

Boeing's payroll is reduced by 8,200; total is 38,100.

In May, fifteen thousand demonstrators organized by the Seattle Liberation Front march from the University District to city hall and the federal courthouse, via Interstate 5, to protest the invasion of Cambodia.

Also in May voters turn down a $615 million bond package including rapid transit. The Boeing recession and the opposition of the highway lobby are blamed.

1971

Friends of the Market are successful in an initiative establishing the Pike Place Market as a historic preservation district.

Burke Building and the Rivoli Theater are razed.

Boeing begins gradually adding employees.

Man calling himself D. B. Cooper hijacks Northwest 727 and leaps out somewhere near Portland with $200,000. He has never been found.

A King County grand jury indicts fifty-five policemen said to be involved in police payoffs in the late 1960s. Eventually there are fourteen guilty pleas, six convictions, and twenty-two case dismissals. Assistant Chief M. E. "Buzz" Cook and former captain Lyle La Pointe receive the only convictions of the nineteen charged with police conspiracy. Earlier, Cook had been convicted of perjury before a federal grand jury, then cleared on appeal.

1972

In February residents vote against the R. H. Thomas Expressway and the Bay Freeway, an elevated highway over Mercer St. between Eastlake Ave. and Seattle Center.

First of at least thirty-six women murdered by Ted Bundy is found.

The city law against topless dancing is found to be an unconstitutional infringement on free expression by a King County court. A year later the state supreme court overturns the decision.

City forms an Office of Women's Rights.

1973

Bruce Lee, actor in seven martial arts movies and a Seattle resident, dies in Hong Kong and is buried in Seattle's Lake View Cemetery.

Police Chief George Tielsch resigns in a dispute over an officer disciplined for brutality.

A six-month study by three hundred citizens is completed on the goals and policies to be achieved by the year 2000.

The Seattle Seven's conviction for property damage at the U.S. courthouse where they were protesting the Chicago Seven conspiracy trial is overturned on appeal.

1974

Police Chief Robert Hanson blurts out something about intelligence files on local activists, then denies that such files are kept. Five years of squabbling between civil libertarians and police follow. The 1978 election of Mayor Charles Royer, who as a KING-TV newsman had objected to police intelligence records, leads to restrictions on police activities.

Residents long for rain during an extremely dry summer.

Topless dancing is found harmless by 50.4 percent of King County voters.

1975

Voters defeat schools' special levy twice. The school district sues the state, arguing that the state constitution gave the state the "paramount duty" of educating citizens. The courts agree to open the way for eventual 100 percent funding of basic education by the state.

Mayor Wes Uhlman wins recall election by a wide margin.

The Reverend Keith Rhinehart, founder of the Aquarian Foundation on Capitol Hill, sponsors an international spiritualists' convention at the Olympic Hotel, promising "famous miracles and scenes right out of the Bible." Since founding the Aquarian Foundation in the 1950s, Rhinehart has had legal problems and spends most of his time in Honolulu, although he keeps in touch with his congregations in Seattle and elsewhere.

1976

Judge Boldt's decision on Indian fishing rights stirs a storm of protest that goes on over the coming decade.

In April, fifteen hundred fans shiver in Sick's Stadium to hear presidential candidate Ronald Reagan.

1977

A national magazine ranks Seattle as the nation's "most livable city" to the dismay of "Lesser Seattle" proponents.

Survey shows the city has only eighty-five cobblestone streets left.

1978

King Tut exhibition from July to November draws 1.3 million visitors to the Seattle Center and sparks a wave of "Tutmania." Seattle Art Museum receipts total $3,039,000. Overall revenue gain by city merchants is $60 million.

Freighter *Chavez* rams Spokane Street Bridge, thus reducing by one-half the highway connection between downtown and West Seattle.

1979

Population is up 1.5 percent, the first gain since 1970.

Seattle SuperSonics win the National Basketball Association championship by defeating the Washington Bullets.

The Fifth Avenue Theatre reopens.

1980

With 506,492 residents in Seattle counted in the 1980 census, Seattle now ranks twenty-first among American cities. It ranks fourth in the percentage of Asian-descendant residents, fifth in the percentage of Indians, and forty-fourth in the percentage of Jews. Seattle does not rank among the first fifty cities in its percentage of black residents, although there was a 71 percent increase between 1950 and 1960 against a 3 percent increase in the white population.

Thirteen billboards come down after a twelve-year legal battle over a city ordinance.

Pike St. improvement program gets under way.

1981

A *Seattle Times* story reveals that most Seattle policemen live outside the city limits because it is safer out there.

Eleven climbers die on Mount Rainier on June 21, making it the worst climbing accident in American history.

Michigan beats the University of Washington 23 to 6 in the Rose Bowl.

Olympic Hotel closes for massive renovation.

1982

The first of the Green River murder victims is found. So many more are found south of the Sea-Tac Airport area that a special Green River Task Force is formed, and the bodies of young women continue to be found over the next four years.

The population of Seattle decreases again after peaking in the late 1970s. A major factor is school busing for racial balance.

Dr. Barney Clark, 61, of West Seattle becomes the world's first artificial-heart recipient. Dr. Clark survives 112 days at the University of Utah hospital.

University of Washington beats Iowa 28 to 0 in Rose Bowl.

Catholic Archbishop Raymond Hunthausen announces he has withheld one-half of his federal taxes to protest the arms race.

1983

Thirteen persons—twelve men and one woman—are slain in the Wah Mee Club gambling club at 507A Maynard Alley S. in Chinatown. It is the largest mass homicide on a single day in the state's history. The three convicted killers are quickly caught, except for Wai Chin Ng, who escapes to Alberta and is not found until October 1984. Ben Ng is sentenced to life; Kwan Willie Mak is given the death sentence; and Wai Ng is also sentenced to life in prison.

Senator Henry M. Jackson dies on September 1. The Port of Seattle quickly renames Sea-Tac International Airport in his honor but rescinds the change when so many people object to it, not out of disrespect for the late senator, but from the way the Port Commission acted without due process.

BankAmerica acquires the deeply troubled Seattle–First National Bank.

The Seattle Breakers hockey team trades the rights to Tommy Martin of Victoria for a new team bus. Martin went on to the NHL. Nobody seems to have tracked the bus's career.

1984

Seattle's Metro transit system is voted the best transit system in the nation by the Public Transit Association.

Construction begins on the Columbia Center, which will be seventy-six stories, or 943 feet high, and the tallest building not only in Seattle but also west of the Mississippi.

1985

Rand McNally's *Vacation Places Rated Almanac* ranks Seattle as the nation's No. 1 recreational city for the fourth year in a row.

An entire family—Charles and Annie Goldmark and their two sons, Colin and Derek—are murdered by David Lewis Rice, who mistakenly believed they were communists. Goldmark was a prominent attorney in Seattle, and his parents were falsely accused of being communists during the McCarthy Era witch hunts.

William Allen, who guided the Boeing Company through World War II and safely into the jet era, dies at the age of 85.

The winter is weird this year and dumps 17½ inches of snow on Seattle in November, closing schools, freezing traffic, and putting 385 Metro buses out of commission.

Yoshiyuki Takada, a member of the ethereal Japanese dance troupe Sankai Juku, falls to his death while suspended from a rope over Pioneer Square.

Ivar Haglund, Seattle's most beloved waterfront character and multimillionaire restaurateur, dies and leaves most of his fortune to the University of Washington and Washington State University.

1986

Boeing sets another record by selling 341 jets for $19.25 billion, of which 213 are 737s.

The Vatican strips the liberal and outspoken Archbishop Raymond Hunthausen of responsibilities in areas dealing with worship, moral issues, liturgy, and instruction of clergy.

Eddie Bauer, founder of the famous outdoor-gear stores and inventor of several sports-related items, including quilted-down sleeping bags and coats, dies at the age of 86.

Brock Adams, the underdog, defeats Slade Gorton for the Senate seat.

1987

Only 2 inches of rain fall in Seattle between June and October.

After many hearings and much pressure from the public and the press, most of Archbishop Raymond Hunthausen's powers are restored.

An estimated 150 members of Los Angeles's street gangs now live in Seattle, as violence and drug sales expand.

Downtown Seattle sometimes resembles Berlin in late 1945 as three major construction projects are underway at the same time: the Metro bus tunnel, completed in 1990; the Washington State Trade and Convention Center over Interstate 5, completed in 1988; and the Westlake Mall project, also completed in 1988.

1988

The Seattle City Council pays Walt Disney Imagineering, Inc., and the Harrison Pice Co. $335 million for a master plan to improve the Seattle Center. Residents aren't impressed, especially when they suggest moving the International Fountain and demolishing the Center House, the Arena, the Memorial Stadium, and the Flag Pavilion.

King County Superior Court Judge Gary Little, 49, commits suicide when a newspaper confronts him with evidence that he had coerced teenage boys into having sex with him. The controversy continues throughout the year as the state's Commission on Judicial Conduct refuses to make public its file on Little.

By a 2-to-1 margin, voters approve a rail-transit system to improve the traffic situation in Seattle.

While some Boeing employees suffer memory loss, skin rashes, and breathing problems, the company reports another record year in sales, 636 total during the year for nearly $30 billion.

Since 1985 sea lions have been eating salmon and steelhead as they congregate around the fish ladder at Ballard Locks. The first one there was named Herschel, and several other Herschels quickly heard of the good deal. Nothing has worked, including catching the sea lions and transporting them elsewhere, stretching nets to let the fish in but keep sea lions out, and underwater firecrackers. Fisheries officials say the sea lions consume 43 percent of the steelhead trying to get through.

1989

The long-awaited completion of Interstate 90 occurs on June 4, when the second floating bridge between Seattle and Mercer Island is opened. But the traffic situation is improved only slightly, as the old floating bridge is closed for a two-year repair job. In the meantime, it takes only three days for the first accident to occur—at 6:47 A.M., June 7, in the new tunnel. Five cars are in a chain-reaction accident that causes no injuries and damages only one car badly enough to be towed away.

When Samoans adopted the staid English game of cricket, they adapted it to their own unstaid culture, then brought it with them to Seattle. After complaints by people living near Genesee Park, the Samoan community agrees to move their noisy version of cricket to Jefferson Park. They also agree to cheer their teams without the use of noisemakers.

Popular KIRO-television personality Larry Sturholm is murdered in July along with a friend, Debra Sweiger. A man who allegedly was in love with Sweiger is found at the scene with his wrists and throat slashed and is charged with the murder.

The late Ferdinand Marcos, dictator of the Philippines, is found liable in the 1981 murders of Silme Domingo and Gene Viernes, cannery workers in Seattle. His estate is ordered to pay $15 million to the survivors.

Drive-by shootings become a major problem in Seattle, with more than 150 reported. In spite of this, Seattle's murder rate, compared with other cities, remains moderate, with an average of fifty-five a year. In 1989 there were only thirty-eight murders. The most in the past decade was sixty-four in 1980, and the fewest occurred in 1982, when thirty-two persons were murdered.

Steve Largent, Seattle's most popular athlete, retires as wide receiver for the Seattle Seahawks after his fourteenth season. He held six National Football League records: receptions (819), receiving yards (13,089), receiving touchdowns (100), consecutive games with a reception (177), fifty-catch seasons (10), and 1,000-yard seasons (8).

1990

Norm Rice is elected mayor. He is the city's first black mayor, although blacks constitute only about 10 percent of the total population.

After lots of attention in the press, the beloved old dive, The Blue Moon Tavern in the University District, is saved from the wrecking ball.

The housing market, for awhile the hottest in the country, slowly cools down after the average price rises 18 percent. At the peak of the rush, the average house costs $180,833.

Seattle makes more "Best" lists. CEOs of 400 of the nation's largest corporations select Seattle as America's best business location. *Money* magazine names it the second-best place to live

(Bremerton is first). The 1989 *Places Rated Almanac* rates it first in livability. *Savvy* magazine rates it the best place to raise kids. *Conde Nast Traveler*'s poll lists it the eighth-best city in the world, behind (in order) Paris, Rome, San Francisco, Florence, Vienna, Lucerne, and London, and the second-best city to visit in the U.S., behind San Francisco. Alaska Airlines is voted best airline in America and twelfth-best in the world by the same poll.

On November 25 during heavy storms that cause the worst flooding in western Washington's history, sections of the original Lake Washington Floating Bridge (nee Lacey B. Murrow), closed for renovations, fill with water and sink.

1991

"Hammering Man," a 48-foot statue being placed in front of the new Seattle Art Museum, topples over into the street damaging only the statue and the installation crew's egos.

A Spam carving contest is held in Pioneer Square, and first place goes to the "Three Spams of the I–90 Bridge," showing slabs of the bridge sinking into Lake Washington.

The New York-based investor group that tried to take over the Pike Place Public Market loses its court case and management remains in local hands.

The city's overall crime rate is the seventh-highest in the nation.

1992

Seattle chocolate lovers prepare themselves for withdrawal when the venerable department store Frederick & Nelson closes, and the future of its Frango mints is uncertain. Fortunately, the candy factory keeps going, and the candy is sold out of a shop at the corner of Fifth and Pine.

The city suffers its worst drought in history and citizens respond with dramatic cuts in water consumption. Citizens worry about melanoma while KOMO–TV sponsors a brown lawn contest.

New York's *Spy* magazine reports that the "Wellness Permission League" has picked September 16 as "Stay Away From Seattle Day," with the explanation that on that day they will try to keep the appeal of Seattle from "haunting us with its siren call."

About half the calls to the United Negro College Fund telethon on KING–TV in January are hate calls.

James Ellis, the man who brought Seattle Forward Thrust, the Lake Washington clean-up, the Convention Center, and numerous other civic accomplishments, has thrown his support and expertise to the Mountains to Sound Greenway, a plan to ensure that Interstate 90 from Cle Elum to Seattle remains beautiful.

Paul Allen, co-founder of Microsoft, announces he will under-write a museum in the Seattle Center for the late Seattle musician Jimi Hendrix.

Bibliography

GENERAL HISTORY

Bass, Sophie. *When Seattle Was a Village*. Seattle: Lowman & Hanford, 1947.
Binns, Archie. *Northwest Gateway*. Portland: Binfords & Mort, 1941.
Broderick, Henry. *The "HB" Story*. Seattle: Frank McCaffrey, 1969.
Clark, Norman. *The Dry Years: Prohibition and Social Change in Washington*. Seattle: University of Washington, 1965.
Grant, Frederick. *History of Seattle*. New York: American, 1981.
Hanford, Cornelius. *Seattle and Environs*. Chicago: Pioneer Historical, 1924.
Jones, Nard. *Seattle*. New York: Doubleday, 1972.
Morgan, Murray. *Skid Road*. New York: Viking, 1962.
Nelson, Gerald R. *Seattle: The Life and Times of an American City*. New York: Knopf, 1977.
Newell, Gordon R. and Sherwood, Don. *Totem Tales of Old Seattle*. Seattle: Superior, 1956.
Potts, Ralph. *Seattle Heritage*. Seattle: Superior, 1955.
Sales, Roger. *Seattle Past to Present*. Seattle: University of Washington, 1976.
Sayre, J. Wilkes. *This City of Ours*. Seattle: Seattle School District, 1936.

ARCHITECTURE, MUSIC, AND ART

Campbell, Esther W. *Bagpipes in the Woodwind Section*. Seattle: Symphony Women's Association, 1978.
Steinbrueck, Victor. *Market Sketchbook*. Seattle: University of Washington, 1968.
———. *Seattle Cityscape*. Seattle: University of Washington, 1962.
Tobey, Mark. *World of a Market*. Seattle: University of Washington, 1964.

ASIAN SEATTLE

Burke, Edward. *Seattle's Other History: Our Asian-American Heritage*. Seattle: Profanity Hill, 1979.
Chin, Art. *Golden Tassels: A History of the Chinese in Washington, 1857-1977*. Seattle: Art Chin, 1977.

Daniels, Roger. *Concentration Camps and USA: Japanese Americans and World War II.* New York: Holt, Rinehart and Winston, 1972.
Hildebrand, Lorraine Barker. *Straw Hats, Sandals and Steel: The Chinese in Washington State.* Tacoma: The Washington State American Revolution Bicentennial Commission, 1977.
Hosokawa, Bill. *Nesei Daughter.* Seattle: University of Washington Press, 1953.
Ito, Kazuo. *Issei: A History of Japanese Immigrants in North America.* (Translated by Shinchiro Nakumura and Jean S. Girard.) Tokyo: Japan Publications, 1973.

BIOGRAPHIES

Cornish, Nellie. *Miss Aunt Nellie.* Seattle: University of Washington, 1964.
Hynding, Alan. *Public Life of Eugene Semple.* Seattle: University of Washington, 1973.
Nesbit, Robert C. *"He Built Seattle:" A Biography of Judge Thomas Burke.* Seattle: University of Washington, 1961.
Potts, Ralph. *Counsel for the Damned: A Biography of George Vanderveer.* Philadelphia: Lippincott, 1953.
Shefferman, Nathan. *Man in the Middle.* New York: Doubleday, 1961.
Speidel, William C. *Sons of the Profits.* Seattle: Nettle Creek, 1967.
———. *Doc Maynard.* Seattle: Nettle Creek, 1978.
Thomson, Reginald Heber. *That Man Thomson.* Seattle: University of Washington, 1950.

CRIME

Chambliss, William J. *On the Take.* Bloomington: Indiana University, 1978.
McNeal, Violet. *Four White Horses and a Brass Band.* New York: Doubleday, 1947.
May, Luke S. *Crime's Nemesis.* New York: Macmillan, 1936.

ENGINEERING AND PLANNING

Blanchard, Leslie. *Street Railway Era in Seattle.* Forty Fort, PA: Harold Cox, 1968.
Bogue, Virgil G. *Plan of Seattle.* Seattle: Lowman & Hanford, 1911.
Brambilla, Roberto. *What Makes Cities Livable? Learning from Seattle.* New York: Institute for Environmental Action, 1979.
McWilliams, Mary. *Seattle Water Department History, 1854–1954.* Seattle: Dogwood Press, 1955.

Phelps, Myra L. *Public Works in Seattle: A Narrative History of the Engineering Department 1875–1975.* Seattle: Engineering Department, 1978.

Thomson, R. H. See "Biographies."

RADICAL HISTORY

Chaplin, Ralph. *Wobbly.* Chicago: University of Chicago, 1948.

Freidheim, Robert L. *Seattle General Strike.* Seattle: University of Washington, 1964.

O'Connor, Harvey. *Revolution in Seattle: A Memoir.* New York: Monthly Review Press, 1964.

Potts, Ralph. See *Counsel for the Damned,* under "Biographies."

Rader, Melvin. *False Witness.* Seattle: University of Washington, 1969.

Strong, Anna Louise. *I Change Worlds.* New York: Holt, 1935.

OTHER

Ames, William E. and Simpson, Roger A. *Unionism or Hearst: The Seattle Post-Intelligencer Strike of 1936.* Seattle: Pacific Northwest Labor Association, 1978.

Carter, Glen. *My Waterfront.* Seattle: Seagull, 1977.

Droker, Howard. *Seattle's Unsinkable Houseboats.* Seattle: Watermark, 1977.

Higman, Harry W. and Larrison, Earl J. *Union Bay.* Seattle: University of Washington, 1951.

Morgan, Brandt. *Enjoying Seattle's Parks.* Seattle: Greenwood, 1979.

Morgan, Murray. *Century 21: The Story of the Seattle World's Fair.* Seattle: Acme, 1963.

Rue, Walter. *Weather of the Pacific Coast.* Mercer Island: Writing Works, 1978.

Schmid, Calvin F. *Social Trends in Seattle.* Seattle: University of Washington, 1948.

UNIVERSITY OF WASHINGTON HISTORY

Gates, Charles. *The First Century at the University of Washington.* Seattle: University of Washington, 1961.

Hines, Neal O. *Denny's Knoll: A History of the Metropolitan Tract of the University of Washington.* Seattle: University of Washington, 1980.

Rader, Melvin. See "Radical History."

Index